W9-BPS-278

The Politics of Civil Rights
in the Truman Administration

Ohio State University Press

The Politics of Civil Rights
in the Truman Administration

William C. Berman

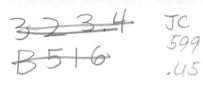

For Debbie

TABLE OF CONTENTS

	Preface	ix
Chapter One:	The Rhetoric of Politics	3
Chapter Two:	The Civil Rights Committee Delivers Its Report	41
Chapter Three:	Presidential Politics of Civil Rights: 1948	79
Chapter Four:	The Congress, the Coalition, and the Federal Executive	137
Chapter Five:	Presidential Politics of Civil Rights: 1952	183
	Conclusion	237
	Bibliography	241
	Index	253

PREFACE

Among the most significant domestic developments in the years Harry Truman served as president was the emergence of the civil rights movement. The genesis of this challenge to the institutional framework of a racist society had, of course, antedated the Truman era; but during the immediate post–World War II period, the incipient civil rights movement was gathering sufficient strength and momentum to pose a serious threat to the cohesiveness of the Democratic party. Thus, the issue of the politics of civil rights in the Truman administration relates the growing political influence of American Negroes to the structure of the Democratic party.

The politics of civil rights first arose as an issue in the 1930's when large numbers of black voters, living in northern urban areas, joined the Democratic party to support Franklin Roosevelt's New Deal. Their presence in the party sparked some northern Democratic liberals into advocating passage of civil rights legislation, a move which was bitterly resented, and actively opposed, by congressmen from the South. Thereafter, the intraparty conflict between proponents and opponents of this legislation slowly grew in intensity. President Roosevelt, who was afraid of offending southern congressmen, tried to sidestep the issue. But in June, 1941, Negro pressure compelled him to issue an executive order creating a Federal Fair Employment Practices Committee. The president's action signified that a new political situation had developed: black Americans were now capable of playing an influential role in national politics.

President Harry Truman inherited the unresolved civil rights conflict from the Roosevelt administration, without at the same time inheriting the good will and affection that most Negroes felt for his predecessor. By 1948 it was clear that Truman would need their votes in order to retain control of the White House. Out of that need emerged the Truman administration's civil rights program. The purpose of this study is to reconstruct and analyze the origins and development of that program, to examine its impact on the internal politics of the Democratic party, and to assess and to evaluate the contributions which the Truman administration made on behalf of Negro aspirations for freedom and justice.

The initial encouragement I received from Professor Robert Bremner of the Ohio State University History Department has been much appreciated. I am grateful for the research assistance and travel grant provided by the Harry

S. Truman Library Institute. Dean George Roadman and Dr. George Hart of California State College, California, Pennsylvania, helped me at an early point in this undertaking. Thanks to their critical reading of the manuscript, Dr. James Morrill of the History Department of the University of Louisville and Professor William Read of the University of Louisville Law School saved me from many errors, stylistic and otherwise. I am of course solely responsible for whatever mistakes in judgment or errors in fact that may still exist. Generous grants from the Research Committees of the University of Louisville and the University of Toronto facilitated the final preparation of the manuscript.

Finally, it must be noted that this work would never have been completed without the support and faith of my wife, Deborah. The travail was hers, the publication mine.

**The Politics of Civil Rights
in the Truman Administration**

Chapter **1**

THE RHETORIC OF POLITICS

For almost two generations following the Civil War, Negro voters remained loyal supporters of the Republican party. In the 1920's that bond appeared to weaken because of Republican neglect and indifference.[1] This development was borne out in the 1928 presidential election when an unprecedented number of Negroes voted for the Democratic party's

---

1. Richard B. Sherman, "The Harding Administration and the Negro: An Opportunity Lost," *Journal of Negro History* XLIX (1964), 151–68.

candidate, New York's Governor Alfred E. Smith.[2] Yet most Negroes supported Herbert Clark Hoover's bid for the presidency. And in 1932, in the depths of the depression, a majority of Negroes once more voted for Hoover.[3] On this occasion, though, Hoover's margin was substantially reduced: he carried black wards in Chicago and Cleveland by the customary substantial Republican margins but lost the black vote in Manhattan, Pittsburgh, Detroit, and Kansas City, Missouri, to his victorious opponent, Governor Franklin Roosevelt of New York.[4] In 1936 Negroes deserted the Republican party en masse to vote for Roosevelt.[5] Despite the strong effort made by Wendell Willkie in 1940 to bring black voters back to the Republican party, Roosevelt retained their support in his successful third-term campaign.[6] The 1940 election demonstrated clearly that the Negro vote had become part of the Roosevelt political coalition.

Negroes voted for Roosevelt in 1936 and 1940 largely because their economic deprivation, stemming from unemployment and discrimination, had been lessened through the work of such New Deal agencies as the Works Progress Administration and the Farm Security Administration. The favorable treatment accorded Negroes by these agencies

---

2. Henry Lee Moon, *Balance of Power: The Negro Vote* (Garden City, N.Y.: Doubleday, 1948), pp. 18–34; also see David Burner, *The Politics of Provincialism: The Democratic Party in Transition, 1918–1932* (New York: Alfred A. Knopf, 1968), pp. 237–39.

3. Moon, *Balance of Power*, pp. 18–34; also see Samuel Lubell, *White and Black: Test of a Nation* (New York: Harper & Row, 1966), p. 57.

4. Moon, *Balance of Power*, pp. 18–34.

5. For an examination of the issue in the context of the Republican campaign of 1936, see Donald McCoy, *Landon of Kansas* (Lincoln: University of Nebraska Press, 1966), pp. 311–12.

6. Gunnar Myrdal, *An American Dilemma* (New York: Harper & Bros., 1944), p. 496.

was evidence enough that for the first time in the twentieth century, government had taken on "meaning and substance for the Negro masses." [7]

Perhaps the most important action taken by the Roosevelt administration in the field of civil rights, prior to the period of defense mobilization, was initiated by Attorney General Frank Murphy. On February 3, 1939, he authorized the establishment of a Civil Rights Section within the Justice Department as a means of defending the civil rights of all citizens. This step was necessary, Murphy felt, because:

> In a democracy, an important function of the law enforcement branch of government is the aggressive protection of fundamental rights inherent in a free people.
> In America these guarantees are contained in expressed provisions of the Constitution and in acts of Congress. It is the purpose of the Department of Justice to pursue a program of vigilant action in the prosecution of infringement of these rights.
> It must be borne in mind that the authority of the Federal Government in this field is somewhat limited by the fact that many of the constitutional guarantees are not guarantees against infringement by individuals or groups of individuals.[8]

The Justice Department subsequently instituted suits in the federal courts to expand the federal government's jurisdiction in the field of civil rights. For example, it petitioned the

---

7. *Crisis*, XLVII (1940), 18.

8. Quoted in Robert K. Carr, *Federal Protection of Civil Rights: Quest for a Sword* (Ithaca, N.Y.: Cornell University Press, 1947), p. 2; see J. Woodford Howard, Jr., *Mr. Justice Murphy: A Political Biography* (Princeton, N.J.: Princeton University Press, 1968), p. 206, for the following: "In retrospect, creation of the Civil Liberties Unit was Murphy's single most significant contribution as Attorney General."

Supreme Court to declare unconstitutional those statutory provisions denying Negroes the right to vote in southern primaries.[9] Such a move placed the political power of the United States government behind legal attempts to modify or nullify laws sanctioning discrimination, particularly as they applied to voting rights.

Although Murphy's order was scrupulously divorced from politics, President Roosevelt's Executive Order 8802, creating a federal Fair Employment Practices Committee (FEPC), was the product of much political controversy.[10] Roosevelt issued his order on June 25, 1941, in the period of defense mobilization in an effort to placate A. Philip Randolph, a leader of the March on Washington movement, who was threatening to bring 100,000 black Americans to Washington to agitate for an FEPC.[11] The fact that Roosevelt released this executive order had twofold significance: Negroes demonstrated that they could function as an effective pressure group; and the government gave notice to the country that Negro labor would now be utilized in defense production.

Once northern Negroes obtained jobs in defense plants, southern Negroes began to migrate to the North and West in order to find similar employment. Between 1941 and 1946 over a million southern Negroes settled in such cities as

9. Francis Biddle, *In Brief Authority* (New York: Doubleday, 1962), p. 159.

10. Louis Kesselman, *The Social Politics of FEPC: A Study in Reform Pressure Movements* (Chapel Hill: University of North Carolina Press, 1947), p. 14.

11. Herbert Garfinkel, *When Negroes March* (Glencoe, Ill.: Free Press, 1959), p. 27; for a persuasive analysis suggesting that Roosevelt really scored a political victory of sorts with this order, see Richard Dalfiume, *Desegregation of the U.S. Armed Forces: Fighting on Two Fronts, 1939–1953* (Columbia: University of Missouri Press, 1969), pp. 117–22.

Chicago, Detroit, Cleveland, and Los Angeles, thereby increasing both numerical strength and political influence of northern Negroes, who, according to the 1940 census figures, had comprised 4 to 5 percent of the potential voters in the major industrial states of New York, New Jersey, Pennsylvania, Ohio, Michigan, and Illinois.[12] This internal migration was an important political development, the long range implications of which did not escape John Temple Graves, a southern journalist:

It means from now on the Democratic party will be competing for what has heretofore belonged to the Republicans. And because the vote represents something near a balance of power in balance-of-power states, it means also that Northern Negroes may become more important than Southern whites in the party of the white South's long allegiance.[13]

Despite the creation of the Civil Rights Section and the establishment of the FEPC, President Roosevelt rarely supported or endorsed any civil rights legislation.[14] Nor was he willing to attack rhetorically the manifold forms of discrimination pervading American society.[15] Roosevelt pursued

12. Jasper B. Shannon, "Presidential Politics in the South," *Journal of Politics* X (1948), 469–89.

13. Quoted in Moon, *Balance of Power*, p. 22.

14. There was an exception however: on the day of his death, April 12, 1945, he publicly endorsed a bill calling for the creation of a permanent Fair Employment Practices Commission; see Louis Ruchames, *Race, Jobs, and Politics* (New York: Columbia University Press, 1953), p. 126.

15. It must be noted that at a press conference on February 13, 1942, Roosevelt attacked the poll tax; see Samuel I. Rosenman, ed., *The Public Papers and Addresses of Franklin D. Roosevelt*, 13 vols. (New York: Harper & Co., 1950), XI, 96.

this policy of non-involvement in order to avoid open political conflict with the majority of congressional Southern
Democrats, whose votes he needed to assure the success of
his economic program. In other words, his political alliances
in Congress made it tactically impossible for him to become
the spokesman for, let alone the initiator of, a federally
sponsored civil rights campaign; and thus he capitulated to
what he construed to be the politics of necessity even while
the conservative coalition was being organized to thwart his
New Deal program.[16]

Roosevelt's acute awareness of his political situation
helps to explain why he spurned the pleas of his liberal
associates to endorse an anti-lynching bill under consideration by the Congress in the middle and late 1930's. However,
one member of the United States Senate who generally
embraced Roosevelt's New Deal program but also went beyond it to support proposed civil rights legislation was
Harry S. Truman, the junior senator from Missouri. It was
no accident that Truman took an active interest in this
issue. Almost from the beginning of his career as an aspir-
ing politician from Jackson County, Missouri, Truman recognized the significance and importance of the black vote in
Kansas City, thanks to Boss Tom Pendergast (Truman's
benefactor), who had enlarged his base of power in the
early 1920's by courting and winning the loyalty of Negro
voters.[17] As Roy Wilkins, onetime journalist for the Negro
newspaper the *Kansas City Call,* and later a power in national civil rights politics, suggests: "Truman was politi-

---

16. Frank Freidel, *FDR and the South* (Baton Rouge: Louisiana
State University Press, 1965), pp. 71–102; for additional information
see James T. Patterson's *Congressional Conservatism and the New
Deal* (Lexington: University of Kentucky Press, 1967), pp. 156–57.

17. Lyle Dorsett, *The Pendergast Machine* (New York: Oxford
University Press, 1968), p. 82.

cally astute on the race question before he ever came to Washington, because the Pendergast machine was politically astute." [18]

When Truman ran for a local office in his home town of Independence, Missouri, in 1924, the Kansas City chapter of the National Association for the Advancement of Colored People (NAACP) refused to endorse him (perhaps because of the rumor that he had been briefly affiliated with the Ku Klux Klan) ; [19] but in 1926—as a beneficiary of Pendergast votes and patronage—he received strong Negro backing in his campaign for a county-wide judgeship.[20]

Grateful for the assistance which the Negro electorate gave him in his successful 1934 senatorial campaign, Truman joined the liberal bloc in the Senate whenever a civil rights question arose. It was good politics because the black vote in Missouri represented approximately 130,000 ballots, strategically concentrated in its two largest cities, St. Louis and Kansas City.[21] The strength of the Negro bloc was such that, as Truman knew, candidates for public office in Jackson County, as well as the state, would be politically handicapped if that support was denied.[22]

Yet Truman's position was not all that unambiguous—he represented a state with southern prejudices and values, and, therefore, he had to step delicately in regard to the civil rights issue. His own political and personal ambiva-

---

18. Cited in the unpublished comments of Alonzo Hamby, delivered at the American Historical Association meeting in New York on December 29, 1966.

19. Franklin D. Mitchell, *Embattled Democracy: Missouri Politics, 1919–1932* (Columbia: University of Missouri Press, 1968), p. 182.

20. Dalfiume, *Desegregation of the U.S. Armed Forces*, p. 135.

21. Myrdal, *An American Dilemma*, p. 488.

22. For an interesting analysis of how the Missouri Democratic party moved to capture that black vote, see Mitchell, *Embattled Democracy*, pp. 124–39.

lence on the matter was apparently revealed in a remark he made to a southern senator about the 1938 anti-lynching bill: "You know I am against this bill, but if it comes to a vote, I'll have to vote for it. All my sympathies are with you but the Negro vote in Kansas City and St. Louis is too important." [23]

Although Truman was prepared to cast his vote for anti-lynching legislation, he never had the opportunity, as a southern filibuster frustrated all attempts to bring the bill to a floor vote. Nevertheless, during the Seventy-fifth Congress, Truman joined northern liberals by signing cloture petitions and endorsing motions to close debate on an anti-lynching bill.[24] Even though cloture was not obtained, his signature on those petitions suggests that he favored such legislation. During the Seventy-sixth Congress, in 1940, he supported an amendment to the Selective Service Act to prevent discrimination against members of minority groups who wished to volunteer for service in the armed forces.[25] Here, then, was the extent to which Truman was able to create a civil rights voting record while serving his first term in the Senate.

Combining that slight civil rights record with a strong endorsement of New Deal economic legislation, Harry Truman appeared ready in 1940 to seek reelection, which first required him to win renomination in the Democratic primary. His chances were not particularly good because Tom Pendergast—the man most responsible for his earlier success in politics—had lost control of Jackson County, the county which had provided Truman with his margin of

---

23. Samuel Lubell, *The Future of American Politics* (New York: Doubleday & Co., Anchor Books, 1956), p. 8.

24. *Congressional Record*, 75th Cong., 1st Sess., 1938, LXXXIII, 1166, 2007.

25. Ibid., 76th Cong., 2d Sess., 1940, LXXXVI, 10895.

victory in 1934.[26] Truman, furthermore, failed to obtain the endorsement of President Roosevelt, who privately supported Governor Lloyd Stark in the Democratic party senatorial primary.[27] It was rumored that the president, thinking Truman's party position was weak, offered him a federal sinecure as an inducement to withdraw quietly from the race.[28]

Thus faced with bleak prospects, Truman entered the fray knowing that his political future could conceivably rest on whatever decision the voters made in the primary. He campaigned indefatigably throughout the state; entered into, and withdrew from, alliances in an attempt to build a working coalition to defeat Governor Stark and the other candidate, Maurice Milligan; and defended his record with the vigor and salty humor for which he later became famous. Thanks to the assistance of Robert Hannegan, who organized the St. Louis Negro vote on his behalf, Truman squeezed out a tight primary victory over his two opponents.[29] In the general election Truman won by a margin of 44,000 votes.

In light of later developments, one of the more significant civil rights pronouncements Truman made during that election year was delivered on June 15, 1940, at Sedalia, Missouri:

I believe in the brotherhood of man; not merely the brotherhood of white men; but the brotherhood of all

26. Pendergast had been indicted and convicted by the federal government of falsifying his income tax returns, thereby terminating his political hold over Kansas City; see Maurice Milligan, *Missouri Waltz* (New York: Charles Scribners & Sons, 1948), p. 166.

27. Cabell Phillips, *The Truman Presidency: The History of a Triumphant Succession* (New York: Macmillan, 1966), p. 30.

28. Ibid.

29. Ibid.

men before the law. I believe in the Constitution and the Declaration of Independence. In giving to the Negroes the rights that are theirs, we are only acting in accord with ideas of a true democracy. If any class or race can be permanently set apart from, or pushed down below the rest in political and civil rights, so may any class or race when it shall incur the displeasure of its more powerful associates, and we may say farewell to the principles on which we commit our safety.[30]

By limiting his speech to a discussion of the principle of equality, he skirted any programmatic commitment which might have threatened the Jim Crow structure of his native state. The Sedalia address was a quiet affirmation of his devotion to the cause of political democracy and was evidence of his respect for the power of the black vote in Missouri.

A fuller exposition of Truman's civil rights views was contained in a speech he gave to the National Colored Democratic Association in Chicago on July 14, 1940:

I wish to make it clear that I am not appealing for social equality of the Negro. The Negro himself knows better than that, and the highest types of Negro leaders say quite frankly that they prefer the society of their own people. Negroes want justice, not social relations.

We all know the Negro is here to stay and in no way can be removed from our political and economic life and we should recognize his inalienable rights as specified in our Constitution. Can any man claim protection of our laws if he denies that protection to others? [31]

This speech, when measured against typical southern utterances on civil rights, is a model of sobriety and good taste.

---

30. *Congressional Record*, 76th Cong., 3d Sess., 1940, LXXXVI, Appendix 4546.

31. Ibid., Appendix 5367–69.

Truman at least recognized that there was considerable disparity between the professed beliefs of the American people and their actual behavior. Moreover, he understood that the lessening of this disparity required the acceptance and the steady application of the legal principle of equal justice under the law. Again, as at Sedalia, he neglected to offer any concrete recommendations to implement such a principle. A more specific commitment from him could have alienated many of his white Missouri constituents.

During Truman's second term in the Senate, he became nationally prominent through his chairmanship of the Senate Special Committee Investigating the National Defense Program.[32] In the early months of his chairmanship, he was unexpectedly embroiled in a dispute with the NAACP having to do with the subject of racial discrimination in the defense program. The issue arose after a small group of liberal senators, led by Senator Robert F. Wagner of New York, introduced Senate Resolution 75 calling for the creation of an autonomous committee to investigate precisely the problem the Truman committee would have preferred to ignore.[33] Although S.R. 75 was later approved by a subcommittee of the Senate Education and Labor committee on April 24, 1941, its opponents, mostly Southern Democrats working on behalf of Senator James F. Byrnes of South Carolina, successfully tabled it in full committee; they wanted the Truman committee to handle the matter, thereby assuring that no meaningful investigation would take place.[34] Then, suddenly, at a time when the March on

---

32. Phillips, *The Truman Presidency*, pp. 34–37.

33. A brief description of Wagner's work on behalf of S.R. 75 can be found in J. Joseph Huthmacher, *Senator Robert Wagner and the Rise of Urban Liberalism* (New York: Atheneum, 1968), p. 275.

34. NAACP press release, July 3, 1941, Folder S.R. 71, Box 359, NAACP Papers, Library of Congress (hereafter cited as L.C.).

Washington movement was emerging as a possible threat to the administration, the Truman committee announced that hearings on the subject of racial discrimination in defense industries would be scheduled in late June or early July.[35] The NAACP at once charged that the proposed hearings represented "a frenzied and hasty attempt to dodge a real investigation into discrimination against the Negro in national defense work." [36]

Aware of the possible disengenuousness of the Truman move and still hoping to salvage the objectives of S.R. 75, Walter White, executive secretary of the NAACP, wrote President Roosevelt on July 7 (a copy of the letter having also been sent to Senator Truman) suggesting the need for a brief delay in the Truman hearings.[37] Such a delay, White felt, would provide time to lay the groundwork for a more thorough and substantial investigation into the problem, by allowing for the appearance of many more witnesses than the several contemplated by the committee. In seeming compliance with White's request, Hugh Fulton, chief counsel of the Truman committee, wired White that "at your suggestion committee hearings on race discrimination have been postponed but no definite date has been determined for hearings." So much, then, for the fate of S.R. 75.[38]

Shortly thereafter, in what could be construed as an act of political fence-mending at home, a Truman subcommittee stopped in Kansas City and St. Louis to investigate racial discrimination in defense-related employment.[39] In both cit-

---

35. Ibid.

36. Ibid.

37. Walter White to Franklin Roosevelt, July 7, 1941, Folder S.R. 71, Box 359, NAACP Papers, L.C.

38. Telegram to Walter White from Hugh Fulton, July 11, 1941. Folder S.R. 71, Box 359, NAACP Papers, L.C.

39. Roy Wilkins to Ira Lewis, September 10, 1941, Folder S.R. 71, Box 359, NAACP Papers, L.C.

ies black delegations were courteously received and their various complaints carefully noted. But the true character and spirit of the investigation is best captured in a short paragraph contained in a letter Roy Wilkins, assistant secretary of the NAACP, wrote to Ira Lewis, president of the Pittsburgh Courier Publishing Company, concerning the hearing in St. Louis:

> After the hearing was concluded, word filtered back to a member of the Negro committee through a sympathetic white connection that one of the secretaries of the committee had made the remark that the Truman committee was "accepting the Negro complaints, but did not intend to do anything about them; and if anybody thought the committee was going to help black bastards into $100-a-week jobs, they were sadly mistaken." [40]

In his letter Wilkins further observed that "we have felt all along that the Truman committee was not going to do very much on this matter. . . . This remark in St. Louis, if true, would seem to indicate that the committee does not take the whole business very seriously." [41] (Harry Vaughn, a Truman aide, was subsequently identified as the individual responsible for the remark Wilkins quoted in his letter.) [42]

During the same period (1941–44), Truman also gave his unqualified support to all legislation designed to finance the activities of the FEPC. In 1941 he introduced a bill calling for a combat command for Negro General Benjamin Davis; in 1942 he voted for cloture to terminate debate on the poll tax filibuster; and in 1943 he supported a resolution "that would have provided for an investigation of the effect of

40. Ibid.
41. Ibid.
42. Walter White to Chester Stovall, September 11, 1941, Folder S.R. 71, Box 359, NAACP Papers, L.C.

segregation on the opportunities of Negroes in the armed services." [43] It must also be noted that on August 25, 1942, Truman voted against an anti–poll tax amendment to the soldier's vote bill for national elections; the amendment carried by a vote of 33 to 20 (with 43 senators present but not voting), and was thus included in the bill that became the law of the land.[44] Here was an occasion when Truman had a direct opportunity to vote against the poll tax but refused to do so. Joining Senator Alben Barkley of Kentucky, a fellow border-state politician, and many southerners, he obviously voted in support of the political biases of his fellow white Missourians. Whether Truman's vote was a reflection of their views or his own prejudices, or both, is difficult to determine.

The 1944 Democratic national convention took place in the middle of Senator Truman's second term. That convention was for Senator Truman an example of political serendipity at work. As the convention approached, Truman was asked by James F. Byrnes, wartime defense mobilizer, to nominate him as Roosevelt's vice-presidential running mate.[45] Truman was assured by Byrnes that his candidacy had received the approval and blessing of President Roosevelt.[46] In reality Byrnes stood little chance of obtaining the nomination because his racist views were unacceptable to the strong liberal bloc still committed to Henry Wallace, the incumbent vice-president. But unbeknown to Wallace's fervent supporters, their hopes for his renomination had been undermined by the big city bosses—particularly Edward J.

---

43. Dalfiume, *Desegregation of the U.S. Armed Forces*, p. 136.

44. *Congressional Record*, 77th Cong., 2d Sess., 1942, Vol. LXXXVIII, Part 5, p. 6971.

45. Phillips, *The Truman Presidency*, p. 39.

46. Ibid.

Flynn of the Bronx—and other leaders of the party, including Robert Hannegan, now the chairman of the Democratic National Committee and a Truman man.[47] They helped convince Roosevelt before the convention started that his election chances would be jeopardized if Wallace remained on the ticket. Roosevelt had to find a suitable replacement for Wallace, that is, someone who would not antagonize the party liberals and yet could calm southern fears about the race question.

After some deliberation Roosevelt chose Truman because his views and record, unlike those of Wallace and Byrnes, could best preserve party harmony and unity. As a member of the centrist faction of the Democratic party, Truman was a New Dealer by necessity and a political moderate by inclination: hence, his selection would be in the best interest of the party. Truman did not really want the nomination; he was very happy in his role as senator, his life was uncomplicated, and he and his family enjoyed their privacy in the hectic political surroundings of Washington. It was only after Roosevelt had informed Truman that his refusal to co-operate could lead to "the breakup of the Democratic party in the middle of a war" that he consented to join the ticket.[48] As Samuel Lubell suggests, echoing Roosevelt's own fear, it was the nomination of Truman or someone like him which may have prevented the dissolution of the Democratic party into two permanently warring groups.[49]

Conversely, Wallace's reputation as a militant advocate of racial justice played a major role in his defeat in 1944. (He had not established a liberal record in race relations in

47. Edward J. Flynn, *You're the Boss* (New York: Viking Press, 1947), p. 181; Phillips, *The Truman Presidency*, pp. 41–42.

48. Phillips, *The Truman Presidency*, p. 47.

49. Lubell, *The Future of American Politics*, p. 21.

the years he served as secretary of agriculture;[50] but by 1944 his evolving views had made him a threat to the South.) When Wallace addressed the convention to second the nomination of Roosevelt, he did not equivocate on this issue. He said:

> The future belongs to those who go down the line unswervingly for the liberal principles of both political democracy and economic democracy regardless of race, color, or religion. In a political, educational and economic sense there must be no inferior races. The poll tax must go. Equal educational opportunities must come. The future must bring equal wages for equal work regardless of sex and race.[51]

Such strong opinion further intensified the South's hatred for him, thereby making his political demise that much more predictable once the roll call of the states began. It was no surprise, then, that Truman received the nomination by an overwhelming margin.

Although the South was delighted with Truman's nomination, black delegates to the convention were most unhappy with what had happened; in every delegation caucus, so it was reported, they had been Wallace's strongest supporters.[52] As a reflection of obvious Negro disappointment with the results of the convention, Negro newspapers caustic ly appraised the new vice-presidential nominee. The *Norfolk Journal and Guide* wrote: "Senator Truman is a conservative Democrat, who, it appears, was given the

---

50. Allen F. Kifer, "The Negro Under the New Deal," (Ph.D. dissertation, University of Wisconsin, 1961), pp. 223–25; for a strong defense of Wallace's civil rights record in the years he served in the Roosevelt cabinet, see Curtis D. MacDougal, *Gideon's Army*, 3 vols. (New York: Marzani & Munsell, 1965), III, 656–61.

51. *Pittsburgh Courier*, July 29, 1944, p. 6.

52. Ibid.

nomination for Vice Presidency for reasons of political expediency." [53] The *Pittsburgh Courier* opined that "Truman is a long way from being a Henry Wallace," and that his nomination was an "appeasement of the South which must rank in cowardice and shortsightedness with the ineptitude shown by Chamberlain at Munich." [54]

To counteract the disillusionment and bitterness which could have quickly spread through the ranks of Negro Democrats, Senator Truman allowed himself to be interviewed on August 3, 1944, by a journalist from the widely circulated and influential *Pittsburgh Courier*. Among the statements made by Truman was:

I have always been for equality of opportunity in work, working conditions and political rights. I think the Negro in the armed forces ought to have the same treatment and opportunities as every other member of the armed forces. I think this should also be true of Negro women in the armed forces. . . . I have a record for fair play toward my Negro fellow citizens that will stand examination.

When asked whether he had heard Wallace's convention speech, Truman commented that he had not, but "no honest American can disagree with Henry Wallace. What he said was gospel." [55]

In a later interview, this time with Morris Milgram, national secretary of the Worker's Defense League, Truman discussed the race issue in an unabashedly candid manner. He asserted that if Negroes sat down to eat in a drugstore in Independence, Missouri, "they would be booted out" because the management of these places had the right to refuse to serve anyone they pleased; that Negroes in St.

---

53. Aug. 5, 1944, p. 6.
54. *Pittsburgh Courier*, July 29, 1944, p. 1.
55. Ibid., Aug. 5, 1944, p. 1.

Louis had started a "push day once a week" to shove white people out of the bars there; and that such a day also existed in Washington, which explained why his daughter was not allowed to go downtown on the street car on Thursday anymore. "It is not safe," Truman declared, "they push people off the street cars." [56] Apparently, Milgram had touched a sensitive nerve, giving Truman an opportunity to express his abhorrence of the theory and practice of social equality. At the time this interview was published, Truman denied having made these remarks.[57]

/ As the campaign progressed, it became evident that Truman's presence on the Democratic ticket was inspiring little or no confidence among black Americans, who still were lamenting the loss of Henry Wallace/ A survey of Negro editorial opinion indicated that a number of Negro newspapers, including the *Pittsburgh Courier* and the *Kansas City Call*, had endorsed the Republican Dewey-Bricker ticket because, among other reasons, they resented the selection of Truman as Roosevelt's running mate and, further, feared the prospect that Roosevelt, if elected, would not serve out a fourth term.[58] The *Courier* even went so far as to present sworn affidavits that Truman had been a member of the Ku Klux Klan for a brief period in 1922.[59] This report must have pleased the Republican party, since it was busily promoting a whispering campaign in Harlem to the effect that "Roosevelt is old and may die and you will then have a KKK man in the White House." [60] The Republicans may have been exploiting a canard, but unless Truman handled the matter

---

56. Ibid., Oct. 21, 1944, pp. 1, 4.
57. Ibid., Oct. 28, 1944, p. 1.
58. Ibid., Nov. 4, 1944, pp. 1, 5.
59. Ibid., pp. 5–6.
60. *Norfolk Journal and Guide*, Nov. 11, 1944, p. 1.

forthrightly, the Democratic party could have been seriously embarrassed on the eve of the election.

The issue exploded with dramatic suddenness in the late stages of the 1944 campaign, at a time when Truman was in Los Angeles campaigning for the party's ticket. While there, he endorsed Hal Styles, a local Democratic candidate for Congress, who, though he had liberal credentials, had been a one-time member of the Klan.[61] Though Truman was apparently aware of Styles's past, he still offered him his support and claimed that he was "one of ours." [62] Immediately after this pronouncement from the senator, David O. Selznick, a powerful West Coast movie mogul, wired Walter White on October 17, demanding to know how he could still support the national Democratic ticket in light of Truman's endorsement.[63] Obviously troubled by the Selznick telegram, White asked Truman on October 19 to explain his support for Styles and, further, to respond to the remarks of Governor Chauncey Sparks of Alabama which had been quoted in the *Birmingham News* of July 23. The Sparks quote, which White included in his telegram, read as follows: "I think the South has won a substantial victory in securing the defeat of Vice President Wallace. I find him (Senator Truman) safe on states rights and the right of the state to control qualifications of its electors. In the matter of race relations Senator Truman told me he is the son of an unreconstructed rebel mother. I think the South has won a victory." [64]

On October 30 Truman dispatched a telegram to White in

61. Telegram to Walter White from David O. Selznick, October 17, 1944, Truman Folder (1944), Box 359, NAACP Papers, L.C.

62. Ibid.

63. Ibid.

64. Telegram to Harry Truman from Walter White, October 19, 1944, Truman Folder (1944), Box 359, NAACP Papers, L.C.

which he defended his voting record on civil rights, argued that he had been misquoted, and stated that Styles himself had had the support of many liberals in Southern California. About the issue of the Klan, Truman suggested that the matter had been raised by Republicans merely for the purpose of partisan politics, and thus the charges were without foundation. He assured White that "the Klan fought me and I fought the Klan. The Klan is repugnant to every policy and every principle I have advocated and struggled for all my life." [65] Interestingly, Truman ignored White's request for a comment on the remarks of Governor Sparks of Alabama.

During the last weekend of the campaign, Truman publicly confronted his critics. Speaking at a Liberal party rally in New York on October 31, 1944, where he was joined by Vice-President Wallace, Truman affirmed that "in supporting the President in these broad programs for human liberty and tolerance, no man in the United States Senate has a more consistent voting record than myself." That record, he noted, included a vote for cloture in order to terminate a southern filibuster against a proposed anti-lynching law, support for federal legislation to outlaw the poll tax, and an endorsement for FEPC appropriations.[66]

On election day Roosevelt won a fourth term with the help he received from Negro voters. Yet that support was not so generously given as in the past; some blacks, including such prominent spokesmen and leaders as W. E. B. DuBois, Channing Tobias, William Hastie, and Charles Johnson, had been upset by Roosevelt's failure to support Wallace for renomination and by his reluctance to press for

---

65. Telegram to Walter White from Harry Truman, October 30, 1944, Truman Folder (1944), Box 359, NAACP Papers, L.C.; also see *New York Times*, Oct. 27, 1944.

66. Senatorial Speech File, Truman Papers, Harry S. Truman Library (hereafter cited as HSTL).

more than a token civil rights plank in the 1944 Democratic party platform.[67] However strong their reservations might have been, they still voted for Roosevelt, as did many hundreds of thousands of other Negroes. Here, perhaps, was the margin of difference between success and failure. It has been estimated that if there had been a shift of 303,414 votes in fifteen non-southern states, Governor Thomas E. Dewey would have captured the 175 electoral votes he needed to win the presidency; in eight of those fifteen states, it was the Negro vote which placed them in the victory column of the Democratic party.[68]

Upon the death of Franklin Roosevelt on April 12, 1945, Harry S. Truman became president, thereby inheriting many of Roosevelt's unresolved domestic problems, not the least of which was civil rights. At his first presidential press conference on April 17, 1945, he was queried about his civil rights position by a representative of the Negro Newspaper Publishers Association.

Q: Mr. President, probably as much as any group, the passing of President Roosevelt is very keenly felt by the Negroes in America, as they looked upon him as sort of a symbol of justice and equal opportunity. I wonder if you would comment on the things that they were so specifically interested in and felt they knew where the President stood: on the fair employment practice, the right to vote without being hampered by poll taxes, and all that?

A: I will give you some advice. All you need to do is read the Senate record of one Harry S. Truman.[69]

---

67. Moon, *Balance of Power*, p. 34.

68. Ibid., p. 35.

69. *Public Papers of the Presidents: Harry S. Truman, 1945*, (Washington: United States Government Printing Office, 1961), pp. 10–11; for editorial opinion critical of Truman's civil rights views at the time of his elevation to the presidency, see the *Pittsburgh Courier*, Apr. 21, 1945, p. 6; and *Norfolk Journal and Guide*, Apr. 21, 1945, p. 10.

And to Walter White, who pledged him his aid, Truman wrote, "I have received a great heritage from my lamented predecessor. I shall strive to attain the ideals for which he fought and am strengthened by the assurance of your support in that effort." [70]

A significant aspect of Truman's record, which has already been indicated, was his endorsement of FEPC, one of the most controversial of the federal wartime agencies. FEPC had been created by Executive Orders 8802 in 1941 and 9346 in 1943, and was financed until 1944 out of the President's Emergency Fund. The president's authority to grant funds to specific executive agencies without congressional approval had been curtailed, however, with the attachment of the Russell Amendment of 1944 to the Independent Offices Appropriation Act of 1945.[71] This amendment was designed to destroy the executive autonomy of FEPC, as well as other governmental agencies created by executive order, since it required the president to seek congressional appropriations for all executive expenditures. Unless the president could wheedle funds from a recalcitrant Congress to support such agencies as FEPC, they soon would be faced with extinction. Congress, after much debate, did appropriate $500,000 for the FEPC in 1944, but in 1945 the agency's future was seriously threatened when all of the funds President Roosevelt had requested for its operation were deleted by the House Appropriations Committee from the Wartime Agencies Appropriations Bill.[72] Only after a series of House

---

70. Harry Truman to Walter White, April 26, 1945, Truman Folder (3), Box 359, NAACP Papers, L.C.

71. *United States Civil Rights Commission Report 3, Employment* (Washington: United States Government Printing Office, 1961), p. 173.

72. Ibid., p. 122.

and Senate compromises—which drastically reduced the Roosevelt request—did the FEPC receive the token sum of $250,000 to continue its work for no longer than one additional year, since the bill, which became law on July 13, 1945, stipulated "that in no case shall this fund be available for expenditure beyond June 30, 1946." [73] Clearly, then, Congress had sounded the death knell for the wartime FEPC by passing the Wartime Agencies Appropriations Bill for the fiscal year 1946.

To his credit, President Truman tried to reverse the decision of the Appropriations Committee; but having failed to win his way in the House, he accepted, without demur, the ultimate compromise the House and Senate made with respect to the wartime agency.[74] On the other hand, Truman did endorse all congressional efforts to create a permanent FEPC; his views on this matter were contained in a letter of June 5, 1945, sent to Congressman Adolph Sabath, chairman of the House Rules Committee and a friend of FEPC. The president declared: "To abandon at this time the fundamental principle upon which the FEP committee was established is unthinkable. . . . The principle and policy of fair employment practice should be established permanently as a part of our national law." [75] On the same day, Truman also wrote to Senator Dennis Chavez, the leader of the FEPC bloc in the Senate, informing him that "as soon as it becomes appropriate in the Senate, let me

---

73. Ibid., p. 129.

74. Will Maslow, "FEPC—A Case History in Parliamentary Maneuver," *University of Chicago Law Review* XIII (1946), 407–45.

75. Harry S. Truman to Adolph Sabath, June 5, 1945, Truman Papers, OF 40, HSTL; on June 1, 1945, White had written Truman asking him to request a vote from Sabath: Walter White to Harry Truman, June 1, 1945, Truman Folder (3), Box 359, NAACP Papers, L.C.

know and I shall send you a similar letter." [76] Yet, in spite of this presidential endorsement, the House Rules Committee by a tie vote succeeded in blocking, on June 12, 1945, all attempts to obtain a floor vote on a permanent FEPC bill which had been introduced by Congresswoman Mary Norton, a Democrat from New Jersey.

Although the House had pigeonholed a permanent FEPC bill, the president stood to gain additional political support from liberals who had been favorably impressed with his June 5 letter to Congressman Sabath; and according to a White House mail analysis, the several thousand messages he received in reference to the letter indicated that it "had established him as a liberal in the eyes of liberals. Prior to the letter, letter writers asked him to follow in President Roosevelt's footsteps. Afterward, they praised him for his independent and courageous stand." [77]

Whether Truman deserved these plaudits of liberals is another question. Louis Ruchames, a historian of FEPC, suggests otherwise:

> In passing, it may be mentioned that although the President's letter was acclaimed as an important contribution to the struggle for an FEPC appropriation and for the creation of a permanent FEPC, the hosannahs which greeted it were not entirely merited. Although it did urge passage of permanent FEPC legislation, it made no request for an appropriation for the existing FEPC which was then fighting for its life. One wonders whether it was the President's intention to speak out on behalf of a bill which had little chance of passing and at the same time do nothing to secure the funds for the existing FEPC, which would have been materially aided by his efforts.

---

76. Harry S. Truman to Dennis Chavez, June 5, 1945, Truman Papers, OF 40, HSTL.

77. Analysis of Presidential Mail on FEPC, Truman Papers, OF 40, HSTL.

Was it perhaps an attempt to curry favor with liberal groups in and out of Congress while at the same time not antagonizing those who opposed FEPC? [78]

This hypothesis points up Truman's dilemma vis-à-vis FEPC in the last half of 1945. Perhaps Truman could have mustered the requisite votes to increase the appropriation for the wartime agency, but if he had resolutely battled the foes of FEPC, in all probability many moderates in Congress whose support he needed on other issues would have deserted him. Yet, by ignoring the issue of a permanent FEPC bill, his uneasy friendship with the liberal bloc in Congress would have been threatened. Hoping to avoid conflict and preferring the politics of stalemate, Truman chose to dodge all firm commitments that might have taken him off dead center. For some time to come, he would do nothing to upset the precarious political equilibrium which had helped to elevate him to the White House.

As Congress continued to debate the FEPC question, President Truman submitted on September 6, 1945, a twenty-one point message to Congress to provide it with guidelines for action on pressing social and economic matters, thereby facilitating America's transition from a wartime to a consumer-based peacetime economy. Included in the various proposals was another suggestion that Congress create a permanent FEPC:

In the reconversion period and thereafter, we should make every effort to continue this American ideal. It is one of the fundamentals of our political philosophy, and it should be an integral part of our economy.

The FEPC is continuing during the transition period. I have already requested that legislation be enacted placing

---

78. Ruchames, *Race, Jobs, and Politics,* p. 126.

the FEPC on a permanent basis. I repeat that recommendation.[79]

Truman's endorsement of FEPC legislation provoked some sharp comments from the *Pittsburgh Courier:* "President Truman asserts that he favors such legislation but there is as yet no evidence that he has tried to use any of his great power to bring pressure on the recalcitrant Southern Senators and Representatives who persist in using every device at their command to sabotage the measure." [80] Also in the same spirit, A. Philip Randolph wrote to Matthew Connelly, the president's appointment secretary: "Unless the President takes a hand in mobilizing the administrative forces in the House and the Senate behind these bills, the opposition, as in the past through filibuster and power politics and other devious tactics, will make a farce out of this whole thing." [81] Speaking for leading advocates of an FEPC, including Bishop G. Bromley Oxnam, William Green, president of the American Federation of Labor (AFL), and Rabbi Stephen J. Wise, Randolph sought in September and October, 1945, to arrange an appointment with the president to discuss with him the need for prompt White House action on behalf of the stalled FEPC legislation. Randolph met with no success, for Truman refused to meet with him about such an explosive matter.[82]

---

79. *Public Papers of the Presidents: Harry S. Truman, 1945,* p. 282.

80. *Pittsburgh Courier,* Sept. 22, 1945, p. 6; also see *Norfolk Journal and Guide,* Oct. 6, 1945, p. 1.

81. A. Philip Randolph to Matthew J. Connelly, October 10, 1945, Truman Papers, OF 40, HSTL. Randolph was international president of the Brotherhood of Sleeping Car Porters and cochairman of the National Committee for a Permanent FEPC.

82. Truman Papers, OF 40, HSTL. Walter White, too, was rebuffed in his efforts to speak privately with Truman, presumably about the same problem; see Charles G. Ross to Walter White, August 14, 1945, Truman Folder (3), Box 359, NAACP Papers, L.C.

The president was reluctant to embrace a political cause that might have damaged him, unless the potential political return for such a move promised to be as great, if not greater, than the risks involved. But when it was politically expedient to act, he did so; e.g., reportedly at the request of Negro Congressman William Dawson, he appointed in early October, 1945, Irvin C. Mollison, a Chicago lawyer, to a judgeship on the United States Customs Court, thereby making him the first Negro appointed to a federal judgeship within the United States.[83] Generally, however, caution and prudence characterized the president's behavior on questions involving race relations in 1945. More specifically, he wanted to remain on good terms with Congress, and not move beyond the limits of what was politically acceptable or permissible as defined by his centrist relationship with both factions of the party and the party organization he now headed.

Truman's handling of the Capital Transit Company strike illustrates this last point. Members of the Amalgamated Association of Street, Electric, Railway, and Motor Coach Employees of America, Division 689, in November 1945, had called a strike against the Capital Transit Company of Washington, D.C. According to the president, the strike was not authorized since it violated a written contract between the union and the employer that was not due to expire until June 30, 1946.[84] Hence, on November 21, 1945, Truman, operating under still existing wartime authority, seized the company to restore transportation facilities for commuters in the District of Columbia. On November 23, 1945, the FEPC, under the chairmanship of Malcolm Ross, prepared to issue a directive authorizing the company "to cease and desist from practices and policies which have

---

83. *Norfolk Journal and Guide*, Oct. 6, 1945, pp. 1, 8.
84. Truman Papers, OF 272, HSTL.

resulted in the denial of employment to Negroes, because of race, as conductors, motormen, bus operators, and traffic checkers." [85] On the same day the president received a telegram from Walter White, asking him to put into immediate practice the "stated policy of hiring qualified Negroes." [86] Ignoring White's request, Truman, on November 24, 1945, ordered the committee not to issue its directive. [87]

This action so angered Charles Houston, a Negro member of FEPC, that he resigned from the committee on December 3, 1945. In his letter of resignation to the president, Houston asserted that as long as the company was under governmental control "the Federal Manager of the Capital Transit system is not only empowered to, but must enforce the national policy of non-discrimination in employment." [88] Furthermore, he suggested that there was more at stake in this case than the question of fair employment of Negroes by the Capital Transit Company: "The failure of the Government to enforce democratic practices and to protect minorities in its own capital makes its expressed concern for national minorities abroad somewhat specious, and its interference in the domestic affairs of other countries very premature." [89] On December 7, 1945, the president in accepting Houston's resignation wrote:

The law requires that when the Government seizes a property under such [wartime] circumstances it shall be operated under the terms and conditions of employment

---

85. Ibid.

86. Telegram to Harry Truman from Walter White, November 23, 1945, Truman Papers, OF 272, HSTL.

87. Truman Papers, OF 40, HSTL; also see *Pittsburgh Courier*, Dec. 8, 1945, pp. 1, 8.

88. Truman Papers, OF 40, HSTL.

89. Ibid.

which were in effect at the time possession of such plant, mine, or facility was so taken.

The property was not seized for the purpose of enforcing the aims of the FEPC, laudable as these aims are, but to guarantee transportation for the citizens of Washington and vicinity.

As anxious as I am for Congress to pass legislation for a permanent FEPC, I cannot contravene an Act of Congress in order to carry out the present Committee's aims.[90]

As the Capital Transit issue began to fade away, President Truman issued on December 20, 1945, Executive Order 9664 reducing the operating authority of the FEPC. Executive Order 9664, which had been drafted by the FEPC agency itself, stated:

As part of its duties the Committee shall investigate, make findings and recommendations, and report to the President, with respect to discrimination in industries engaged in work contributing to the production of military supplies or to the effective transition to a peacetime economy.[91]

Now functioning under a new directive, the FEPC was no longer empowered to release "cease and desist" proclamations; the Truman order had effectively reduced it to a mere fact-finding agency. It is safe to assume that Truman had to sacrifice FEPC in order to secure the cooperation of the South for at least part of his domestic program. Clearly, Truman was finding it difficult to reconcile the liberal principles espoused and votes taken in the years when he was still a senator from Missouri with the more complex political realities that confronted him as president.

---

90. Ibid.
91. Executive Order 9664, 10 Federal Register 15301.

Among those political realities Truman could not ignore was the omnipresent conservative Democratic-Republican coalition which had effectively throttled most of Truman's legislative program. That program had been drafted largely to resolve problems created by the demobilization and reconversion process. By the winter of 1946, however, the country was plagued by such intense labor-management conflict that Truman had no choice but to seek congressional assistance to cope with the emergency.[92] But Congress rejected the president's recommendations, forcing him to go to the people, via radio, on January 3, 1946, to explain to them why these "grave problems" were not being adequately handled. One of the problems Truman singled out for discussion was FEPC. He suggested in his talk that "a small handful of Congressmen in the Rules Committee of the House" had prevented the Norton FEPC bill from reaching a vote by the Congress.[93]

In his State of the Union message of January 21, 1946, Truman once more referred to the need for a permanent FEPC.[94] And he continued to endorse the bill whenever it was politic to do so. For example, writing to A. Philip Randolph on February 6, 1946, Truman reaffirmed his comitment to the principle of a permanent FEPC. "I want you to know," wrote the president, "that I regard FEPC legislation as an integral part of my re-conversion program and shall contribute my efforts to give the Congress a chance to vote on it." [95] On February 28, 1946, a Truman spokesman, Louis

---

92. *Public Papers of the Presidents: Harry S. Truman, 1946* (Washington: United States Government Printing Office, 1962), pp. 1–8.

93. Ibid., p. 3.

94. *New York Times*, Jan. 22, 1946, p. 17.

95. Harry Truman to A. Philip Randolph, February 6, 1946, OF 40, HSTL; also see *Norfolk Journal and Guide*, Feb. 23, 1946, pp. 1–2.

Schwellenbach, secretary of labor, appeared before a huge
FEPC rally at Madison Square Garden to endorse the Norton
bill, which was then tied up in a House committee.[96]
In spite of his many public commitments to FEPC, the
president rarely exerted pressure on Congress to act on this
legislation. Throughout January and February, 1946, only
once did Truman indirectly criticize the Senate filibuster
which made it impossible to obtain a floor vote on a permanent FEPC bill that had successfully cleared committee.[97]
And, more important, he failed to rally support for the
projected cloture vote designed to terminate the debate on
this issue, a move which would have surely angered the
South.[98] Thus, aware of the realities of power on Capitol
Hill, Truman simply refused to climb into the political
arena on behalf of such a potentially divisive cause. In other
words, Truman preferred to stand on the sidelines where he
could play the role of benevolent spectator rather than run
the risk of doing battle for what he felt was a losing effort.
While avoiding a bruising fight, he could still make certain
ritualistic gestures on behalf of a good cause. A speech here
and a letter there would assure him of some liberal support
and gratitude for his efforts. In this manner he could keep
his lines of communication open with all factions while
retaining a free hand to do exactly as he pleased in any
given situation.

As the Senate prepared to vote on cloture, Roy Wilkins,
assistant secretary of the NAACP, wrote Robert Hannegan,
the chairman of the Democratic National Committee, that
"the Democratic party has promised the passage of an FEPC
bill and if the party permits a minority of its members in

---

96. *Norfolk Journal and Guide*, Mar. 9, 1946, pp. 1–2.

97. *Public Papers of the Presidents: Harry S. Truman, 1946*, p. 94.

98. See I. F. Stone, "Where There Is No Vision," *Nation* CLXII
(1946), 111–19.

the Senate to prevent this bill from even being considered by the Senate, it is certain that the failure will be noted in the 1946 and 1948 elections." [99] On February 9, 1946, the advocates of cloture, needing support from at least two-thirds of all those members of the Senate present and voting, lost their battle. Forty-eight senators, including 22 Democrats, 25 Republicans, and 1 Progressive (Robert M. La Follette, Jr., of Wisconsin), voted for cloture; 36 senators, including 28 Democrats and 8 Republicans, rejected it.[100]

If Truman appeared to be almost as politically cautious as Roosevelt, for somewhat similar reasons, his liberal rhetoric served to distinguish him from his immediate predecessor. Truman never hesitated to pronounce his steadfast loyalty to the ideas of justice and equality. For instance, speaking spontaneously to a group of Negro newspaper editors at the White House on March 1, 1946, the president remarked:

> There are things that are necessary today of course—it is a pity that they have to be done—but there are certain things that are necessary to be done to give us the Bill of Rights as it is written in the Constitution of the United States. We want to see equal opportunity for everybody, regardless of race, creed or color.[101]

Nevertheless, because of political pressure or personal whim, Truman sometimes reaffirmed an equivocal stand which he had taken as a Senator, as is indicated by his

---

99. *Norfolk Journal and Guide*, Feb. 16, 1946, p. 2.

100. *Congressional Record*, 79th Cong., Vol. XCII, part 1, p. 1219; also see Maslow, "FEPC—A Case History in Parliamentary Maneuver," pp. 407–45.

101. Transcript of Press Conference, March 1, 1946, Records of the White House Official Reporter, Truman Papers, HSTL.

remarks about poll tax legislation. Discussing the matter on April 6, 1946, in Chicago, he suggested that poll tax legislation was a question of state responsibility.[102] However, at a White House press conference on April 11, 1946, Truman, attempting to blunt possible public criticism of his April 6 comment, modified his earlier remark by suggesting that there was a legitimate need for both state and federal action on the problem of the poll tax and FEPC—as far as he was concerned, state and federal action complemented each other.[103] The sudden change from the April 6 position to the one of April 11 indicates that Truman wanted to avoid—if possible—alienating liberal public opinion.

But because a de facto political coalition—essentially conservative in character—controlled Congress, the Truman administration had no hope or intention of rescuing FEPC from oblivion. This organization, one of the uniquely successful creations of the wartime period, finally had to be dissolved. On May 18, 1946, President Truman informed Malcolm Ross, the committee's chairman, that funds were no longer available to sustain further activity.[104] Consequently, on June 28, 1946, Ross and his fellow committee members submitted their resignations to the president. Accompanying this letter was a report which summarized and analyzed the committee's activity subsequent to the period of its first published statement of 1943.[105]

The committee's letter, published as the preface to its survey, *Final Report,* declared that "in the majority of

---

102. *Public Papers of the Presidents: Harry S. Truman, 1946,* p. 185.

103. Ibid., pp. 192–93.

104. Truman Papers, OF 40, HSTL.

105. United States Fair Employment Practice Committee, *Final Report* (Washington: United States Government Printing Office, 1946).

cases discriminatory practices by employers and unions can be reduced or eliminated by simple negotiation when the work of the negotiator is backed up by firm and explicit national policy." "However," the letter continued, "executive authority is not enough to insure compliance in the face of stubborn opposition. Only legislative authority will insure compliance in the small number of cases in which employers or unions or both refuse after negotiation to abide by the national policy of nondiscrimination." The committee's findings further indicated that in the period following V-J Day the wartime gains of Negro, Mexican-American, and Jewish workers "are being dissipated through an unchecked revival of discriminatory practices." In the committee's opinion only federal legislation could prevent a complete collapse of those humane employment standards that had been established because of the emergency.[106] The chief executive, in accepting the committee's letter and report, stated: "The degree of effectiveness which FEPC was able to attain has shown once and for all that it is possible to equalize job opportunity by governmental action, and thus eventually to eliminate the influence of prejudice in the field of employment." [107]

Following the demise of FEPC, the president felt that, "in the absence of FEP statute, . . . steps should be taken to insure compliance with this policy of nondiscrimination in Federal service and by government contractors." [108] On July 22, 1946, in an attempt to initiate some action on this mat-

---

106. Ibid., p. v–vi.

107. *Public Papers of the Presidents: Harry S. Truman, 1946*, p. 334. At the time Truman penned this reply, his administration, specifically, the Veterans Bureau and the Department of Agriculture, was discriminating against Negroes; see *Pittsburgh Courier*, May 18, 1946, p. 6.

108. Memorandum to David K. Niles from Harry S. Truman, July 22, 1946, Philleo Nash Files, Box 21, HSTL.

ter, Truman authorized David Niles, his administrative assistant on minority problems, to prod the various federal agencies into investigating all alleged charges of discrimination and to rectify all legitimate grievances.[109] There is no record to indicate that the president's instructions were implemented, nor is there any evidence to suggest that Truman himself inquired why a report from Niles was not forthcoming. It can be assumed that owing to the indifference of Mr. Niles, or to his own lack of concern, Truman failed to challenge discriminatory employment practices carried on by the government.[110]

Truman did score a political triumph of sorts (that was related to civil rights) with his successful "purge" of Representative Roger Slaughter of Missouri's Fifth Congressional District, i.e., Kansas City and environs. As a member of the House Rules Committee, Slaughter had broken a tie vote on the Norton FEPC bill by voting with the opposition, thus preventing the bill from reaching a floor vote.[111] Apparently this act so incensed the president that on July 18, 1946, at a White House press conference, he proclaimed his opposition to Slaughter's renomination in the Democratic primary. "If Slaughter is right, then I am wrong," said the irate president, who then announced that he and James Pendergast, the heir to Tom Pendergast's political estate, would support Enos A. Axtell, a political unknown, for the

109. Philleo Nash Files, Box 21, HSTL.

110. Presidential Committee on Civil Rights, *To Secure These Rights* (New York: Simon & Schuster, 1947), p. 57; see also letter from Henry A. Wallace to Louis Schwellenbach, secretary of labor, in the *New York Times*, Aug. 21, 1946, p. 48. At the annual convention of the NAACP, meeting in Cincinnati on June 29, 1946, a resolution was passed attacking the segregationist policy of the Veterans Bureau "as one of the most disappointing developments of the post war era" (1946 Resolutions File, Box 335, NAACP Papers, L.C.).

111. *Crisis* LIII (1946), 265.

Democratic nomination.[112] Axtell, thanks to the public support of the president and the efforts of Pendergast, won the primary by 2,300 votes; of Axtell's 12,168 votes, nearly 7,000 came from black wards.[113] His victory, however, was sullied by evidence of voter irregularities and fraud stemming from the unscrupulous activity of the Pendergast machine working in his behalf. He was defeated by his Republican opponent, A. L. Reeves, in the November general election.[114]

In summary it can be said that throughout his first year in office, President Truman, according to an editorial in the *Pittsburgh Courier,* had manifested "friendship for the Negro people" but "had produced but little in racial advancement." [115] Other than to nominate Negro judge William Hastie as the governor of the Virgin Islands, appoint Irwin C. Mollison to a judgeship, and occasionally proclaim his support of FEPC legislation, Truman evinced no willingness to fight for the principles he espoused. With the exception of the Slaughter case, which really had local rather than national significance, he avoided, with political skill and verbal dexterity, any direct confrontation with civil rights issues that could have split his party and further undermined his position as party leader.

Meanwhile, a burgeoning social crisis was beginning to grip America. Responsible and politically conscious Negro leaders were asking in the spring and summer of 1946 that the president of the United States take cognizance of, and do something about, the rapidly deteriorating racial situa-

112. *Public Papers of the Presidents: Harry S. Truman, 1946,* pp. 351–51.

113. *Norfolk Journal and Guide,* Sept. 21, 1946, p. 5.

114. Milligan, *Missouri Waltz,* p. 258.

115. *Pittsburgh Courier,* Apr. 20, 1946, p. 4.

tion, north and south, as indicated by the fresh outbreak of lynching and other forms of violence.

President Truman was to answer this plea with a surprising display of executive initiative that in time was destined to create even more complex problems and difficult choices for him. Suddenly, because of the complex interaction of international with domestic pressures, the White House was to be touched by one of the great currents of the twentieth century: an incipient domestic counterpart of "the revolution of rising expectations."

Chapter 2

THE CIVIL RIGHTS COMMITTEE
DELIVERS ITS REPORT

During World War II the civil rights movement slowly gathered the strength and momentum needed to challenge a Jim Crow society. Such breakthroughs as the establishment of FEPC had given Negroes reason to hope that perhaps life for them in America might take a turn for the better. With that hope acting as a goad, black Americans had become increasingly militant and outspoken in their demands for racial justice and equality of treatment and opportunity in and out of the armed forces.[1]

---

1. H. C. Brearley, "The Negro's New Belligerancy," *Phylon* V (1944), 339–45; for an excellent analysis of the problem of Negro morale and developing militancy in the World War II period, see Richard Dalfiume, *Desegregation of the U.S. Armed Forces*, pp. 105–32.

Of some importance in furthering this development was the role of Negro newspapers; by directing a barrage of criticism against forces in American society bent on preserving the status quo in race relations, they stimulated and encouraged the black community to adopt a more aggressive attitude.[2] Proclaiming a need for a "Double Victory"—that is, a victory against Nazism and on the home front as well—these newspapers, led by the *Pittsburgh Courier*, turned the "Four Freedoms" slogan of Franklin Roosevelt into an ideological weapon to be used against the supporters of domestic racism.[3] Declared the *Chicago Defender:* "We pledge ourselves to fight segregation, discrimination and all forms of racial bigotry and Hitlerism, which impede our war effort and give aid and comfort to the enemy." [4] "War on two fronts" had become the new call to arms, the tocsin which sounded in black America between 1941 and 1945.

A counterattack soon developed. White critics of Negro militancy challenged the "Double Victory" proposition, with some arguing that the war had to be won first before changes could be effected, others committing themselves to holding the line at all costs. Given this polarization of feeling between the races, it is not surprising that racial tension and conflict quickly spread throughout American society, culminating in 1943 in the ugly race riots in Detroit.[5] In the South conflict fed on rumors about the existence of armed bands of young blacks and of "Eleanor Clubs" al-

---

2. Lester M. Jones, "The Editorial Policy of the Negro Newspapers of 1917–1918 As Compared with That of 1941–1942," *Journal of Negro History* XXIX (1944), 24–31.

3. Ibid.

4. *Chicago Defender*, Sept. 26, 1942.

5. Langston Hughes, *Fight for Freedom* (New York: W. W. Norton, 1962), pp. 95–98.

legedly founded by Mrs. Eleanor Roosevelt for the purpose of removing Negro domestics from white kitchens.[6]

With the racial cauldron bubbling, Virginius Dabney, editor of the *Richmond Times Dispatch* and known for his racial moderation, wrote in January, 1943:

> A small group of Negro agitators and another small group of white rabble rousers are pushing this country closer and closer to an interracial explosion which may make the race riots of the first World War and its aftermath seem mild by comparison. Unless saner councils prevail, we may have the worst internal clashes since Reconstruction, with hundreds if not thousands, killed and amicable race relations set back for decades.

Among the "Negro extremists" singled out by Dabney were A. Philip Randolph and the leadership of the NAACP.[7]

It was in this context of increased racial tension that in 1943 Jonathan Daniels, a White House administrative assistant, and Howard Odum, a noted sociologist from the University of North Carolina, approached President Roosevelt and urged him "to create a commission of race relation experts to advise him on what steps the government should take to improve matters." [8] The president rejected the idea on the grounds that the war had to be won before there could be planning in the future; later, after the Detroit riots, he appointed Daniels to gather information from all government departments about what they were doing to

---

6. Howard Odum, *Race and Rumors of Race* (Chapel Hill: University of North Carolina Press, 1943), pp. 73–90.

7. Virginius Dabney, "Nearer and Nearer the Precipice," *Atlantic Monthly* CLXXI (1943), 94–100.

8. Dalfiume, *Desegregation of the U.S. Armed Forces*, pp. 129–30.

improve race relations.[9] There, for the time being, matters stood.

Racial violence, often producing bloodshed and death, extended into the immediate postwar period. An already tense situation had been further exacerbated by the return of black veterans who were demanding the right to register and vote in Mississippi, Alabama, and Georgia.[10] Their efforts were repeatedly frustrated and their rights denied by a revived Ku Klux Klan, and more respectable proponents of white supremacy, determined to prevent even a token liberalization of southern political institutions.[11]

An extreme example of what was happening to Negroes in the South took place in Batesburgh, South Carolina. There, on February 13, 1946, Issac Woodward, a newly discharged black veteran, still in military uniform, was removed from a bus after a verbal tiff with the driver and was assaulted and blinded by the chief of police of that town.[12] News of this crime received wide publicity, which in turn eventually produced demands for a federal investigation. The Justice Department brought an indictment against the alleged perpetrator of this deed, but he was

---

9. Ibid., pp. 130–31.

10. The impetus for this drive for greater enfranchisement had been provided by the landmark decision of the Supreme Court in *Smith* v. *Allwright*, 1944. The Court ruled that the white primary—a key institutional prop of the Jim Crow political system—no longer could be constitutionally justified, thereby removing one of the major legal obstacles preventing Negroes from voting in primary elections; for a discussion of the political implications of this case, see V. O. Key, Jr., *Southern Politics in State and Nation* (New York: Random House, Carvelle Edition, 1962), pp. 624–28.

11. McWilliams, *Brothers under the Skin*, pp. 29–35.

12. Florence Murry, ed., *The Negro Handbook*, 1949 (New York: Macmillan, 1949), p. 102.

acquitted in federal court in Columbia, South Carolina, on grounds of self-defense.[13]

Another incident occurred in Columbia, Tennessee, on February 24 and 25, 1946. In that two-day period, the Negro population of the town was terrorized by the Ku Klux Klan, the local police, and National Guardsmen.[14] Twenty-eight Negroes were arrested on the charge of attempted murder; two others were shot and killed while they were in jail.[15] So deplorable was the situation that the NAACP, which had actively intervened in the case, sought an appointment with President Truman in order to discuss developments in Columbia with him. He failed to comply with this request, but Attorney General Tom Clark agreed to investigate the case.[16] A grand jury was later impaneled, but no indictment was presented against those white officials who had patently violated the civil rights of these black citizens. After months of tortuous litigation, supported by the NAACP in the person of the Negro attorney Thurgood Marshall, the twenty-eight people were freed of the charges brought against them.[17] Meanwhile, a national emergency committee was created to protest the Columbia incident. Headed by Mrs. Eleanor Roosevelt and Dr. Channing Tobias, it would in time evolve into the National Emergency Committee against Mob Violence, a broadly based and influential liberal pressure group destined to play

---

13. Ibid., p. 103; also see the Issac Woodward File, Box 62, NAACP Papers, L.C.

14. Hughes, *Fight For Freedom*, pp. 102–6.

15. *Norfolk Journal and Guide*, Mar. 16, 1946, p. 1.

16. Hughes, *Fight For Freedom*, pp. 102–6. Also see telegram to David Niles from Walter White, March 28, 1946, Department of Justice Folder, Box 342, NAACP Papers, L.C.

17. Boxes 333, 342, NAACP Papers, L.C.

an important, though short-lived, role in the civil rights drama of 1946.[18]

While violence in the South continued, the efforts of Negroes to obtain their political rights received the warm support of President Truman. He made this quite explicit in a message sent to the annual convention of the NAACP on June 26, 1946: "The ballot is both a right and a privilege. The right to use it must be protected and its use by everyone encouraged. Lastly, every veteran and every citizen, whatever his origins, must be protected from all forms of organized terrorism." [19] How to provide that protection and in what form would soon become a matter of highest governmental concern.

The nightriders of the South were to bring the issue of violence to the doors of the White House more quickly than the President may have wanted. On July 25, 1946, two Negro couples in the company of a white farmer (who was transporting them to work on his farm) were shot to death by an armed mob near Monroe, Georgia.[20] Evidently one of the Negroes, Roger Malcom, had earlier stabbed his white farm employer because the latter had made advances to Malcom's wife.[21] It was after Malcom had been released from jail on bond that the murders took place. Harold Hinton, a *New York Times* reporter, discovered that the Ku Klux Klan, fearing that returning Negro veterans "were getting out of their place," committed the murders because "one of the men had come back from the war a bad

---

18. See Minutes of Executive Committee against Mob Violence, August 21, 1946, Box 332, NAACP Papers, L.C.

19. *New York Times*, June 27, 1946, p. 19.

20. *To Secure These Rights*, p. 22. Also see Box 236, NAACP Papers, L.C.

21. *New York Times*, Aug. 4, 1946, p. 7E.

Negro." [22] The presumed killers were later tried and acquitted of the charge.[23]

This act of vigilante violence, when coupled with a number of earlier incidents, aroused the American liberal conscience. Allied Negro and white liberal organizations besieged President Truman with demands that he authorize the Justice Department to arrest and indict the individuals responsible for the Monroe murders.[24] In addition, he was asked by the president of the Negro Newspaper Publishers Association to seek congressional action on anti-lynching legislation so as "to restore and preserve law and order in America." [25] On July 30, 1946, fifty women from the NAACP picketed the White House while carrying banners which read: "Speak! Speak! Mr. President!" and "Where is Democracy?" [26]

Responding to the pressure created by the news of the Monroe murders, President Truman released on July 30, 1946, a statement through the office of Attorney General Tom Clark, informing the country that he was horrified by the Monroe murders and that he had instructed the Justice Department to investigate "this or any other crime of oppression, and to ascertain if any Federal statute can be applied to the apprehension and prosecution of the criminals." [27] The president added emphasis to his July 30 statement when he remarked at his press conference of

---

22. Ibid., Sept. 1, 1946, p. 4E.

23. *The Negro Handbook*, 1949, p. 94. For a listing of fourteen major acts of violence directed at Negroes in 1946, see *Pittsburgh Courier*, Aug. 17, 1946, p. 1.

24. *New York Times*, July 31, 1946, p. 28; by November, 1946, 30,000 pieces of mail had been received by the Justice Department on this case (*New York Times*, Nov. 14, 1946, p. 33).

25. *Norfolk Journal and Guide*, Aug. 3, 1946, p. 1.

26. *New York Times*, July 31, 1946, p. 48.

27. Ibid.

August 1, 1946, that as a senator he had always voted for proposed anti-lynching legislation; [28] and when questioned once more about the Monroe case at his August 9 press conference, Truman indicated that the Justice Department investigation was moving ahead "with all possible energy." [29]

Despite the administration's willingness to prosecute the Monroe murderers, the Justice Department actually lacked the jurisdiction to deal with such crimes. Title 18 of the federal criminal code contained only three sections, 51, 52, and 441, making it possible for the Justice Department to function as a defender and protector of individual civil rights.[30] Section 51 secured against state interference all civil rights created by federal statute, e.g., social security and labor's right to organize for collective bargaining.[31] It did not provide the federal government with the proper statutory authority to protect the individual or members of a racial minority from mob activity or violence. As Attorney General Tom Clark himself noted: "While such attacks may amount to a deprivation of freedom of speech or other rights guaranteed by the Bill of Rights, these rights are rights protected *only* against official action, not private action." [32]

Section 52 was also of limited utility, having application only in those cases where it could be shown that federal or state officials willfully misused their power of office to de-

---

28. *Public Papers of the Presidents: Harry S. Truman, 1946*, p. 368.

29. Ibid., p. 409.

30. *To Secure These Rights*, pp. 116–17.

31. Ibid., p. 118.

32. From an address by Attorney General Tom C. Clark delivered to the Chicago Bar Association on June 21, 1946: Philleo Nash Files, Box 21, HSTL.

prive individuals of rights guaranteed by the Bill of Rights and the Fourteenth Amendment.[33] To prove that a federal or state official had deliberately compromised the rights of private citizens was an immensely difficult task, complicated even more by a 1945 Supreme Court decision which declared that a person could not be prosecuted under Section 52 unless there was evidence that he was aware of a specific federal right and had acted willfully to deprive his victim of it.[34] Thus Section 52 failed to protect the individual against mob activity unless it could be demonstrated that an official in some way played a part in mob action. Section 441 was limited to antipeonage cases.[35] Clearly, then, these statutes, even when broadly construed, could frustrate even the best-intentioned federal official, leaving him without the requisite legal tools to protect the civil rights of both Negroes and whites.

Yet the growing political strength of northern Negroes required that something be done to cope with the likelihood of further violence in the South. In mid-August, 1946, Attorney General Clark announced that he would seek action on an anti-lynching bill in the next session of Congress.[36] It was already too late for the administration to move for such a measure in the Seventy-ninth Congress, then preparing

---

33. *To Secure These Rights*, p. 118; compounding the difficulties of the Justice Department was the Supreme Court's 1945 ruling in *Screws* v. *United States*, which further narrowed the legal grounds on which alleged violators of Section 52 could be prosecuted. In the Screws Case, the Court said that a person could not be prosecuted under Section 52 unless there was evidence that he knew of the existence of a specific federal right and wilfully intended to deprive his victim of that right (see *United States Commission on Civil Rights, Report 5, Justice* [Washington: United States Government Printing Office, 1961], pp. 45–51).

34. *To Secure These Rights*, p. 118.

35. Ibid.

36. *Pittsburgh Courier*, Aug. 24, 1946, pp. 1, 4.

for its preelection adjournment. Furthermore, this Congress had already refused to enact FEPC and anti–poll tax legislation, a fact President Truman could not ignore. In addition, his personal unpopularity was such that he could ill afford to offend the political sensibilities of the Southern Democrats, whose support he might need on other issues in the new Eightieth Congress. The postponement of anti-lynching recommendations might give him a chance to find a fresh solution to the difficult political problem of placating aroused Negroes and their white liberal supporters, including Mrs. Eleanor Roosevelt, without giving umbrage to the South.

An opportunity presented itself on September 19, 1946, the day the president met at the White House with the National Emergency Committee against Mob Violence, whose chief spokesman was Walter White, executive secretary of the NAACP.[37] The committee delivered to the president a petition requesting that he call a special session of Congress to consider laws against mob violence, to concentrate efforts to apprehend lynchers, and to "rouse the American people by radio, press and other media to oppose actively every form of violence." [38] In addition, members of the committee, including Dr. Channing Tobias of the Phelps-Stokes Fund and James Carey of the CIO, apprized the president of the details of racial violence occurring in the South and informed him that hate literature of all sorts was spreading across the country. At the conclusion of the

---

37. Walter White, *A Man Called White* (New York: Viking Press, 1948), pp. 331–32. Included in the group that was scheduled to meet with Truman was Franklin Roosevelt, Jr. He, however, could not attend, a point which White brought to Truman's attention the day after their meeting; see telegram to White from Roosevelt, September 19, 1946, Box 367, NAACP Papers, L.C.; and White to Truman, September 20, 1946, Box 367, NAACP Papers, L.C.

38. White, *A Man Called White*, pp. 330–31.

committee's report of these recent developments, the president exclaimed, "My God! I had no idea that it was as terrible as that! We have to do something. . . . Everybody seems to believe that the President by himself can do anything he wishes on such matters as this, but the President is helpless unless he is backed by public opinion." [39] David K. Niles, a Truman administrative assistant, then suggested that a committee be created to investigate the problem and to recommend a program of corrective action. When Walter White remarked that Congress might not be amenable to such a proposal, the president replied that he would act by creating the committee by executive order and finance it out of the president's contingent fund.[40]

Walter White and his associates were quite pleased with what appeared to be the president's spontaneous offer to create a civil rights committee, but, in fact, Truman and Niles had planned beforehand to introduce this proposal at a propitious moment of the September meeting.[41] (It is possible that Henry Wallace's forced resignation from the cabinet on September 20, 1946—a move tentatively agreed upon before Truman's meeting with White's group— spurred the administration into making that promise; and it is also possible that Mrs. Roosevelt's close friendship with Walter White and her active support of his cause had something to do with the decision.) Here was an ingenious solution that would serve Truman's political needs by allow-

---

39. Ibid.

40. *Pittsburgh Courier*, Oct. 5, 1946, pp. 1, 4.

41. Author's interview with Philleo Nash on June 29, 1962. This proposal sounds very much like the one advanced in 1943 by Jonathan Daniels and Howard Odum, which President Roosevelt rejected. Niles had been a member of the White House during this period, and he may have picked up the idea of creating a civil rights committee either from Daniels or Philleo Nash, who had worked with Daniels on questions affecting race relations and the federal government.

ing him through symbolic action to improve his standing among northern liberals while, conversely, avoiding the alienation of the South. After all, Truman's pledge to create this committee was not a commitment in advance to any legislative program the committee might recommend.[42]

The president's unwillingness to antagonize the South was revealed in a discussion he had with representatives of the National Conference on Lynching on September 23, 1946. When Paul Robeson, the committee's spokesman, requested that the chief executive issue a formal statement protesting lynching, and also support a definite legislative and educational program to end mob violence, Truman indicated the political situation made it difficult to issue a statement of his views at that time. In order to obtain passage of an anti-lynching law, suggested the president, political timing was important.[43]

Despite Truman's reluctance to initiate legislative action on civil rights, he continued to speak out in favor of the principle of equal justice under the law. In a message sent on September 24, 1946, to an Urban League convention at St. Louis, the president stated that "if the civil rights of even one citizen are abused, government has failed to discharge one of its primary responsibilities." He further declared that "we as a people must not, and I say to you we

---

42. White was well aware of this possibility; hence, he wrote Truman on September 20, 1946, that "with respect to the proposal made by Mr. Niles . . . , I hope this will not be considered a substitute for stronger federal legislation against violence, nor handled in such way as to give the Congress an excuse for postponement of action. I mention this because it should be in our thinking" (Box 367, NAACP Papers, L.C.).

43. *New York Times*, Sept. 24, 1946, p. 60. This committee presented to the president a letter from Albert Einstein suggesting that "security against lynching is one of the most urgent tasks of our generation"; see Fiske University Bulletin, *Race Relations* IV, No. 3 (1946) 78; and *Norfolk Journal and Guide*, Sept. 28, 1946, pp. 1–2.

shall not, remain indifferent in the face of acts of intimidation and violence in our American communities." [44]

The first sign that the administration was taking its "primary responsibilities" more seriously, following the Truman message to the Urban League, appeared in a letter sent from Attorney General Tom Clark to the president on October 11, 1946. He suggested that Truman issue an executive order entitled "Establishing the President's Committee on Civil Rights" and emphasized that "the work of the proposed committee would, in my opinion, be of utmost value in the task of preserving and implementing our civil rights." [45]

As work went on both at the White House and the Justice Department on the format and framework of the proposed committee, the country was preparing for the 1946 congressional election. By this time, because of incessant labor-management conflict, the growing shortage of meat (held back from market by cattlemen who were hoping to drive up prices), and erratic leadership from the White House, Truman's political standing had fallen considerably.[46] The Republican opportunities to capture Congress had not seemed so bright in years. Among the groups which began to fall away from the Democratic party was the Negro bloc. Negro leaders in Philadelphia were predicting before the election that there would be sizable black support for Republican candidates because it appeared that Mrs. Roosevelt no longer had a voice in Democratic party councils; because the White House lacked interest in FEPC; because in the highest councils of government there were too many "deep

---

44. *New York Times*, Sept. 25, 1946, p. 38.

45. Tom C. Clark to Harry S. Truman, October 11, 1946, Truman Papers, OF 596A, HSTL.

46. Allen J. Matusow, *Farm Policies and Politics in the Truman Years* (Cambridge, Mass.: Harvard University Press, 1967), pp. 61–62.

Southerners" (men like Secretary of State James Brynes and George Allen, head of the Reconstruction Finance Corporation) who "could not have sympathy for Negro problems and aspirations"; and, finally, because there was the problem of "Bilboism." [47] Senator Theodore Bilbo, a virulent racist from Mississippi, had heaped so much calumny on Negroes from his protected perch in the Senate that they were going to pull the Republican lever in the hope that a newly constituted Republican majority in the Senate might strip him of his Senate seat. (With the convening of the Eightieth Congress, Bilbo's seat was challenged, but before the Senate could resolve the issue, Bilbo died.) [48]

The trend away from the Democratic party was confirmed on election day, as the Republicans won a congressional victory of landslide proportions. Black journalists were pleased with the outcome because they believed the removal of the Southern Democrats from key committee chairmanships made possible the development of a more fluid situation in Congress—conceivably leading to the passage of some civil rights legislation.[49] And Walter White, thinking of possible future political developments, suggested that "if . . . the Republicans keep some of the promises they so eloquently and frequently make to Negroes, the present Negro resentment against the Bilbo-Talmadge-Rankin-Byrnes domination of the Democratic Party may develop into a force strong enough to decide who will occupy the White House and control Congress in 1948." [50]

---

47. *New York Times*, Oct. 18, 1946, p. 13; also see *Norfolk Journal and Guide*, Oct. 26, 1946, p. 1.

48. Key, *Southern Politics*, pp. 244–45; also see Bilbo File, Box 375, NAACP Papers, L.C.

49. *Norfolk Journal and Guide*, Nov. 23, 1946, p. 1.

50. NAACP press release, November 15, 1946, Republican National Committee Folder, Box 359, NAACP Papers, L.C.

On December 5, 1946, subsequent to the defeat suffered by the Democratic party in the 1946 congressional election, President Truman issued Executive Order 9008, creating a presidential civil rights committee modeled after the Wickersham Committee of the Hoover administration.[51] This order authorized the committee "to inquire into and to determine whether and in what respect current law-enforcement measures and the authority and means possessed by federal, state, and local governments may be strengthened and improved to safeguard the civil rights of the people." The committee was also directed to include in its written report "recommendations with respect to the adoption or establishment, by legislation or otherwise, of more adequate and effective means and procedures for the protection of civil rights. . . ."[52]

The administration had established a prestigious committee, whose fifteen members had been selected to represent industry, labor, the legal profession, higher education, the South, the American Negro community, and various religious denominations. Charles Wilson, the president of General Electric, and formerly executive vice-chairman of the War Production Board, was appointed chairman; other members were Mrs. Sadie T. Alexander, a lawyer from Philadelphia and a member of the board of directors of the National Urban League; James Carey, secretary-treasurer of the Congress of Industrial Organization; John S. Dickey, president of Dartmouth College; Morris Ernst, a lawyer and author from New York City; Rabbi Roland Gittlesohn, Jewish chaplain of the Fifth Marine Division at Iwo Jima; Dr. Frank Graham, president of the University of North Carolina; The Reverend Francis Haas, Catholic bishop of

---

51. Executive Order 9809, 11 F.R. 14153; Author's interview with Philleo Nash on June 29, 1962.

52. *To Secure These Rights*, pp. vii–ix.

Grand Rapids, Michigan, and former chairman of the President's Committee of Fair Employment Practice; Charles Luckman (who never served), president of Lever Brothers; Francis P. Matthews, former supreme chairman knight of the Knights of Columbus; Franklin Roosevelt, Jr., chairman of the Housing Committee of the American Veterans Committee; The Reverend Henry Knox Sherrill, presiding bishop of the Episcopal church; Boris Shiskin, an economist for the American Federation of Labor; Mrs. M. E. Tilly, an official of the Women's Society of Christian Service, Methodist Church; Dr. Channing Tobias, director of the Phelps-Stokes Fund and formerly senior secretary of the National Council of the Young Men's Christian Association.[53] Later, upon the recommendation of the Justice Department, the committee selected Professor Robert K. Carr, a Dartmouth College political scientist, as its executive secretary.[54] It was a felicitous choice because Carr had already made an intensive study of the Justice Department's role and responsibility in the defense of civil rights.[55]

The impressive credentials of this committee and the task to which it was committed so impressed the *Norfolk Journal and Guide* that it editorially remarked:

> The action of President Truman in naming a committee on civil rights is salutary and potentially of great value to the welfare of millions of Americans. . . . The committee may be instrumental in bringing about some construc-

53. *Negro Handbook*, 1949 (New York: Macmillan, 1949), pp. 214–15. Four members of this Committee—Mrs. M. E. Tilly, Franklin Roosevelt, Jr., Channing Tobias, and Frank Graham—had been recommended by White to David Niles; see White to Niles, September 26, 1946, Niles Folder, Box 367, NAACP Papers, L.C.

54. Author's interview with Philleo Nash on June 29, 1962.

55. Robert K. Carr, *Federal Protection of Civil Rights: Quest for a Sword* (Ithaca, N.Y.: Cornell University Press, 1947), p. 2.

tive changes in the laws and thereby providing greater protection for millions now denied full civil rights. . . . Its very creation by the executive head of the nation's government is alone a constructive step.[56]

Political considerations, already mentioned, compelled the president to issue his order; but there were other reasons which entered into his decision. As he wrote some years later:

I took this action because of the repeated anti-minority incidents immediately after the war in which homes were invaded, property was destroyed, and a number of innocent lives were taken. I wanted to get the facts behind these incidents of disregard for individual and group rights which were reported in the news with alarmingly regularity, and to see that the law was strengthened, if necessary, so as to offer adequate protection and fair treatment to all our citizens.[57]

He undoubtedly wanted to see "fair treatment" extended to all citizens. It is not likely, however, that he wished to upset his working relations with the South in December, 1946, in order to support such an objective. Yet by establishing a civil rights committee, Truman inadvertently built up political pressure that could spell trouble for him in the future.

President Truman presented his State of the Union address to the Eightieth Congress on January 6, 1947, and included in his remarks were several references to the racial conflict besetting the country in 1946. After pointing out that citizens had been deprived of their constitutional rights, specifically, their right to vote and to engage in

---

56. Dec. 14, 1946, p. 6.

57. Harry S. Truman, *Memoirs*, 2 vols. (Garden City, N.Y.: Doubleday, 1956), II, 180.

lawful callings, Truman declared that "the will to fight these crimes should be in the heart of everyone of us." He felt the Justice Department was doing its best to protect civil rights "to the full extent of the powers conferred upon it," but the lack of legal weapons limited its participation. Perhaps existing laws could be amended, Truman speculated, to extend "the limit of federal power to protect the civil rights of the American people." He then announced that the President's Committee on Civil Rights had been created "to study and report on the problem of federally secured civil rights, with a view to making recommendations to Congress." [58]

The president's remarks on civil rights made little impression on Congress; the South had no reason to be alarmed as long as he did not offer a concrete legislative program.[59] Two days later, however, Truman sent his economic message to Congress, containing a specific proposal calling for the enactment of FEPC legislation:

> We must end discrimination in employment or wages against certain classes of workers regardless of their individual abilities. Discrimination against certain racial or religious groups, against men in late middle age and against women, not only is repugnant to the principles of our democracy, but often creates "artificial labor shortages" in the midst of labor surplus. Employers and unions both need to re-examine and revise practices resulting in discrimination. I recommend that, at this session, the Congress provide permanent Federal legislation dealing with this problem.[60]

---

58. *Public Papers of the Presidents: Harry S. Truman, 1947* (Washington: United States Government Printing Office, 1962), p. 9.

59. *New York Times*, Jan. 9, 1947, p. 15; also see *Norfolk Journal and Guide*, Jan. 18, 1947, p. 2.

60. *Public Papers of the Presidents: Harry S. Truman, 1947*, pp. 31–32.

This recommendation, wrote a *New York Times* reporter, "seemed to dispel the relief among Southern Democrats that was manifest after delivery of the State of the Union message." [61] In all likelihood Truman's pleas for an FEPC was designed not to offend the South but, rather, to take the issue away from liberal Republicans in the ranks of the majority party now controlling the Congress.

The Republican party, however, had no serious intention of committing itself to this cause, as was indicated by the remarks of Joseph Martin, the newly designated Speaker of the House, to a group of Negro Republican leaders.

The FEPC plank in the 1944 Republican platform was a bid for the Negro vote, and they did not accept the bid. They went out and voted for Roosevelt. I'll be frank with you. We are not going to pass a FEPC bill, but it has nothing to do with the Negro vote. We are supported by New England and Middle Western Industrialists who would stop their contributions if we passed a law that would compel them to stop religious as well as racial discrimination in employment. I am not saying that I agree with them, but that is the situation we face, so we may as well be realistic. We intend to do a lot for the Negroes, but we can't afford to pass the FEPC bill. . . . We have a number of mavericks in our party who may not go along with us on needed labor legislation, so we may need some voters from the other side until this issue is taken care of. After the labor legislation is out of the way, we may be able to pass the poll tax bill.[62]

Meanwhile, Thomas Richardson, vice-president of the CIO United Public Workers, disclosed on January 10, 1947, that nine federal agencies within the administration re-

---

61. Jan. 9, 1947, p. 15.

62. *Pittsburgh Courier*, Jan. 4, 1947, p. 6; also see *Norfolk Journal and Guide*, Jan. 4, 1947, p. 6.

fused to hire Negroes.[63] Richardson also revealed that he had previously discussed the matter with David Niles of the White House staff, who not only confirmed the truth of his charges but informed him that his union would be contacted about them; according to Richardson, nothing was heard from Niles after that meeting.[64]

The president paid no heed to Richardson's charges, but he was evidently distressed by the deteriorating situation in race relations in the country. Speaking to the members of his Committee on Civil Rights at its organizational meeting at the White House on January 15, 1947, Truman intimated that the country might be faced with a period of racial and religious hysteria similar to the decade of the 1920's. As he indicated: "I don't want to see any race discrimination. I don't want to see any religious bigotry break out in this country as it did then." Since Truman thought "there are certain rights under the Constitution which . . . the Federal Government has a right to protect," he hoped the committee would be able to inform him "just exactly how far the Attorney General can go legally" in protecting the civil rights of citizens in the event of a breakdown of local law enforcement.[65]

The remarks Truman made during his meeting with this committee suggest that he viewed the problem of civil rights as something more than a political issue; it was, for him at least, a constitutional issue as well.[66] Truman firmly believed that as president of the United States he was obligated to defend the Constitution not only by upholding the laws of the land but by strengthening them as well. He understood

63. *New York Times*, Jan. 11, 1947, p. 7; and *Pittsburgh Courier*, Feb. 15, 1947, p. 4.

64. *New York Times*, Jan. 11, 1947, p. 7.

65. Truman, *Memoirs*, II, 182.

66. Ibid., p. 180.

that it was necessary to protect civil rights, if only to preserve the integrity of the law. Although he was destined to be attacked in the South and elsewhere as a dangerous innovator for his seeming disregard of local customs, Truman actually appears to be a traditionalist who decried acts of injustice because they violated what he thought constituted the American heritage of political liberty and fair play.[67]

On April 9, 1947, Walter White invited the president to address an NAACP rally scheduled to be held in front of the Lincoln Memorial in late June, and Truman accepted his invitation.[68] It may well be that he accepted White's offer because, in the aftermath of his Truman Doctrine pronouncement of March 12, 1947, such a speech would allow him to reaffirm his commitment to the principles of democracy and freedom; to seize the propaganda initiative from the Republican-controlled Eightieth Congress; and to convince skeptical liberals that he was truly in earnest about such matters.

Now that the president was committed to talk, he had to have an appropriate speech. Truman could have accepted advice such as that of David Niles, who suggested that "the closing paragraph of the speech, not to exceed one minute, should be devoted to civil rights." [69] But probably for the reasons already mentioned, Truman decided to use the occasion to make a forthright statement about civil rights; hence, Robert Carr and Milton Stewart, of the President's Committee on Civil Rights, were drafted to write most of the speech he was to read. When the president delivered his speech on June 29, 1947, he spoke not only to an actual

67. Ibid., p. 183.
68. White, *A Man Called White*, p. 347.
69. Memorandum to Matthew J. Connelly from David Niles, June 16, 1947, Clark Clifford File, HSTL.

audience of 10,000—including Mrs. Eleanor Roosevelt, Chief Justice Fred Vinson, Senator Wayne Morse, and Walter White—but also to a nationwide audience over the combined facilities of the major radio networks; in addition, his speech was carried by short wave to all parts of the world.[70]

A major theme of the president's speech dealt with the new role he envisioned for the federal government in the defense of civil rights. He suggested:

> We must keep moving forward with new concepts of civil rights to safeguard our heritage. The extension of civil rights today means, not protection of the people against the government, but protection of the people by the government. We must make the Federal Government a friendly, vigilant defender of the rights and equalities of all Americans. And again I mean all Americans. . . . There is much that state and local governments can do in providing positive safeguards for civil rights. But we cannot, any longer, await the growth of a will to action in the slowest state or the most backward community.
>
> Our national government must show the way. This is a difficult and complex undertaking. Federal laws and administrative machinery must be improved and expanded. We must provide the government with better tools to do the job. . . .
>
> Our immediate task is to remove the last remnants of the barriers which stand between millions of our citizens and their birthright. . . . We cannot wait another decade or another generation to remedy these evils. We must work, as never before, to cure them now. The aftermath of the war and the desire to keep faith with our Nation's historic principles makes the need a pressing one. . . . Every man should have the right to a decent home, the right to an education, the right to adequate medical care, the right to a worthwhile job, the right to an equal share

---

70. White, *A Man Called White*, pp. 330–31.

in making public decisions through the ballot, and the right to a fair trial in a fair court. We must insure that these rights—on equal terms—are enjoyed by every citizen.[71]

The president also spoke of the growing cold war conflict between the United States and the Soviet Union, declaring that the promise of American life had to be realized in order to strengthen the cause of democracy in a world convulsed with crisis and change. He asserted:

> The support of desperate populations of battle ravaged countries must be won for the free way of life. We must have them as allies in our continuing struggle for the peaceful solution of the world's problems. They may surrender to the false security offered so temptingly by totalitarian regimes unless we can prove the superiority of democracy. Our case for democracy should be as strong as we can make it. It should rest on practical evidence that we have been able to put our own house in order.[72]

When Truman finished, he turned to Walter White and said: "I mean every word of it—and I am going to prove that I do mean it." [73]

It was a remarkable speech that Truman delivered. He had provided the country with a searching look into the current situation in race relations by pointing to the barriers of discrimination, and he had challenged the American people to surmount these barriers as quickly as possible. Thus, for the first time in the twentieth century, an American president publicly discussed the problem of racial discrimination with frankness and humanity.

Truman's speech impressed many Negroes, who now felt

---

71. Truman Papers, OF 413, HSTL.

72. Ibid.

73. White, *A Man Called White*, pp. 330–31.

that he meant business.[74] A number of Negro newspapers and magazines praised him for his candid approach. The *Kansas City Call,* for example, wrote on July 4, 1947, that "Truman so strongly denounced race prejudice and discrimination based upon race, creed, color, and national origin that even his enemies were convinced that the Missourian in the White House had left behind him Missouri's tradition of second-class citizenship for Negroes." The *Pittsburgh Courier* said on July 12, 1947, that Truman's words and deeds pertaining to civil rights were more impressive than those of his predecessor, Franklin Roosevelt, "who enjoyed to a far greater degree the affection of colored Americans." The *Courier* also pointed out:

> We cannot recall when the gentleman who now sleeps at Hyde Park made such a forthright statement against racial discrimination. . . . Here we have a President saying that a revolution in American mores must be worked here and now, and this is more remarkable when one considers Mr. Truman's origin and antecedents as contrasted with those of Mr. Roosevelt. . . . President Truman . . . where colored Americans are concerned, is looming, on the record, to greater stature than his predecessor. . . . Mr. Truman deserves high praise for his sincerity and forthrightness after a long era of double talk and political expediency.

The August, 1947, issue of the *Crisis,* the monthly journal of the NAACP, referred to the speech itself as "the most comprehensive and forthright statement on the rights of minorities in a democracy and the duty of the government to secure safeguards that has ever been made by a President of the United States."

---

74. Walter White, "Will the Negro Elect Our Next President?", *Colliers Magazine* CXX (1947), 26.

A moderate white southern response to Truman's speech appeared in Little Rock's *Arkansas Gazette* of July 1, 1947: ". . . Is it in the power of any government to wipe out prejudice? Enforcement of laws against 'discrimination' in fields where the government had not previously entered might only make prejudice more active." Typical, perhaps, of a number of newspapers outside of Dixie was the response of the *St. Louis Star Times* of June 30, 1947. It agreed with the president's support of freedom and justice for all citizens, but questioned Truman's advocacy of FEPC contained in his earlier economic message to Congress.

The president's June 29 speech aroused the hopes of American Negroes, but many individuals, such as Walter White, waited impatiently for him to do something about the situation that he described with such clarity and conviction. Seeking to compel the American government to take a stronger political stand against discrimination, the NAACP turned to the forum of the United Nations to promote its campaign for equality and justice for the Negro citizens of the United States. It submitted a petition of grievances, drafted in part by the historian W. E. B. Du Bois, to the world body on October 23, 1947, calling attention to the long history of cultural deprivation suffered by the black man in America.[75] Included was this statement:

This protest is a frank and earnest appeal to all the world for elemental justice against the treatment which the United States has visited upon us for three centuries. . . . It is to induce the nations of the world to persuade

---

75. Its petition, "A Statement on the Denial of Human Rights to Minorities in the Case of Citizens of Negro Descent in the United States of America and an Appeal to the United Nations for Redress, Prepared for the NAACP," was drafted by Du Bois, with the assistance of Milton Konvitz, Earl B. Dickerson, and Rayford Logan. A copy can be found in Box 354, NAACP PAPERS, L.C.

this nation to be just to its own people, that we have prepared and now present to you this document . . . and we firmly believe that the situation pictured here is as much your concern as ours.[76]

But the United Nations Commission on Human Rights, meeting in Geneva, Switzerland, on December 4, 1947, rejected a Soviet proposal to investigate the charges which the NAACP had placed before it.[77]

The NAACP action received extensive news coverage not only from the American press but from the foreign press as well; India, in particular, was deeply concerned.[78] That the United States government was quite embarrassed by the adverse publicity it received from the NAACP petition was revealed by Attorney General Tom Clark, who, speaking in Boston on October 27, remarked that he was "humiliated" by the fact that a group of Americans could not find equitable treatment at home. He then declared that his department would move "with as great vigor and force as is permitted under the law where States through negligence, or for whatever reason, fail . . . to protect the life and liberties of the individual." He also announced the Civil Rights Section of the Justice Department would be enlarged and strengthened.[79]

The NAACP's claim that widespread discrimination was indeed a basic fact of life in the United States was rein-

---

76. *Crisis* LIV (1947), 362–64.

77. *Norfolk Journal and Guide*, Dec. 13, 1947, p. 1. The minutes of the NAACP's board of directors meeting of February 9, 1948, contains a letter Mrs. Roosevelt sent to Walter White explaining precisely what happened and why, when the NAACP petition was presented to the United Nations Commission; see Minutes of Board of Directors, February 9, 1948, Box A-12, NAACP Papers, L.C.

78. *Race Relations* V (December, 1947—January, 1948), 78.

79. *Norfolk Journal and Guide*, Nov. 8, 1947, pp. 1–2.

forced by the report *To Secure These Rights*, which the Committee on Civil Rights submitted to President Truman on October 29, 1947.[80] Based upon the testimony submitted by forty witnesses, correspondence with nearly 250 private organizations and individuals, as well as information supplied by twenty-five government agencies and numerous state and local public agencies, the report had been carefully prepared in order to make it a reliable study of the shortcomings and failings of American democracy.[81]

The report itself was divided into four sections: (1) The American Heritage: Promise of Freedom and Equality; (2) The Record: Short of the Goal; (3) Government Responsibility: Securing These Rights; (4) A Program: The Committee's Recommendations.

The first section spelled out four essential rights which the committee determined to be characteristic of a free society: the right to safety and security of the person; the right to freedom of conscience and expression; the right to equality; and the right to citizenship and its privileges. Here, then, was a yardstick that could measure America's achievements and failures against its revolutionary heritage of freedom and justice for all men.[82]

Section Two emphasized those incidents of American life which, in the committee's judgment, violated the principles of a free society discussed in Part One. They included the lynchings of 1946 and 1947, constant police brutality directed at Negroes and other minority groups, failure of the judiciary to uphold the principle of equal justice under the law, and infringement of the physical freedom of Japanese-Americans during World War II. The denial of

---

80. *Public Papers of the Presidents: Harry S. Truman, 1947*, p. 479.
81. *To Secure These Rights*, p. 178.
82. Ibid., pp. 3–10.

the ballot to Negroes and Indians and the existence of segregated armed forces was further proof that citizenship rights had not yet been adequately protected. The committee also took care to point out lack of equal opportunity in the fields of employment, public and private education, housing, medical care, public services, and public accommodations. Also condemned was the theory and practice of segregation which, the committee insisted, was incompatible with the values of a free society. The committee also examined the widespread existence of segregation and discrimination in Washington, D.C., which it described as a "graphic illustration of the failure of democracy." [83]

Section Three emphasized the need for the federal government to assume much greater responsibilities as the guardian and protector of civil rights. Only the federal government, in the committee's opinion, had sufficient power and authority to contend with what was a national problem requiring a national solution. The justification for federal involvement in the defense of civil rights was to be found in the powers expressly and implicitly delegated to Congress by the Constitution as defined by the Supreme Court, especially in the Court's civil rights decisions of the 1930's and 1940's. The committee suggested also that precedents for further and stronger federal executive action had been established by the creation of a civil rights section in the Justice Department in 1939. The preparation of *amicus curiae* briefs and the investigation of violations of existing civil rights statutes had represented a novel experiment by the federal executive branch to safeguard civil rights. But without stronger statutory authority, the committee indicated, the federal government would remain severely handi-

---

83. Ibid., pp. 13–95.

capped in its efforts to provide protection for citizens whose rights were either threatened or still non-existent.[84]

In Section Four the committee presented its "program for action" and stressed what it considered to be the several imperatives to justify the federal government's immediate assumption of much greater responsibility for the protection of civil rights in American society, namely: the moral imperative ("The United States can no longer countenance these burdens on its common conscience, these inroads on its moral fiber."); the economic imperative ("The United States can no longer afford this heavy drain upon its human wealth, its national competence."); and the diplomatic imperative ("The United States is not so strong, the final triumph of the democratic ideal is not so inevitable that we can ignore what the world thinks of us or our record.")

The "program for action" called specifically for the improvement in the administrative machinery dealing with civil rights questions; the strengthening of the right to the safety and security of the person; the protection and enlargement of the right to citizenship and its privileges; and the fostering of the conditions for equality. Improvement in the administrative machinery required the elevation of the Civil Rights Section of the Justice Department to the status of a full division within the Justice Department; the establishment of a permanent Commission on Civil Rights, preferably by an act of Congress; and the creation of a Joint Standing Committee on Civil Rights in Congress.

To assure further the safety and security of the person, the committee recommended that Congress enact new legislation making it easier for the Justice Department to prosecute individual violators of civil rights. This would include

---

84. Ibid., pp. 99–135.

enlarging the penalties for violations of Sections 51 and 52 of the Criminal Code and the passage of anti-lynching legislation.

The protection of the right of citizenship required that, in the committee's judgment, Congress or the states abolish poll taxes; that Congress pass legislation protecting the right of qualified persons to participate in federal primaries and general elections; that Congress grant local self-determination and the right to participate in presidential elections to the District of Columbia; and that Congress enact legislation, followed by administrative action, to end immediately all discrimination and segregation in the organization and activities of all branches of the armed services.

To foster the conditions making for equality in American life, the committee deemed it vital that Congress distribute federal funds only to those public and private agencies which did not practice discrimination or segregation; that Congress enact an FEPC law containing legal sanctions; that the president not only issue a mandate against discrimination in government employment but also create adequate machinery to enforce it; that the Justice Department initiate a legal attack upon racially restrictive housing covenants; that Congress prohibit discrimination and segregation in the rendering of all public services by the national government; that Congress enact a law prohibiting discrimination and segregation in interstate transportation; and that Congress remove the blight of segregation and discrimination from both the District of Columbia and the Canal Zone.[85]

Charles Wilson and his colleagues handed to President Truman a document of great political and social importance. In all probability *To Secure These Rights* went far

---

85. Ibid., pp. 139–73.

beyond anything Truman and his advisers had in mind when they initially commissioned an investigation of the problems created by the racial violence of 1945 and 1946. The report contained more than recommendations to improve law-enforcement procedures for the protection of civil rights; it was also an impressively organized, factual presentation of what racism was doing to American life and democratic institutions. It was a comment on the country's history and a challenge to its decency. A number of liberally inclined Americans, working temporarily for their government, had succeeded in bringing about a confrontation between politics and morality. As Richard Neustadt, a student of the modern American presidency, suggests: "It is hardly credible that Truman could have ignored their report, no matter what the politics of his own situation." [86]

As soon as the report was released, it became a source of controversy in and out of Congress. Democratic Senator Scott Lucas from Illinois expressed the opinion that "the President's Committee has dealt courageously with some fundamentals that the people of this country have got to recognize sooner or later and [the] sooner the better"; Democratic Congressman Chet Holifield of California said: "Everything I saw in it was all right. . . . It is the most valuable and complete report that has been published in the field." [87] Republican Representative Charles Eaton of New Jersey slighted the work of the committee by suggesting

---

86. Richard Neustadt, "Congress and the Fair Deal: A Legislative Balance Sheet," in Richard Abrams and Lawrence W. Levine, eds., *The Shaping of Twentieth Century America* (Boston: Little, Brown, 1965), p. 574.

87. Robert C. Albright, "Civil Rights Draws Broad Backing," *Washington Post*, Oct. 30, 1947; for a sample of editorial opinion from white newspapers, see *Norfolk Journal and Guide*, Nov. 8, 1947, p. 11; and from Negro newspapers, see *Norfolk Journal and Guide*, Nov. 15, 1947, p. 11.

that "no legislation can change human nature. That has to be done by religion and thought." [88] Southern legislators were largely quiet, as were a number of possible 1948 Republican presidential candidates. New York's Thomas Dewey, Earl Warren of California, Ohio's Robert Taft, and Harold Stassen of Minnesota failed to respond to the telegrams from the *Norfolk Journal and Guide* asking them their opinion of the report.[89]

When President Truman received his copy of the report, he remarked that "this committee has given us an American charter of human freedom . . . [and] a guide for action." [90] Truman was also aware that *To Secure These Rights* was a political bombshell which had to be either detonated or defused. The choice was his alone. It was relatively easy for him to assert that the report "will take its place among the great papers of freedom," but such rhetoric was no substitute for a hard political decision requiring him to upset the political equilibrium within the Democratic party which he had used to his advantage since taking office in April, 1945. The choice was either to side with the urban liberals by sending the report, or a part of it, to Congress, or support the South by ignoring its recommendations entirely. Either decision would be irrevocable and would profoundly affect his 1948 presidential aspirations.

Truman's unwillingness to discuss the political implications of the report was manifested at a presidential press conference on November 6, 1947.

> Q: What happens to the big report of the Civil Rights Committee? Does it stay here, or do you send that to Congress?

---

88. *Norfolk Journal and Guide*, Nov. 8, 1947, p. 11.

89. Ibid., Nov. 15, 1947, p. 2.

90. *Public Papers of the Presidents: Harry S. Truman, 1947*, p. 480.

A: That report is made to me, and that report can be used as a basis for a part of the message on the State of the Union, which of course in the long run will be sent to Congress.

Q: In other words, you will use it as a part of your message?

A: I did not say that. I said that it could be used as a foundation for part of the message—some of it maybe. I have not read it carefully.

Q: What do you think of it, Mr. President?

A: I think it is a good report.[91]

During the rest of November and early December, 1947, the president discussed with officials of his administration what policy he should pursue with regard to the report. Truman received conflicting advice about the matter from his political associates, whose views were probably shaped by their own environmental background and political predilections.[92] On December 9, 1947, he asked Clark Clifford, his special counsel, to confer with Attorney General Tom Clark before submitting a recommendation to the president.[93]

Even as the administration was arriving at a decision regarding the fate of the civil rights committee's report, other moves on the civil rights front were underway. On June 23, 1947, the Supreme Court accepted for review two cases involving the issue of whether racially restrictive

---

91. Ibid., p. 482. Evidence suggesting that Truman was not entirely pleased with what he received and disagreed with some, if not many, of the recommendations can be found in Brooks Hays, *A Southern Moderate Speaks* (Chapel Hill: University of North Carolina Press, 1959), p. 33.

92. Author's interview with Oscar Chapman, June 25, 1962.

93. Personal memorandum of Clark Clifford, December 9, 1947, Clark Clifford File, HSTL.

housing covenants were enforceable.[94] This move immediately caught the attention of liberals inside and outside of the federal government, who thought it would be a good idea to have the Justice Department submit an *amicus curiae* brief on behalf of those Negroes whose cases had come before the Court. Because of the efforts of these liberals, the Justice Department was soon bombarded with letters and other forms of communication asking it to intervene in these cases.[95] The letters were collected by Solicitor General Philip Perlman, who then spoke to Attorney General Tom Clark about the matter. Clark, in turn, sought and received President Truman's permission to submit a brief. On October 30, 1947, the day after *To Secure These Rights* had been turned over to Truman, the attorney general announced at a press conference that the Justice Department was planning to involve itself in the restrictive covenant cases. It may be assumed that the decision to intervene was made largely for political reasons, that is, to help Truman secure the Negro and white liberal vote for the 1948 presidential election.[96]

On December 5, 1947, the Justice Department submitted a brief to the Supreme Court in the case of *Shelly* v. *Kraemer*.[97] Here, then, was the first of a series of briefs originating in the Solicitor General's Office during the Truman era that in time would profoundly affect American jurisprudence and, in turn, American society. In its brief the government argued that housing covenants merely served to perpetuate "an artificial quarantine of minority

94. Clement Vose, *Caucasians Only* (Berkeley: University of California Press, 1959), p. 157.

95. Ibid., p. 173. An example of that technique were the letters Walter White sent to both Truman and Clark requesting intervention in this case; see White to Truman, September 17, 1947, Attorney General Folder, Box 374, NAACP Papers, L.C.

96. Vose, *Caucasians Only*, p. 173.

97. Tom C. Clark and Philip Perlman, *Prejudice and Property* (Washington: Public Affairs Press, 1948).

groups" and should, therefore, be declared null and void. The Court was also told that "this situation cannot be reconciled with the spirit of mutual tolerance and respect for the dignity and rights of the individual which give vitality to our democratic way of life." [98] And to further emphasize the government's interest in this particular case, Perlman participated in the oral argument before the Court on January 15, 1948, where he made good use of the report of the President's Committee on Civil Rights in his attack on restrictive covenants. It was his contention that their enforcement would hamper the United States "in doing its duty in the fields of public health, housing, home finance, and in the conduct of foreign affairs." [99]

On May 3, 1948, the Supreme Court made known its decision in the restrictive covenant cases. With three justices having earlier disqualified themselves from participating in the cases, the remaining six justices unanimously agreed that racially restrictive housing covenants were not enforceable.[100] Speaking for the Court, Chief Justice Fred Vinson declared that the covenants were directed toward a group "defined wholly in terms of race and color"; and that "among the civil rights intended to be protected from discriminatory state action by the Fourteenth Amendment are the rights to acquire, enjoy, own and dispose of property." [101] Charles Abrams, a knowledgeable and sympathetic friend of urban minorities, later suggested that the government's brief was probably decisive in the adjudication of the restrictive covenant cases.[102]

---

98. Ibid.

99. Vose, *Caucasians Only*, p. 200.

100. Ibid., p. 206.

101. *Shelly* v. *Kraemer*, 334 U.S. 1 (1948).

102. Charles Abrams, *Forbidden Neighbors: A Study of Prejudice in Housing* (New York: Harper & Bros., 1955), p. 220.

The Justice Department's action in regard to *Shelly* v. *Kraemer* was a fresh move by the president to convince Negroes that he was determined to champion their rights. But it would be necessary for Truman to make even more dramatic and far-reaching moves in the field of civil rights if he was to counter a serious challenge to his liberal flank, which developed in the last days of 1947. That challenge came from Henry Wallace, who declared in Chicago on December 29, 1947, that he would be the presidential candidate of the newly formed Progressive party.[103] In announcing his candidacy, Wallace reaffirmed the strong position he had taken on civil rights at the 1944 Democratic national convention. "In speeches in the North and in the South at non-segregated meetings I have stated the simple truth that segregation and discrimination of any kind or character have no place in America." [104] And to emphasize the political impact created by the news of Wallace's candidacy, the Associated Negro Press reported from Los Angeles that "thousands of Negro voters here began lining up behind Henry A. Wallace the day after he announced that he would run for the Presidency." [105] This demonstration of sympathy for Wallace, occurring in one of America's major urban centers, indicated that civil rights would play an important role in determining who was going to win the 1948 election.

---

103. Curtis D. MacDougal, *Gideon's Army* (New York: Marzani & Munsell, 1965), I, 224–305.

104. *New York Times*, Dec. 30, 1947, p. 15. Wallace earlier had endorsed all of the recommendations contained in *To Secure These Rights;* see NAACP press release, December 19, 1947, Wallace Folder, Box 367, NAACP Papers, L.C.

105. *Race Relations* V (December, 1947—January 1948), 107; also see *Norfolk Journal and Guide*, Jan. 3, 1948, pp. 1–2. For a measurement of Wallace's political strength see American Institute of Public Opinion Poll of June, 1947, in *Public Opinion Quarterly* XII (1947), 490.

Long before Henry Wallace entered the presidential sweepstakes, Harry Truman was doing all he could—short of compromising himself in the South—to cultivate Negro voters. From August, 1946, to January, 1948, he tried to win their support primarily through rhetoric and token executive action. In short, Truman publicly condemned discrimination but refused to engage in an overt political struggle to end it. Thus it would appear that he followed a policy which was largely consistent with the one he pursued in his first year in office.

Yet Truman's position in this later period did not exactly conform to the one he had adopted earlier. He was now more strongly committed to a defense of civil rights because the domestic and international situations required him to act in a more forceful manner. Following the defeat of the Democratic party in the 1946 election, Truman soon realized that in order to win the 1948 presidential election he would need the votes of the many Negroes who lived in the key industrial states of the North and the West. And to improve his political standing with them, he created the Committee on Civil Rights, condemned discrimination in his speech to the NAACP rally in June, 1946, and authorized governmental intervention in the case of *Shelly* v. *Kraemer*. Such action, limited as it was, did move Truman beyond his earlier, more passive position of 1945–46, and prepared the way for more daring innovations in 1948.

That Truman acted at all was due not only to the changing domestic situation but to the cold war, which had transformed the civil rights issue into a problem possessing international significance. Truman realized that Soviet propaganda on this subject needed to be challenged by words, if not deeds, in order to protect America's interests in the United Nations and around the world. The treatment henceforth accorded to millions of underprivileged and abused black citizens would more than indirectly affect the outcome of the great power struggle between the United States and the Soviet Union.[106]

These, then, were the major reasons why Truman advocated the cause of equality and justice in 1947. And as the election year approached, Truman made plans to take an even more decisive stand on civil rights. He was aware that, in the words of Walter White, "the party that wins the Negro vote in 1948 will be the one that offers some concrete evidence that it intends at least to help him get a square deal." [107] Fully aware of the dangers which confronted him, Truman headed into the 1948 campaign determined to make the most of his opportunities.

---

106. Robert Cushman, "Our Civil Rights Become a World Issue," *New York Times Magazine,* January 11, 1948.

107. White, "Will the Negro Elect Our Next President?", p. 26.

Chapter **3**

PRESIDENTIAL POLITICS OF
CIVIL RIGHTS: 1948

The growing personal unpopularity of President Harry
Truman and national dissatisfaction with his administration—caused by the problems of mounting inflation and
labor unrest—helped bring about the defeat of the Democratic party in the 1946 congressional election. Fearing that
1946 was a prelude to 1948, a number of Democratic party
liberals, led by Oscar J. Ewing, acting chairman of the
Democratic National Committee and director of the Federal
Security Agency, began meeting informally in December,

1946, to devise ways and means of revitalizing the party.[1] Other members of this group included Leon Keyserling, associated with the President's Council of Economic Advisers, Charles Murphy, a White House administrative assistant, and Clark Clifford, who had been appointed the president's special counsel in mid-1946.[2]

Clifford was especially impressed by the argument advanced by members of the Ewing circle that Truman, if he was to win in 1948, would have to develop a coherent political program appealing to "labor and the urban minorities." [3] Thus, the major task of that group was to put together such a program and then, "quietly and unobtrusively, . . . try to steer the President in that direction." [4] Evidently, the first victory for Clifford and his associates occurred when Truman, after hearing much conflicting advice, decided to veto the Taft-Hartley bill, thus endearing himself to organized labor.

In mid-November, 1947, Clifford, whose responsibility it had been to funnel into the White House the information and insights he received from the liberal strategy group, delivered to Truman a forty-page memorandum dealing expressly with the issues and personalities of the 1948 campaign. Included in the memorandum were the following points: (1) Governor Thomas Dewey of New York would probably be the Republican presidential candidate, and he was "resourceful, intelligent, and highly dangerous . . . with an extremely efficient group of men around him"; (2)

---

1. Author's interview with Oscar J. Ewing on June 27, 1962; also see Phillips, *Truman Presidency*, pp. 162–65; and Irwin Ross, *The Loneliest Campaign: The Truman Victory of 1948* (New York: New American Library, 1968), pp. 18–20.

2. Ross, *The Loneliest Campaign*, pp. 19–21.

3. Ibid., pp. 21–27.

4. Phillips, *Truman Presidency*, pp. 197–98.

Henry Wallace would be a third-party candidate and would draw 5 to 10 percent of the vote in a few "key states which could throw the election to the Republicans"; and (3) the South, as always, could be "considered safely Democratic." [5]

The Clifford memorandum also presented specific policy recommendations which Truman might consider in order to deal with the combined threat of Dewey and Wallace. In the words of Cabell Phillips:

> The number one priority should be the farmers who were enjoying a high rate of prosperity and whose Republican moorings were already loosening. The labor vote was crucial in most big states, and it almost certainly would suffer some inroads from the Wallaceites. The same was true of the Negroes, and strong emphasis would be necessary to hold them in line. Jews held the key to New York, and the key to the Jewish voters was what the administration would do about Palestine.[6]

It was Clifford's conviction, then, that the requirements of 1948 called for the administration to liberalize its domestic program. Such a move could revitalize the Roosevelt political coalition and, at the same time, minimize the defection of voters to Henry Wallace in case he decided to head a third-party ticket.

Among the groups Clifford singled out for special consideration was the Negro bloc, which constituted at least 4 percent of all potential voters in such important states as New York, New Jersey, Pennsylvania, Ohio, Michigan, and Illinois.[7] And because Truman's political needs dictated a

---

5. Ibid., p. 198.

6. Ibid.

7. Jasper B. Shannon, "Political Obstacles to Civil Rights Legislation," *Annals of the American Academy of Political and Social Science* CCLXXV (1951), 53–60.

fresh commitment to the Negro cause, he was receptive to Clifford's advice. Hence, Truman decided to submit a presidential message on civil rights to Congress, a point that was indicated by remarks contained in the State of the Union address he delivered on January 7, 1948: "The recent report of the President's Civil Rights Committee points the way to corrective action by the Federal Government and by state and local governments. Because of the need for effective federal actions, I shall send a special message to Congress on this important subject." [8]

One week after the president addressed Congress, work commenced on that special message. Clark Clifford delegated to his assistant George Elsey the task of writing the first draft, and Elsey in turn secured the assistance of Professor Robert Carr of Dartmouth College, and formerly executive secretary of the President's Committee on Civil Rights. [9] After numerous consultations with Clifford, Elsey and Carr finished the draft and sent it to his office in the White House, where, according to Elsey, minor changes were made. [10] At the same time the draft was being written, other members of the White House staff and the Justice Department were organizing a different but related project: the creation of an omnibus civil rights bill designed to complement the president's message. [11]

Even before the administration completed preparations to send its civil rights message and legislative recommenda-

---

8. *Public Papers of the Presidents: Harry S. Truman, 1948* (Washington: United States Government Printing Office, 1964), p. 3. For an informed discussion of the strategy employed by the administration on this as well as other messages, see Ross, *The Loneliest Campaign*, pp. 60–61.

9. Author's interview with George Elsey on June 28, 1962.

10. Ibid.

11. See Stephen J. Spingarn File, HSTL.

tions to Congress, the civil rights issue became a topic of importance on other political fronts. On January 18, 1948, Henry Wallace released a seventy-four-point program, including demands for anti–poll tax, anti-lynching, and FEPC legislation.[12] Two days later, Governor Fielding J. Wright announced in his inaugural address in Jackson, Mississippi, that he would not tolerate any federal action "aimed to wreck the South and our institutions." As far as he was concerned, "vital principles and eternal truths transcend party lines, and the day is now at hand when determined action must be taken." [13] To emphasize this point, the Mississippi state legislature passed a resolution supporting Wright's threat of a bolt if the White House pressed for civil rights legislation.[14] Whether this resolution represented merely a state uprising or the beginning of a sectional upheaval was not yet clear.

Mindful of Wallace's potential strength with Negro voters and not at all intimidated by Governor Wright's rhetoric, President Truman dispatched his message to Congress on February 2, 1948. Stylistically similar to Truman's earlier NAACP speech, this message was not written to inflame passions; its language was dignified and responsible.

After introducing his theme that the American heritage guaranteed equal rights to all citizens, the president pointed out that "there is a serious gap between our ideals and some of our practices," and "that this gap must be closed." In the event the states and local governments were incapable of rectifying the situation, the president insisted that "the Federal government has a clear duty to see that constitutional guarantees of individual liberties and of equal protec-

---

12. *New York Times,* Jan. 19, 1948, p. 48.
13. Key, *Southern Politics,* p. 330.
14. *Norfolk Journal and Guide,* Jan. 31, 1948, p. 122.

tion under the law are not denied or abridged anywhere in America." [15] Thus, it was imperative, Truman felt, that Congress provide the federal executive with the authority necessary to protect those rights. Specifically, the president requested that Congress:

1. Establish a permanent Commission on Civil Rights, a joint Congressional Committee on Civil Rights, and a Civil Rights Division in the Department of Justice.
2. Strengthen existing civil rights statutes.
3. Provide Federal protection against lynching.
4. Protect more adequately the right to vote.
5. Establish a Fair Employment Practice Commission to prevent unfair discrimination in employment.
6. Prohibit discrimination in interstate transportation facilities.
7. Provide home rule and suffrage in Presidential elections for the residents of the District of Columbia.
8. Provide statehood for Hawaii and Alaska and a greater measure of self-government for our island possessions.
9. Equalize the opportunities for residents of the United States to become naturalized citizens.
10. Settle the evacuation claims of Japanese-Americans.[16]

The president then announced that he was going to release an executive order "containing a comprehensive restatement of the federal non-discrimination policy, together with appropriate measures to insure compliance," and that he had instructed the secretary of defense to have "the remaining instances of discrimination in the armed services eliminated as rapidly as possible." Concluding his message, he

15. *Public Papers of the Presidents: Harry S. Truman, 1948*, p. 122.

16. Ibid., p. 122.

suggested that foreign policy requirements necessitated congressional action on his ten-point program:

> The position of the United States in the world today makes it especially urgent that we adopt these measures to secure for all our people their essential rights. . . . If we wish to inspire the peoples of the world whose freedom is in jeopardy, if we wish to restore hope to those who have already lost their civil liberties, if we wish to fulfill the promise that is ours, we must correct the remaining imperfections in our practice of democracy.
> We know the way. We need only the will.[17]

After the message had been read in Congress, the government, recognizing its propaganda importance, presented it as the story of the day via the Voice of America.[18] In short, the civil rights message now entered the cold war arena as a document of diplomacy. At home it immediately became a source of major political controversy. A number of liberals were disappointed with the moderate, apparently equivocal stand the president had taken on the subject of segregation. Willard Shelton, a reporter for the New York newspaper *PM,* noted, for example, that the message generally ignored the pervasive influence of segregation in American life and that it disregarded almost entirely those recommendations of the Civil Rights Committee which called for the radical repudiation of Jim Crow.[19] Few liberals or moderates were as critical of Truman's position as Shelton; most were pleased with his courageous stand, especially Negroes such as Walter White.

---

17. Ibid., p. 126.

18. Memorandum to Philleo Nash from Howland Sargeant, Philleo Nash Files, Box 24, HSTL.

19. Willard Shelton, "Political Aims May Wreck Truman's Civil Rights Program," *PM,* Feb. 3, 1948; also see *Norfolk Journal and Guide,* Feb. 14, 1948, p. 2.

On the other hand, the message met with predictable disapproval from the South. In Congress, only Florida's Senator Claude Pepper spoke approvingly of the president's action. More typical of southern congressional opinion were the remarks of Mississippi's Congressman John Bell Williams:

> If it were not for Southern Democrats, Henry Wallace would be in the White House today instead of Harry Truman. Southern Democrats have always been the best friends that President Truman or the Democratic Party ever had. May I say . . . that it is a mightly poor way for him to evince his gratitude.[20]

Congressman Eugene Cox of Georgia stated: "When I read his message I wondered if, after all, Henry Wallace is such a bad man. The President attacks the people of that section of the country whose support he must have if he is to hope to be reelected. The whole thing sickens me." [21] And, finally, Senator James O. Eastland demanded that the South refuse to give its electoral votes to the Democratic party's candidate in order to promote the election of a "distinguished Southerner." [22]

Despite Eastland's call for a bolt from the Democratic party, it was reported by C. P. Trussel in the *New York Times* that in certain unspecified congressional quarters such talk was considered to be "just another Dixie flareup which would wind up with Dixie in line." [23] There was a good reason, suggested Arthur Krock, why the Trussel report might be worth considering: "Lavish federal bounties,

---

20. *Congressional Record*, 80th Cong., 2d Sess., 1948, Vol. LXXXVI, Part 2, p. 976.
21. Ibid.
22. Ibid., pp. 1134–37.
23. Feb. 4, 1948, p. 1.

originating with the New Deal, but happily accepted and retained by anti-New Deal Democratic politicians of the South have tied their constituents tightly to Democratic executive power." [24]

Still, this southern "flareup" might have been more serious if the White House's omnibus civil rights bill had been introduced in the Congress. Senate minority leader Alben Barkley of Kentucky, who received the bill from the White House on February 4, refused to sponsor it after he had observed the reaction of the Southern Democrats to the February 2 message.[25] (Barkley himself had not been consulted either about its contents or the designated date for its delivery.)

While the president faced the wrath of the Southern Democrats, the Republicans in Congress—fearing that they had been outflanked by his message—were now prompted to move their civil rights legislation through House and Senate committees to take advantage of whatever Democratic schism might develop. Republican members of the House Judiciary Subcommittee pressed on February 4 for full committee action on proposed anti-lynching legislation.[26] In the upper house, the Senate Labor Committee voted 7–5 to

---

24. *New York Times*, Feb. 5, 1948, p. 2.

25. Author's interview with Philleo Nash on June 29, 1962. The omnibus bill was divided into two sections: (1) Provisions to strengthen federal government machinery, specifically, the establishment of a civil rights commission in the executive branch of government; the reorganization of civil rights activities in the Department of Justice; and the creation of a joint congressional civil rights committee. (2) Provisions to strengthen the protection of individual rights, specifically, anti-lynching legislation; amendments and supplements to existing civil rights statutes; federal anti-poll tax legislation; protection of political rights; a federal FEPC; prohibition against discrimination and segregation in interstate transportation. For a copy of this draft bill, see Stephen J. Spingarn File, HSTL.

26. *New York Times*, Feb. 5, 1948, p. 17.

bring the Ives FEPC bill to the floor, even though the commit-tee's chairman, Senator Robert Taft, voted with the south-ern members to block its discharge.[27] This Republican move at last convinced Senator James Eastland that "organized mongrel minorities control the government. I am going to fight it to the last ditch. They are not going to Harlemize the country." [28] Eastland's call to arms was answered by a num-ber of southern politicians, mostly from Mississippi, Ala-bama, and South Carolina. Mississippi Representative John Bell Williams, for instance, warned the administration not to "brush off" Dixie's threat of secession.[29] But few south-ern congressmen were prepared to lead such a movement, fearing a loss of their patronage claims and seniority privi-leges, if the president decided to take action against them. Hence, most congressmen who favored a bolt requested that local and state officials develop and lead the campaign against the national leadership of the party.[30]

That such a campaign might not sweep the South was indicated by the events taking place during the Southern Governors' Conference at Wakulla Springs, Florida, from February 6 through February 8. A majority of southern governors refused to support the resolution submitted by Governor Wright of Mississippi and Governor James Fol-som of Alabama calling for a meeting at Jackson, Missis-sippi, on March 1 "to formulate plans for activity and adopt a course of action." [31] Georgia's Governor Marvin E. Thompson, though condemning Truman's civil rights mes-

27. Ibid., Feb. 6, 1948, p. 1. Taft later moved to postpone all floor action for at least six weeks; see *Norfolk Journal and Guide*, Mar. 6, 1948, p. 2.

28. Ibid., p. 5.

29. Ibid., p. 17.

30. Ibid.

31. Key, *Southern Politics*, p. 330.

sage as "unnecessary" and "unwise," refused to sanction a secession from the party. He said: "I cannot join in any movement which directly or indirectly would cut the feet from under the Democratic party and its leaders, and thereby deprive the South of its greatest strength. I will support the Democratic party." [32] Governor Millard Caldwell of Florida endorsed the sentiments expressed by his colleague from Georgia, thereby weakening the drive of the "bolters" to sweep the South with an anti-party ticket of their own.[33] On the other hand, the governors' conference did not entirely pigeonhole the issue, deciding instead to postpone action for forty days while a five-man committee headed by South Carolina's Governor Strom Thurmond sought to arrange a compromise solution through direct consultation with the president.[34]

As the various southern governors returned home to await the outcome of their ad hoc committee's meeting with Truman, the civil rights issue remained loaded with political dynamite. Republicans asserted that the president's message had been ingeniously designed to appeal to the Negro vote in such states as New York, Pennsylvania, and Illinois.[35] Ignoring this Republican charge, the White House announced on February 10 that "there will be absolutely no compromise on any point." [36] Two days later, the president further affirmed this point by declaring at his news conference that he would not discuss the matter with any southern group.[37] Subsequently, the Thurmond group scheduled a

---

32. *New York Times*, Feb. 7, 1948, p. 9E.

33. Ibid., Feb. 8, 1948, p. 1.

34. Key, *Southern Politics*, p. 17.

35. *New York Times*, Feb. 8, 1948, p. 9E.

36. Ibid., Feb. 10, 1948, p. 1.

37. *Public Papers of the Presidents: Harry S. Truman, 1948*, p. 138.

meeting with Senator J. Howard McGrath, the chairman of the Democratic National Committee.

The response of the Negro press to the February 2 message was enthusiastic. Davis Niles, a White House administrative assistant, indicated as much in a memo he sent to the president on February 16:

> Strong favorable language was the rule in the editorials. The President was described as the new champion of human freedom. The program as a whole was hailed as the strongest civil rights program ever put forth by any President. The message was referred to as the greatest freedom document since the Emancipation Proclamation. The language of the message was described as Lincolnesque.[38]

Such praise could help Truman undermine Henry Wallace's appeal to urban voters; otherwise, the Republicans would have little trouble capturing the White House.

Wallace's campaign was beginning to take on serious and ominous proportions so far as Democrats were concerned. Although Wallace was not yet receiving a significant endorsement from organized labor, he seemed quite capable of drawing considerable support in an important urban constituency such as New York. Wallace came to New York on February 15 to promote the candidacy of Leo Isacson, the Progressive party's nominee for the vacant Twenty-fourth Congressional District, located in the Bronx. Speaking on behalf of Isacson, Wallace attacked Truman's wavering Palestine position as one which played into the hands of Ameri-

---

38. Memorandum to the President from David K. Niles, February 16, 1948, Philleo Nash Files, HSTL. See *Norfolk Journal and Guide*, Feb. 14, 1948, p. 8, for the following: "Mr. Truman received the report of his Civil Rights Committee on October 29, 1947. That he has so promptly acted on some of its recommendations, and during an election year at that, demonstrates that he has honest and deep convictions and the courage to give official voice to them."

can oil interests; [39] it was an approach especially designed to appeal to the many Jewish voters of that district now disenchanged with Truman's handling of the heated Palestine question. Later that day, Wallace discussed civil rights at a black rally in Harlem. After pointing out that the president's February 2 message had generally ignored the issue of segregation in American life, Wallace went on to say that "Southern Governors and Senators have no more reason to fear action on Mr. Truman's . . . message than we have to expect it. They are angry that the President has paid lip service to the fundamental democratic principles." [40]

To the surprise of many Democrats, Leo Isacson emerged victorious in the February 17 special election, with a vote of 22,697 as compared with the 12,578 given to his Democratic opponent, Karl G. Propper. [41] The Progressive party's triumph was regarded by some observers as a spectacular upset which strongly indicated that President Truman lacked strength in big-city New Deal constituencies. [42] A few days after the election, James A. Hagerty reported the results of a *New York Times* survey which indicated that Wallace's political stock had risen in Michigan, Pennsylvania, Illinois, and California, because of Isacson's victory in New York. [43] The survey concluded with the observation that Truman would be hard pressed to win any of these states in the fall now that Wallace had demonstrated that his party was more than just a potential threat. [44]

It was just subsequent to the Isacson election, at a time

---

39. *New York Times*, Feb. 16, 1948, p. 5. Also see Ross, *The Loneliest Campaign*, pp. 65–66.

40. *New York Times*, Feb. 16, 1948, p. 5.

41. MacDougal, *Gideon's Army*, III, 323.

42. Ibid., pp. 324–35.

43. *New York Times*, February 18, 1948, p. 1.

44. Ibid., p. 15.

when Democratic party officials were "more worried about Wallace than a bolt or a half bolt from the south," [45] that Truman decided to launch his 1948 election drive. Speaking at the traditional Jefferson-Jackson Day banquet in Washington on February 19, he mentioned the magical name of Franklin Roosevelt for the first time since before the 1946 election, intimating, of course, that his administration was the true heir of the New Deal tradition. He further declared that the Democratic party was the party of "progressive liberalism," the Republican, the party of "reactionary conservatism." [46] Truman was now beginning to appropriate the "vital center" of American politics in order to isolate Wallace. Meanwhile, he waited for the reaction on his right to fizzle out.

If the hierarchy of the Democratic party thought the southern response to the February 2 speech was a "tempest in a teapot—a solid front put up for political purposes," [47] they were mistaken, for some southern congressmen were really quite serious about a party revolt. On February 19— the day Truman delivered his Jefferson-Jackson Day speech —52 out of 103 Southern Democrats in the House of Representatives, headed by William Colmer of Mississippi, caucused for the purpose of endorsing the efforts of Governor Strom Thurmond's committee to seek a compromise with the administration on civil rights. While taking steps to have representatives attend the Thurmond-McGrath meeting (McGrath having replaced Truman), they also put the administration on notice that the party would be facing "serious consequences" if a civil rights plank was included in the 1948 platform. [48]

---

45. Ibid., Feb. 22, 1948, p. E3.

46. *Public Papers of the Presidents: Harry S. Truman, 1948*, p. 32.

47. *Norfolk Journal and Guide*, Feb. 14, 1948, p. 2.

48. *New York Times*, Feb. 20, 1948, p. 1.

Even though Southern Democrats such as Senator East-land had already raised the specter of a bolt, the administration stood its ground by refusing to compromise the principles ennunciated in the February 2 message. Senator J. Howard McGrath made this clear in a meeting with Governor Strom Thurmond and other members of the ad hoc committee from the Southern Governors' Conference on February 23.[49] McGrath defended the February 2 message as a moderate statement which did not call for the repeal of the segregationist system except in the case of interstate transportation. At one point in the meeting, however, McGrath indicated that something might be arranged to allay southern hostilities; he suggested that perhaps the 1944 Democratic party civil rights plank could serve as the model for the 1948 plank.[50] Governor Thurmond, the most belligerent member of the southern group, was unwilling to consider any accommodation with the administration as long as it refused to withdraw its civil rights program. Following their unsuccessful meeting with McGrath, the governors released a four-hundred-word statement declaring that "the South was no longer in the bag." [51]

Actually, a good part of the South was already committed to the Truman organization. For instance, Governor R. Gregg Cherry of North Carolina announced on February 28, 1948, that he would support Truman, civil rights program or no civil rights program.[52] But an active, vocal minority of southern politicians refused to hoist the banner of party loyalty, preferring instead to go their own way. In Virginia, Governor William Tuck asked his legislature on February 26 to modify the state election laws in order to

---

49. Key, *Southern Politics*, p. 331.
50. *New York Times*, Feb. 24, 1948, p. 14.
51. Phillips, *The Truman Presidency*, p. 207.
52. Key, *Southern Politics*, p. 331.

permit a state party convention to determine, if necessary, how the state's electoral votes would be cast in November.[53] In Mississippi, the state Democratic executive committee decided on March 1 that its state electors "would stand firmly for states rights and therefore against any nominee for President or Vice President who refuses to take an open and positive stand against civil rights recommendations." The committee also instructed the state's delegation to the Democratic national convention "to withdraw from the convention if the civil rights program was placed in the party platform, and if the party nominees did not give proper assurances." [54]

Because the civil rights issue generated an unseasonable heat, the political temperature of the country started to rise long before the political conventions were scheduled to begin. It was in this context that President Truman announced on March 8, through Senator McGrath, that he would be a presidential candidate in 1948.[55] McGrath remarked: "I have talked to the President with respect to his civil rights message. The President's position remains unchanged since he delivered that message." [56]

Although Truman remained publicly committed to the principles he espoused in the February 2 message, he decided to shelve his omnibus civil rights bill rather than present it formally to Congress as an administration-sponsored measure. He indicated as much at his press conference on March 11.

Q: Mr. President, do you plan to send Congress bills to carry out your civil rights message?

---

53. *New York Times*, Feb. 27, 1948, p. 1.

54. Key, *Southern Politics*, p. 332.

55. John Redding, *Inside the Democratic Party* (Indianapolis: Bobbs-Merrill, 1958), p. 103.

56. *New York Times*, Mar. 9, 1948, p. 15.

A: Congress never feels very happy when the Executive sends them bills and says "this is it." When I was in Congress it was customary for Congress to write its own bill. If they request suggestions from me, I will be glad to make them.[57]

Truman canceled his original plan to send such legislation to Capitol Hill because the South was manifesting much greater resistance to his February 2 message than he or Clifford had anticipated.[58] Unwilling to alienate that section any more than absolutely necessary, Truman now retreated somewhat from his more advanced position in order to protect his flank against the possibility of a southern revolt. Southerners who were inclined to revolt, of course, failed to understand that Truman was engaged in symbolic action, that his rhetoric was a substitute for a genuine legislative commitment.

Truman's temporizing with the rebellious southern states also extended to the executive branch. In his February 2 message he had pledged to issue an executive order "containing a comprehensive restatement of the federal non-discrimination policy, together with appropriate measures to insure compliance." [59] By the end of March a draft of that order was available, but, in the words of George Elsey, it was "weasely and unsatisfactory." [60] No moves were underway either to strengthen it or to prepare it for release. Evidently the southern revolt had frightened Truman and his associates, including Oscar Ewing and Senator McGrath, into deferring, if not permanently suspending,

57. *Public Papers of the Presidents: Harry S. Truman, 1948,* p. 179.

58. Ross, *The Loneliest Campaign,* p. 64.

59. *Public Papers of the Presidents: Harry S. Truman, 1948,* pp. 122–26.

60. Ross, *The Loneliest Campaign,* p. 65.

that action.[61] Aware of this development, Philleo Nash, a White House aide strongly in sympathy with the cause of civil rights, suggested to Clarence Mitchell, a Washington representative of the NAACP's national office, that Walter White write Truman about the delay in releasing the order so as to offset the "negative influences operating around the White House." [62] In his letter to White advancing Nash's suggestion, Mitchell also mentioned that "Philleo made an interesting observation that the present revolt in some respects is not as bad as it was in 1944, but it is hard to get some people around here (the White House) to see that." [63]

If the February 2 message antagonized some southerners, it improved Truman's standing with the black community, a point emphasized by the Democratic party executive committee in its meeting in Washington on March 11. As reported in the *New York Times* of March 12, "Members from the North and Far West, conceding that the Truman administration had reached the depths, asserted that they saw the President's stock picking up." His strong stand on civil rights, in the *Time*'s opinion, had helped to improve his position.[64] Yet the continuing challenge of Wallace and the Republicans would perhaps make it necessary for Truman to adopt new and bold programs to convince Negroes that his administration really intended to protect their rights. How far and how fast he would move with respect to civil

---

61. Ibid.

62. Clarence Mitchell to Walter White, April 5, 1948, Truman Executive Order Folder, Box 419, NAACP Papers, L.C. White dispatched a letter to Truman on this very issue; see Walter White to Harry Truman, April 7, 1948, Truman Executive Order Folder, Box 419, NAACP Papers, L.C.

63. Clarence Mitchell to Walter White, April 5, 1948, Truman Executive Order Folder, Box 419, NAACP Papers, L.C.

64. P. 17.

rights would be determined by the requirements of the forthcoming campaign.

Several prominent Negroes refused to wait for the president's next gambit in this civil rights chess game. Realizing that Truman's political ambitions and needs might make him vulnerable to pressure, A. Philip Randolph and the Reverend Grant Reynolds had organized on October 10, 1947, a Committee against Jim Crow in Military Service and Training.[65] In December, 1947, Randolph and Reynolds received a promise from the Democratic National Committee that a statement against a segregated draft act would be issued, but no action was taken.[66] On February 5, 1948, Randolph informed a representative of the Democratic National Committee that the Committee against Jim Crow wanted the administration to repudiate publicly any legislation perpetuating military segregation. Randolph was told that "careful consideration" would be given his request.[67]

On March 22, 1948, Randolph and other concerned citizens met with the president and requested his support for anti-segregation amendments to the proposed draft bill. During this meeting Randolph informed Truman that his (Randolph's) recent travels around the country convinced him that "Negroes are in no mood to shoulder guns for democracy abroad, while they are denied democracy here at home"; he then announced that unless the government took decisive action to change the current racial policies of the

---

65. The President's Committee on Equality of Treatment and Opportunity in the Armed Forces (hereafter known as the Fahy Committee), Box 10, HSTL.

66. Dalfiume, *Desegregation of the U.S. Armed Forces*, p. 163. For a comprehensive discussion of how segregation and discrimination in National Guard units became an issue of national significance at this time, see pp. 159–62.

67. Ibid., p. 163.

armed forces, a civil disobedience campaign would be launched.[68] Truman made it clear that he was not happy with those remarks. The conference ended with nothing settled.

The Randolph-Reynolds call for racial reform of the armed forces was soon repeated by twenty Negro organizations which had gathered in New York on March 27, 1948, at the request of the NAACP. They released a public statement pointing out that Negro votes could play a "balance of power" role in at least seventeen states in a presidential election, and that their support required the elimination of segregation and discrimination from the armed forces.[69]

Once it was evident that no concessions were forthcoming from the administration, Randolph and Reynolds decided to press the issue before Congress. On March 30, 1948, they appeared before the Senate Armed Services Committee and repeated their threat to lead a civil disobedience campaign if Congress refused to pass legislation outlawing segregation and discrimination in the armed forces. As Randolph put it:

> I personally pledge myself to openly counsel, aid and abet youth, both white and colored, to quarantine any Jim Crow conscription system, whether it bears the label Universal Military Training or Selective Service. From coast to coast . . . I shall call upon all colored veterans to join this Civil Disobedience movement and to recruit their younger brothers in an organized refusal to register.

Randolph further declared, in response to questions from Republican Senator Wayne Morse of Oregon, that he would counsel such action even if the country were at war, trea-

---

68. *Crisis* LV (1948), 140.

69. Declaration of Negro Voters Folder, Box 376, NAACP Papers, L.C.

sonable as it seemed to Morse, "on the theory that . . . we are serving a higher law than the law which applies to the act of treason.[70]

Randolph's threatened use of civil disobedience tactics divided the Negro community. Harlem Congressman Adam Clayton Powell announced he would support the Randolph proposal if Congress passed a draft bill lacking an anti-segregation amendment.[71] Blacks polled in New York City indicated that Randolph would receive considerable support for his campaign as long as the country remained at peace.[72] On the other hand, Walter White and the Negro press generally opposed this move, while admitting that the grievances aired by Randolph and Reynolds were indeed legitimate and that the bitterness inside of the Negro community about which they spoke did exist.[73]

As Randolph continued to press his attack, James Forrestal, the secretary of defense, and Lester Granger, the head of the National Urban League, were laying the groundwork for a "National Defense Conference on Negro Affairs" permitting Negro spokesmen to advise the armed forces how they might best overcome their racial problems.[74] On April 26, 1948, Secretary Forrestal and representatives from the three services met with a delegation of Negroes, headed by Granger. He informed Forrestal and the others that A. Philip Randolph had been warmly praised for his efforts by "what may easily be a majority of Negroes throughout the

---

70. U.S. Senate, Committee on Armed Services, *Hearings . . . on Universal Military Training* (Washington: United States Government Printing Office, 1948), pp. 688–89.

71. *Pittsburgh Courier*, Apr. 10, 1948, pp. 1, 4.

72. *Congressional Record*, 80th Cong., 2d Sess., 1948, XCIV, 4314–18.

73. *Pittsburgh Courier*, Apr. 10, 1948, pp. 1, 4.

74. Ibid.

country." [75] Furthermore, Granger asserted, it was necessary to desegregate the armed forces in order to prevent irreparable damage to the national interest. Navy and Air Force officials present informed Granger and his associates that they were formulating plans to eliminate segregation and discrimination in their respective branches. But Army Secretary Kenneth Royall, who was at the meeting, refused to countenance any such move; he strongly endorsed the position taken by Chief of Staff General Omar Bradley of favoring continued military segregation. [76] Disgusted by Royall's stand, the Negro delegation refused to serve further as Pentagon advisers. The battle for a desegregated defense establishment was now headed for Congress. [77]

Meanwhile, anti-Truman elements of the Southern Democracy were making bold moves in the direction of a walkout. On March 13, in Washington, seven out of fifteen southern governors, upon receiving Strom Thurmond's report of his committee's fruitless negotiations with Chairman McGrath, repudiated Truman and his civil rights program, called for the restoration of the two-thirds rule in the convention, and urged southerners to cast their electoral college votes for those candidates who did not support civil rights legislation. [78] Later, the chairmen of the Mississippi and Arkansas state Democratic committees arranged to have a states' rights conference assemble in Jackson, Mississippi, on May 10 to promote further the aims and interests of "states' rights" Democrats. [79]

---

75. Fahy Papers, Box 11, HSTL.

76. Ibid.

77. Dalfiume, *Desegregation of the U.S. Armed Forces*, pp. 166–67.

78. Key, *Southern Politics*, p. 333.

79. Ibid., p. 335. Senator McGrath was not happy with this development; attempting to placate these potential rebels, he remarked that "the people simply don't realize that the President has never said

Before the states' rights convention opened, a primary election was held in Alabama on May 4 to determine whether loyal party Democrats, represented by Senator Lister Hill and Governor James Folsom, could prevent the Dixiecrat faction from seizing control of the party machinery.[80] The voters of Alabama, as was indicated by the returns of May 4 and June 1, decided that the state electors would be pledged to vote against Truman or any other so-called civil rights candidate. Half of the elected Alabama delegation to the Democratic national convention was committed to a bolt if the national convention adopted a civil rights plank.[81] Despite these results, "the administration," according to Arthur Krock, "was not worried about the Southern uprising." [82]

The May 10 meeting in Jackson, Mississippi, illuminated the fact that the rebellion had its deepest roots in Mississippi and South Carolina.[83] During the proceedings Governor Wright of Mississippi and Governor Thurmond of South Carolina vehemently attacked Truman and his civil rights program. In his remarks Thurmond distorted what the President had actually recommended in his February 2 message by making it appear that Truman had called for the abolition of segregation from American life.[84] But more

---

a single word about invading State's rights. There is not and never has been any intention to upset or invade the rights of the States under the constitution" (see *Norfolk Journal and Guide*, May 8, 1948, p. 1).

80. Key, *Southern Politics*, p. 333.

81. *New York Times*, May 6, 1948, p. 3.

82. Ibid., May 7, 1948, p. 22.

83. Key, *Southern Politics*, p. 334.

84. Ibid. The Dixiecrats were intent on stigmatizing the Truman program as a direct threat to the Jim Crow system; see Alexander Heard, *A Two Party South?* (Chapel Hill: University of North Carolina Press, 1952), p. 181.

than bombast issued from this meeting: plans were prepared for the calling of a states' rights nominating convention to meet in Birmingham, Alabama, on July 17, in the event the Democratic national convention adopted Truman's civil rights program.[85]

Throughout the spring of 1948 President Truman refused to discuss publicly the issue of a bolt; and at a press conference on May 13 he denied that the administration was preparing an executive order to end the practice of discrimination in the federal executive branch.[86] By taking this position Truman hoped to placate as much of the South as possible before the start of the Democratic national convention. Arthur Krock, writing in the *New York Times* of June 8, confirmed that the Truman administration "was feverishly working to prevent a walkout by some Southern delegations." [87] What the administration offered them was a 1948 civil rights plank comparable to the one included in the party's 1944 platform. The 1944 plank, which Walter White four years earlier had called a splinter, was a rather innocuous statement:

> We believe racial and religious minorities have the right to live, develop and vote equally with all citizens and share the rights that are guaranteed by our Constitution. Congress should exert its full constitutional powers to protect those rights.[88]

But whether the die-hard Dixiecrats would be satisfied with it was not certain. And quite possibly, liberals might not find it acceptable either.

---

85. Key, *Southern Politics*, p. 335.

86. *Public Papers of the Presidents: Harry S. Truman, 1948*, p. 254.

87. P. 24.

88. Kirk H. Porter and Donald Johnson, *National Party Platforms: 1840–1964* (Urbana: University of Illinois Press, 1966), p. 404.

While Truman tried to unite the torn factions of the Democratic party behind his candidacy, the Republican party met in Philadelphia during the third week of June and selected Governor Thomas E. Dewey of New York and Governor Earl Warren of California to carry the party's banners. With respect to civil rights, Dewey's record was clearly superior to that of any previous New York governor.[89] In 1945 he helped to push through the legislature a bill creating a State Commission against Discrimination (a state FEPC law); and throughout his years as governor, he appointed Negroes to positions in the state government they had never before held.[90]

Perhaps the best public expression of Dewey's 1948 civil rights views were contained in the civil rights plank of the Republican party's 1948 platform:

> Lynching or any other form of mob violence anywhere is a disgrace to any civilized state, and we favor the prompt enactment of legislation to end this infamy.
>
> One of the basic principles of this Republic is the equality of all individuals in their right to life, liberty and the pursuit of happiness. This principle is enunciated in the Declaration of Independence and embodied in the Constitution of the United States; it was vindicated in battle and became the cornerstone of the Republic. This right of equal opportunity to work and to advance in life should never be limited in any individual because of race, religion, or country of origin. We favor the enactment and just enforcement of such Federal legislation as it may be necessary to maintain this right at all times in every part of this Republic.
>
> We favor the abolition of the poll tax as a requisite to voting.
>
> We are opposed to the ideal of racial segregation in the armed forces of the United States.[91]

---

89. Lubell, *The Future of American Politics*, p. 100.
90. Moon, *Balance of Power*, p. 209.
91. Porter and Johnson, *National Party Platforms*, pp. 452–53.

Although this plank was not as inclusive or as far-reaching as the position Truman took in his February 2 message, it placed the Republican party on record as opposed to segregation in the armed forces.

But if Dewey intended to compete for a substantial part of the Negro vote, he would find it necessary to publicize his commitment to that civil rights plank and to discuss as well his achievements in New York State. But such a campaign could focus attention on the failure of the Republican Eightieth Congress to pass any civil rights legislation, a point which Walter White had already made in his testimony delivered to representatives of the resolutions committee of the Republican national convention:

> We would be less than honest if we did not say frankly that the members of our organizations have been disappointed by the complete failure of the Republican controlled Eightieth Congress to enact any of the civil rights legislation pledged in the 1944 platform.[92]

If Wallace appeared to be a millstone around Truman's neck, then the domestic record of the Eightieth Congress was a weight which could sink Dewey.

After the Republicans left Philadelphia, the Democrats prepared to hold their convention in the City of Brotherly Love. In the weeks preceding the opening of that convention, the president continued to extend the olive branch to the southern malcontents. On June 22 Truman met with Congressman John Rankin of Mississippi and apparently persuaded him that a compromise on civil rights could be arranged. Following his discussion with the president, Rankin informed the press, "I am not without hope that the

---

92. Republican National Committee File, Box 1951, NAACP Papers, L.C.

Democratic convention will reach a satisfactory agreement on the civil rights issue. If that convention adopts the same plank that was inserted in the platform of 1944, I am assured that it will be adhered to." [93] With these remarks Rankin seemingly implied that if the 1944 plank was written into the 1948 platform, the president would not sponsor future civil rights legislation.

Following the publication of Rankin's comments, Henry Wallace, speaking in Washington, charged the president with hypocrisy on the civil rights issue.

If we ever had any hesitancy before, Mr. Rankin has dispelled our doubts. We can now say of President Truman's civil rights message that the views in the message are not necessarily those of the sponsor. We can go further. We can say positively that they are not the views of Mr. Truman.[94]

Nevertheless, the NAACP, holding its annual convention in St. Louis, Missouri, during the last week of June, refused to condemn the president. Truman was praised for the stand he had taken on civil rights, while Wallace was attacked, particularly by Walter White, for his failure to fight discrimination or segregation during the years he had served as vice-president and secretary of agriculture and commerce.[95] It was evident that the leadership of the NAACP preferred Truman to Dewey or Wallace. (Apparently, a rift that existed in March between Truman and Wallace supporters within the organization had been healed by late June.) [96]

---

93. *New York Times*, June 23, 1948, p. 14.
94. Ibid., June 26, 1948, p. 4.
95. Walter White Folder, Box 376, NAACP Papers, L.C.
96. *New York Times*, Mar. 20, 1948.

Outwardly unperturbed by Wallace's statement, and probably comforted by the support he was receiving from the NAACP, Truman, with the help of his aides, pushed on with his efforts to achieve a compromise with the South. While Truman tried to mend his southern fences, he was faced with another revolt, this time from Democrats of various political persuasions who were organizing a "Draft Eisenhower" movement. The Eisenhower boom was born of the despair and fear of many Democrats that Truman's nomination would produce a shattering defeat for the party in November. Included in this variegated movement were liberals such as Senator Claude Pepper of Florida, Walter Reuther, president of the United Automobile Workers union, Chester Bowles and Wilson Wyatt of Americans for Democratic Action, a recently formed private liberal organization, and southern conservatives such as Senator Richard Russell of Georgia and South Carolina's Governor Strom Thurmond.[97] But their hopes of capturing the convention with General Dwight Eisenhower were dashed on July 10, 1948, when he declared that he would not "accept even if nominated." [98]

Earlier, on July 5 fifty members of the "Draft Eisenhower" group, who were meeting in Minneapolis, made it clear that they were going to fight for the inclusion of Truman's civil rights program in the party platform. For them:

> The report of the President's Committee on Civil Rights is one of the most important measures of moral

---

97. MacDougal, *Gideon's Army*, II, 473–75; for additional material, plus a thoughtful evaluation of this phenomenon, see Ross, *The Loneliest Campaign*, pp. 72–75, 112–14.

98. MacDougal, *Gideon's Army*, II, 475.

strategy devised by the United States of America in modern times. . . . Its sponsorship will remain a landmark in the history of this Democratic administration.

As active members of the Democratic party and as citizens, we support this program. Many of us will be delegates to the national convention of our party in Philadelphia. The issue of civil rights is in the worthiest tradition of our party. We hereby declare that we shall actively seek, at Philadelphia, to make the accomplishment of this program a part of our party's platform for 1948.[99]

This statement was endorsed by "Eisenhower Democrats" like Congressman James Roosevelt, Cook County boss Jacob Arvey, and a newly arrived liberal spokesman, Hubert Humphrey, mayor of Minneapolis; and it also received the backing of Truman stalwarts, including former New York governor Herbert Lehman, Mayor David Lawrence of Pittsburgh, and Boss Edward J. Flynn of the Bronx.[100]

Thus, by the time the drafting committee of the Democratic national convention assembled in Philadelphia on July 7 to begin work on the party's platform, it was clear that there would be a fight if the liberals pressed their civil rights campaign. Pennsylvania's Senator Francis Myers, the chairman of the platform committee, would have to deal with the problem at first hand; but any civil rights plank drafted by his committee for presentation to the convention would surely have the backing of the president and his advisers through their prior approval.

Before the platform committee began its work, its members received testimony from people representing various organizations and points of view. Among those who addressed them was Walter White, spokesman for not only the

---

99. *New York Times*, July 6, 1948, p. 26.
100. Ibid.

NAACP but twenty other Negro organizations, with a combined membership of 6,084,000. White told the committee that the 1944 Democratic civil rights plank would be wholly unsatisfactory in 1948 because "human events not only within the continental United States but throughout the world have moved measurably forward in the past four years. The party must move forward or perish." He pointed out that Negro voters, numbering as many as three million, would be a "vital factor" in some 75 out of 435 congressional districts in at least seventeen border states and northern states with a total of 295 electoral college votes. "Issues," said White, "instead of party labels will determine how these votes will be cast." [101]

White's statement had little impact on the men who had the authority and power to decide what would go into the party's civil rights plank. To insure compliance with the president's will, Clark Clifford, Truman's special counsel, came to Philadelphia on July 10 to consult with Senator Myers about the language and content of the committee's civil rights draft.[102] Clifford, it was reported, presented Myers with a virtual rewrite of the 1944 plank, containing none of the specific recommendations demanded by Walter White or the Americans for Democratic Action.[103]

But complicating Clifford's task was Hubert Humphrey, a member of the drafting committee, who announced that he intended to fight for the inclusion of such specific civil rights recommendations as an anti-lynching law, abolition of the poll tax, an FEPC, and the abolition of segregation in

101. Box 367, NAACP Papers, L.C.

102. *New York Times*, July 12, 1948, p. 31. Members of Myers's committee included Senators Scott Lucas of Illinois, Theodore Francis Green of Rhode Island, John Sparkman of Alabama, plus Philip Perlman, the solicitor general of the United States.

103. Ibid. For a slightly different description of how the document reached Myers, see Ross, *The Loneliest Campaign*, pp. 120–21.

the armed forces.[104] But given the preponderant Truman majority on this committee, Humphrey was not likely to succeed in his attempt to strengthen the plank, unless, of course, he was prepared to take the question of the plan to the convention floor. As expected, a majority of the platform committee approved a plank articulating the Truman position, a move which still failed to placate the most intransigent southerners, who wanted not only the restoration of the two-thirds rule but a resolution in favor of "states' rights" as well. Liberals were offended by the plank's equivocal language; they wanted specific civil rights propositions, not bland generalities. A floor fight was now in prospect.

On July 14 the civil rights issue precipitated a dramatic confrontation between the anti-administration liberals, administration supporters, and southern delegates. On behalf of the 108 members of the platform committee, Senator Myers presented to the convention that version of the civil rights plank which a majority of his committee approved:

The Democratic party is responsible for the great civil rights gains made in recent years in eliminating unfair and illegal discrimination based on race, creed or color.

The Democratic party commits itself to continuing its efforts to eradicate all racial, religious and economic discrimination.

We again state our belief that racial and religious minorities must have the right to live, the right to work, the right to vote, the full and equal protection of the laws, on a basis of equality with all citizens as guaranteed by the Constitution.

---

104. For the role played by Americans for Democratic Action, see Clifford Brock, *ADA* (Washington: Public Affairs Press, 1962), p. 97; also see *Norfolk Journal and Guide*, July 17, 1948, p. 2. A shrewd account of Humphrey's indecision about leading this fight, and his desire to retain organizational roots, can be found in Ross, *The Loneliest Campaign*, pp. 123–24.

We again call upon the Congress to exert its full authority to the limit of its constitutional powers to assure and protect these rights.[105]

After Senator Myers had finished reading the text of the platform, other members of the drafting committee submitted their minority resolutions. Dan Moody of Texas, Cecil Sims of Tennessee, and Walter Sillers of Mississippi, respectively, presented three different versions of the states' rights plank. The Moody plank, the only one of the three to receive a roll call vote, read as follows:

> . . . The Democratic Party stands for the principle that the Constitution contemplated and established a Union of indestructible sovereign states and that under the Constitution the general Federal Government and the separate states have their separate fields of power and of permitted activities. Traditionally it has been and it remains a part of the faith of the Democratic party that the Federal Government shall not encroach upon the reserved powers of the states by centralization of government and otherwise.
>
> Within the reserved powers of the states, to be exercised subject to the limitations imposed by the Fourteenth and Fifteenth Amendments to the Constitution on the manner of their exercise, is the power to control and regulate local affairs and act in the exercise of police powers.[106]

Congressman Andrew J. Biemiller of Wisconsin, speaking for Hubert Humphrey, Esther Murray, and himself, submitted a liberal civil rights plank to the convention for its consideration:

---

105. C. Edgar Brown, ed., *Democracy at Work* (Philadelphia: Local Democratic Committee, 1948), p. 167.

106. Ibid., p. 178.

We highly commend President Harry Truman for his courageous stand on the issue of civil rights. We call upon the Congress to support our President in guaranteeing these basic and fundamental principles: The right of full and equal political participation, the right to equal opportunity of employment, the right of security of persons, and the right of equal treatment in the service and defense of our Nation.[107]

Hubert Humphrey, in defending this substitute plank, exhorted the convention:

Friends, delegates, I do not believe that there can be any compromise on the guarantees of the civil rights which we have mentioned in the minority report. . . . There can be no hedging. The newspaper headlines are wrong.

There will be no hedging, and there will be no watering down, if you please, of the instruments and the principles of the civil rights program.

My friends, to those who say that we are rushing this issue of civil rights, I say to them, we are 172 years late.

To those who say that this civil rights program is an infringement on states rights, I say this, that the time has arrived in America for the Democratic party to get out of the shadows of states rights and to walk forthrightly into the bright sunshine of human rights. . . . I ask this Convention to say in unmistakable terms that we proudly hail and we courageously support our President and leader, Harry Truman, in his great fight for civil rights in America.[108]

Subsequently, a floor vote was held on the Moody resolution, which was defeated by a vote of 925 nays to 309 yeas, as only eleven votes outside of the Solid South were cast for it. The Sims and Sillers resolutions were defeated by a voice

107. Ibid., p. 181.
108. Ibid., p. 189.

vote. Finally, the moment arrived for the crucial vote on the Biemiller resolution. As Sam Rayburn, the permanent chairman of the 1948 Democratic national convention, was about to put it also to a voice vote, a California delegate, acting more quickly than Rayburn, requested a roll call.[109] By a vote of 651½ to 582½ the Biemiller plank was written into the platform, largely because of the support it received from the big city bosses in New York, Illinois, and Pennsylvania.[110] They voted for it out of fear that unless provisions were made to hold the black vote, their local and state tickets would go down to defeat in the "prospective GOP landslide." [111] Missouri voted against it, as did Rhode Island, whose state delegation was controlled by Senator McGrath. Outside of the South the administration controlled votes in only sixteen states—not enough to defeat the resolution. (As Arthur Krock wrote, "Cynical politics was never better served than today. The President's spokesmen tried to reject specific endorsement of him and his program in an effort to prevent total revolt in the South.") [112] Thus, Truman's efforts to preserve harmony came to naught, for immediately after the final civil rights vote was taken, half of the Alabama delegation, including Eugene Connor of Birmingham, followed by the entire Mississippi delegation, walked out of the convention.[113] But, other southern delegates refused to join them, preferring instead to remain seated despite the convention's stand on civil rights.

Most southerners refused to bolt, but, incensed by their

109. *Norfolk Journal and Guide*, July 24, 1948, p. 2.

110. *Democracy at Work*, p. 202. Truman, years later, was to take full credit for the action taken by the convention on the civil rights plank; see Truman, *Memoirs*, II, 182.

111. *New York Times*, July 15, 1948, p. 8; also see Robert Bendiner, "Rout of the Bourbons," *Nation* CLXVII (1948), 1–3.

112. *New York Times*, July 15, 1948, p. 22.

113. Key, *Southern Politics*, p. 335.

defeat on the civil rights vote, they overwhelmingly rejected Truman as the party's candidate. They supported instead Senator Richard Russell of Georgia, who received 263 southern votes to 13 for Truman. Truman easily won the nomination with 947½ votes, with another half-vote going to Paul V. McNutt.[114]

After nominating Truman, the convention selected Senator Alben Barkley of Kentucky, a border-state moderate, as the party's vice-presidential candidate. He had not been Truman's first choice. Truman wanted Supreme Court Justice William Douglas to be his running mate, perhaps thinking that if Douglas were the party's vice-presidential candidate, the liberal-labor bloc might be more inclined to work for the ticket.[115] But Douglas rejected Truman's entreaties, thereby opening the way for Leslie Biffle, former secretary of the Senate and a backstage power in Democratic circles in Washington, to promote the candidacy of Barkley, a popular figure in Congress but not in the White House.[116]

A feeling of despair gripped the delegates as they prepared to listen to the president's acceptance speech. (It was, after all, the judgment of most political pundits that come November, Truman was practically a sure loser.) [117] But Truman quickly dispelled the convention's gloom with a

---

114. *New York Times*, July 15, 1948, p. 9. Also see *James Forrestal's Diary*, ed. Walter Millis and E. S. Duffield (New York: Viking, 1951), p. 458, for the following: "He [Truman] made the observation that he himself had not wanted to go as far as the Democratic platform went on the civil rights issue. He said that he had no animus toward the delegates from the Southern states, who had voted against the civil rights plank and against his nomination. 'I would have done the same thing myself,' [he said], 'if I were in their place and came from their states.'"

115. Jules Abels, *Out of the Jaws of Victory* (New York: Henry Holt & Co., 1959), p. 92.

116. Author's interview with Oscar Ewing on June 25, 1962.

117. See Morris Ernst and David Loth, *The People Know Best* (Washington: Public Affairs Press, 1948).

fighting talk attacking the record of the Eightieth Congress —a Congress which, he said, would be recalled on July 27 for the purpose of enacting into legislation the high-sounding resolutions contained in the Republican party platform.[118] Referring to civil rights, the president commented:

> Everybody knows that I recommended to the Congress the civil rights program. I did so because I believe it to be my duty under the Constitution. Some members of my own party disagreed with me violently on this matter, but they stand up and do it openly. People can tell where they stand. But the Republicans all professed to be for those measures, but the Eightieth Congress did not act. They had enough men to do it and they could have had cloture. They didn't have to have a filibuster. There are enough people in that Congress that would vote for cloture.[119]

Truman neglected to mention that he had not offered to cooperate with them in any attempt to secure cloture.

While Truman lambasted the Republicans, he himself was under attack by former Democrats. On July 17 a states' rights conference met in Birmingham, Alabama, and selected South Carolina's Governor Strom Thurmond and Governor Fielding Wright of Mississippi to head a states' rights ticket.[120] It was the hope of the conference that this ticket would attract enough political support in the form of electoral college votes to force the House of Representatives to pick the next president.[121] In order to throw the election into the House, where the South could then bargain with the

---

118. For a good account of the strategy that lay behind Truman's recalling of Congress, see R. Alton Lee, *Truman and Taft-Hartley: A Question of Mandate* (Lexington: University of Kentucky Press, 1966), pp. 120–25. See Ross, *The Loneliest Campaign*, pp. 133–35.

119. *Democracy at Work*, p. 300.

120. Key, *Southern Politics*, p. 335.

121. Abel, *Out of the Jaws of Victory*, p. 147.

various candidates on the civil rights issue, the Dixiecrats needed strong backing not only in the deep South but in those border states where white supremacist politics was no longer quite so fashionable. Hence, Thurmond, in the course of the conference, attacked lynching and advocated state abolition of the poll tax in an attempt to persuade southern moderates that his political organization was in reality defending the noble heritage of Jeffersonian Democracy.[122] Yet lurking behind the scenes, where they were exerting real influence, were racist politicians like Senator James Eastland of Mississippi and former Alabama governor Frank Dixon, whose presence revealed the party's true character.[123] The conference's platform exposed the States Rights party for what it was: a vehicle for privilege and prejudice.[124] Thus the third political convention of 1948 ended as the fourth was about to begin.

On July 20 the Progressive party held its convention in Philadelphia; it was the one in which blacks played a prominent role. Lankin Marshall Howard, a Negro attorney from Des Moines, was the convention's keynote speaker. There were approximately 150 other Negroes, including W. E. B. Du Bois and Paul Robeson, who attended the convention as delegates or alternates. (Robeson was later designated co-chairman of the party.) Black delegates were among those who approved the party platform, which "was more detailed in proposals affecting Negroes than were those of the major parties, reflecting the Progressives' efforts to capitalize on Negro discontent." Evidently, the Progressive party's militant espousal of civil rights partly reflected the quasi-Communist control of the party machinery. By working through the Progressive party, American Communists hoped to in-

---

122. *New York Times*, July 18, 1948, p. 3.
123. Key, *Southern Politics*, p. 335.
124. Ibid.

corporate Negroes into a coalition of "labor and the people against war and fascism." [125]

Months before the Progressive party convention, Henry Wallace and Idaho's Senator Glenn Taylor, the party's nominees, had been outspoken critics of Jim Crow. For this reason many Negroes considered them attractive candidates. Whether Wallace and Taylor could enlist substantial numbers of Negroes and white liberals in "Gideon's Army" (as the movement was known) was another matter. Their party had been stigmatized by Truman and Dewey as a Communist front; and Wallace himself was labeled a "Communist dupe." Still, Wallace's potential strength was such that he could materially weaken Truman's support in the big cities, thus enhancing Dewey's opportunity to win a landslide victory.

On July 26, the day before Congress was scheduled to reconvene in special session, President Truman issued two executive orders pertaining specifically to civil rights.[126] Both orders—9980 and 9981—had been under careful consideration by the White House for at least six months prior to July 26; [127] in fact, an early version of 9980 had been

---

125. Wilson Record, *The Negro and the Communist Party* (Chapel Hill: University of North Carolina Press, 1951), pp. 280–81. For a different view of the role played by the Communists at that convention, see MacDougal, *Gideon's Army*, II, 506–83.

126. Executive Orders 9980, 9981, in F.R. 4311, 4314. Immediately following the Democratic convention, representatives of organizations such as the NAACP, the American Veterans Committee, and the American Jewish Congress renewed pressure on Truman by asking him to issue those orders; see, for example, Walter White to Harry Truman, July 23, 1948, Box 367, NAACP Papers, L.C.

127. Author's interview with George Elsey on June 27, 1962, and Philleo Nash on June 29, 1962. Executive Order 9981 had been originally part of the omnibus draft bill which the White House failed to introduce; for evidence see Dalfiume, *Desegregation of the U.S. Armed Forces*, p. 157.

available since March, 1948.[128] Only Truman's signature was needed to authorize their release, and when that was forthcoming, the Republican-controlled Congress would be under pressure, perhaps, to produce equivalent civil rights legislation. The Truman orders were timed perfectly, then, to focus attention on Congress, and, concurrently, to undercut Wallace's standing with many Negroes. In all probability, Executive Order 9981 was also designed to reduce the possibility of an immediate confrontation between the administration and A. Philip Randolph. Randolph had announced on June 26 that unless the president issued an executive order desegregating the armed forces before August 16, the day the new draft law went into effect (it contained no desegregation proviso), then he and his followers "would work in the big east coast cities in behalf of a campaign of civil disobedience, non registration, and non induction." [129]

Executive Order 9980 authorized the creation of a review board in each department and agency of the federal executive branch to whom government employees could appeal if they felt victimized by discriminatory employment practices. The Fair Employment Board, attached to the Civil Service Commission, was designed "to coordinate the practices and procedures of the various departments and agencies, to maintain overall supervision of their compliance with the policy and to serve as a final review body to hear appeals from the decision of departmental heads on complaints of discrimination." [130]

Executive Order 9981 provided the framework that could make possible a major breakthrough in race relations.

---

128. *Norfolk Journal and Guide*, Apr. 3, 1948, p. 18.

129. *Pittsburgh Courier*, July 3, 1948, p. 1.

130. Philleo Nash Files, Box 6, HSTL. The FEB had no power to enforce its decisions; all it could do was appeal to the president.

It is hereby declared to be the policy of the President that there shall be equality of treatment and opportunity for all persons in the armed services without regard to race, color, religion or national origin. This policy shall be put into effect as rapidly as possible, having due regard to the time required to effectuate any necessary changes without impairing efficiency or morale.[131]

It also authorized the creation of the President's Committee on Equality of Treatment and Opportunity in the Armed Forces to study and resolve the problem of discrimination and segregation in the armed forces in accordance with the president's stated policy. Of the two orders, 9981 was considerably more important, because if it were properly implemented, its results would be more far-reaching. Professor Milton Konvitz does not exaggerate its significance when he suggests that "in the history of civil rights in the United States, this order ranks among the most important steps taken to end racial discrimination." [132]

Truman's action prompted criticism from different sources for a variety of reasons. The *Baltimore Sun* suggested that "the timing of President Truman's executive orders against racial discrimination in civilian government employment and in the armed forces strongly suggests that they were politically inspired." [133] The *Montgomery Advertiser* stated that "Truman's army program is of more raw and repugnant character than that urged for the civilian provinces." [134] The *Shreveport Times* accused the president of "grandstanding to try to get back some of the Roosevelt

---

131. *Freedom To Serve* (Washington: Government Printing Office, 1950), pp. xi–xii.

132. Milton Konvitz, *Expanding Liberties: Freedom's Gains in Postwar America* (New York: Viking, 1966), p. 260.

133. July 27, 1948.

134. July 29, 1948.

Negro vote which seems to be swinging to the Wallace-Communist Progressive banner in some areas." [135]

Henry Wallace was also critical of the president's efforts to fight discrimination in the federal ranks:

> Mr. Truman's nightmares over the rapid growth of the Progressive party have forced him to face the issue of discrimination, but once again he has made only an empty gesture. He has written in the executive order the language of the South. He talks glibly of "equal opportunity" and "equal treatment," dodges always used to avoid action, but fails utterly to attack the heart of the matter—segregation.
>
> The President's order on equality of treatment in the armed forces says nothing, promises nothing, does nothing—and leaves segregation intact.[136]

Senator Richard Russell, a powerful member of the Senate Armed Services Committee, charged that Truman's executive orders were "articles of unconditional surrender to the Wallace convention, and to the treasonable civil disobedience campaign organized by the Negroes, by A. Philip Randolph and Grant Reynolds." Russell further asserted that Truman was unwilling to prosecute those men who were defying the Selective Service Act because "such action would alienate the few Negroes who remain loyal to him in the present political campaign." [137]

Although General Omar Bradley, chief of staff, had not read the president's order, he declared at Fort Knox, Kentucky, on July 28 that "the Army is not out to make any social reforms. The Army will put men of different races in different companies. It will change that policy when the

---

135. Aug. 1, 1948.

136. *New York Times*, July 28, 1948, p. 4.

137. Ibid., p. 8.

Nation as a whole changes it." [138] This startling statement
had to be refuted at once if the president's order was to be
taken seriously. In order to clarify the situation, Truman
pointed out at his press conference of July 29 that the
language of his executive order would compel the armed
forces eventually to abolish the practice of segregation and
discrimination.[139] That the White House had no intention of
equivocating on this issue was further reaffirmed by Senator McGrath, who told A. Philip Randolph and Grant Reynolds on August 2 that the seven-man presidential committee, which was designed to supervise the program of
desegregation, would "initiate its activities and functions
on the basis of non segregation." [140] Randolph, apparently
satisfied that the president was sincere in his advocacy of a
non–Jim Crow military service, announced on August 18
that the civil disobedience campaign he and Reynolds had
organized was going to be terminated.[141]

On July 27 the president addressed the special session of
Congress, and near the end of his speech, he made a specific
reference to civil rights.

Finally, I wish to urge upon the Congress the measures I
recommended last February to protect and extend the
basic civil rights of citizenship and human liberty. A
number of bills to carry out my recommendations have
been introduced in the Congress. Many of them have
already received careful consideration by Congressional
committees. Only one bill, however, has been enacted, a

138. *Washington Post*, July 29, 1948.
139. *Public Papers of the Presidents: Harry S. Truman, 1948*, pp.
422–23.
140. Grant Reynolds, "Triumph for Disobedience," *Nation* CLXVII
(1948), 228.
141. *Norfolk Journal and Guide*, Aug. 21, 1948, p. 1; Aug. 28, 1948,
p. 2.

bill relating to the rights of Americans of Japanese origins. I believe that it is necessary to enact the laws I have recommended to make the guarantees of the Constitution real and vital. I believe they are necessary to carry out our American ideals of liberty and justice for all.[142]

The Republican leadership—now on the spot—responded to the president's request by bringing to the floor of the Senate H.R. 29, the anti–poll tax bill, which had cleared the House on July 21, 1947, by a vote of 290 to 112.[143] This bill immediately ran into that well-known verbal buzz saw, a southern filibuster. Moreover, it became the focus for an important procedural wrangle over Rule Twenty-two, a rule providing the only available means of terminating Senate debate. That rule authorized the limitation of discussion on a given issue if two-thirds of all those present and voting agreed to support cloture.

On August 2 the Republican leadership presented a cloture petition—requesting a cloture vote—to the Senate's president pro tempore, Michigan's Arthur Vandenberg. At this point Senator Richard Russell, the de facto leader of the southern bloc, raised a point of order, contending that according to Rule Twenty-two, cloture might only be invoked when a "pending measure," not a "motion," was before the Senate. He argued that the move to make the anti–poll tax bill the immediate business of the Senate came through a motion that automatically precluded the introduction of a cloture petition.[144] Although Senator Vandenberg spoke in favor of anti–poll tax legislation, he sustained Russell's point of order, predicating his decision on the fact

142. *Public Papers of the Presidents: Harry S. Truman, 1948*, pp. 420–21.

143. *Congressional Record*, 80th Cong., 2d Sess., 1948, XCIII, 9551–52.

144. Ibid., 80th Cong., 2d Sess., XCIV, Part 8, pp. 9598–9600.

that there was no existing authority to justify any other ruling.[145] In other words, Vandenberg argued that Rule Twenty-two failed to specify whether cloture applied to motions. His ruling also meant that unlimited debate on the anti–poll tax bill could rightfully continue, and that there was no legal way for the Senate to terminate it until the rules under which the Senate operated were changed. On August 4 Nebraska's Senator Kenneth Wherry, the Republican majority leader, announced that it was necessary to shelve the anti–poll tax bill. He also revealed that his party had decided to make a determined effort in the new session of Congress, beginning in January, 1949, to change Rule Twenty-two, thereby making it possible to deal with the problems raised by the Vandenberg ruling.[146] On August 7 the special session adjourned, with little accomplished.

The fact that Congress produced next to nothing in the way of significant legislation gave President Truman a ready-made issue: the domestic record of the Eightieth Congress. And once the campaign was in full swing, Truman constantly played on that theme. At the same time, he solicited the support of labor, the farmer, the consumer, and the Negro. In other words, "though not a New Dealer at heart," wrote Walter Lippmann, Truman was a politician "who appreciates the voting strength of the Roosevelt combination." [147] Whatever hopes Truman had of victory depended largely on the support he would receive from that powerful political coalition. The question was: Would it remain intact for one more election campaign?

By early September, Truman was solidifying his support among black voters. The southern walkout at the Demo-

---

145. Ibid., pp. 9603–4.
146. Ibid., p. 9736.
147. Cited in Abels, *Out of the Jaws of Victory*, p. 82.

cratic national convention had dramatized his differences with the Dixiecrats, hence convincing many Negroes that his advocacy of civil rights legislation was genuine. Executive Order 9981 also had made a distinct impression upon the Negro community, a fact confirmed by Donald Dawson, a White House aide, in a memo he sent to Truman on September 9:

1) Since your executive order was issued all important opposition to the draft on the basis of the Army's race policy has disappeared. Philip Randolph and Grant Reynolds have withdrawn from their Committee Against Jim Crow, and only a few C.O.'s and other war resisters remain in the movement.

2) Negro leaders and their white friends have been universal in the praise of the order and in their support of the proposed committee.

3) The Committee will have complete minority press support. The Negro press, which had been conducting a vigorous campaign against the Army's racial policy has now abandoned it.[148]

In order to enhance further his position with Negroes, the president on September 18 designated the seven men who were to become members of the President's Committee on Equality of Treatment and Opportunity in the Armed Services. They were Charles Fahy, former solicitor general of the United States; Lester Granger, executive secretary of the Urban League; John H. Sengstacke, editor of the influential Negro newspaper the *Chicago Defender;* Dwight Palmer and Charles Luckman, industrialists; William Stevenson, educator; and Alphonsus J. Donahue, a prominent Catholic layman.[149] This committee, subsequently known as

---

148. Memorandum to the President from Donald Dawson, September 9, 1948, Philleo Nash Files, Box 6, HSTL.

149. Philleo Nash Files, Box 28, HSTL. Luckman and Donahue contributed no work to the committee.

the Fahy Committee, was scheduled to begin its work in January, 1949, assuming, of course, that Truman was still in the White House.

While Truman was reaping the benefits that accrued from the release of his executive orders, Henry Wallace toured the South and spoke before racially integrated audiences, wherever possible, to convince Negroes of the sincerity of his egalitarian convictions.[150] It was a courageous effort which Truman had no intention of matching. During his campaign swing through Texas, Oklahoma, Kansas, and Missouri in late September, Truman ignored the issue of civil rights, because, among other reasons, the Democratic leaders in the states he visited discouraged any discussion of the subject. They felt that it was "too hot"; its discussion would only succeed in driving many Democrats away from the regular organization into the "states' rights party," thus making it difficult for them to elect their own local candidates.[151] Finally, though, after arriving in Carbondale, Illinois, on September 30, Truman did make brief mention of the fact that his administration had fought "to expand our civil liberties by new measures against discrimination." [152]

That Truman's measures were influencing Negro voters was also confirmed by Carl T. Rowan, a journalist for the *Baltimore Afro-American*. On October 2 he reported the results of a poll the *Afro-American* had conducted in four widely separated Negro districts in Baltimore: Truman received 43.7 percent of the votes; Dewey, 26.5 percent; and Wallace, 22 percent.[153] On the basis of this sample it could be

---

150. *Norfolk Journal and Guide*, Sept. 4, 1948, p. 1; MacDougal, *Gideon's Army*, III, 707–44.

151. *Pittsburgh Courier*, Oct. 2, 1948, pp. 1, 4.

152. *Public Papers of the Presidents: Harry S. Truman, 1948*, p. 650.

153. P. 11.

ascertained that Truman held a comfortable lead over his two rivals at least in the black wards of predominantly Democratic Baltimore. But Truman was not carrying these wards by a sufficiently large margin; Wallace was evidently still cutting into his strength.

Truman was compensating for the inroads Wallace was making in the North by doing well in the South, because the Dixiecrat rebellion seemed to have jelled in only four southern states: South Carolina, Alabama, Mississippi, and Louisiana.[154] Elsewhere in the South, there was no real opposition to Truman's candidacy. Even Senator Richard Russell of Georgia, Dixie's candidate at the Philadelphia convention, endorsed the Democratic standard-bearer a few days before the election because he felt the South was safer with Truman.[155] As the chairman of the Democratic state committee of North Carolina suggested: "What can we accomplish? . . . The Republicans are committed to a more determined civil rights program than our party is and Governor Dewey has already put into effect in the New York government many of the proposals to which we in the South most vigorously object." [156]

During the last few weeks of the campaign, Truman concentrated on the key industrial states in the North and East. While making that final swing, Truman at first completely muted the civil rights issue; but on October 23 he toured the Negro slums of Philadelphia, which no previous president had visited, and was well received. On October 25 he informed an audience at the Chicago Stadium:

Dangerous men, who are trying to win followers for their war on democracy, are attacking Catholics, Jews and

154. For a preelection state-by-state survey, see Key, *Southern Politics*, pp. 337–44.
155. Cited in Abels, *Out of the Jaws of Victory*, p. 219.
156. Ibid., p. 220.

Negroes and other minority races and religions. . . . We must do everything we can to protect our democratic principles against those who foment racial and religious prejudice. This evil force must be defeated. I shall continue the fight. And I pledge to you that I shall never surrender.[157]

On October 26 Truman asserted in South Bend, Indiana, that the creed of the Democratic party was predicated on the idea "that all men are created free and equal, and that everyone deserves an even break. It is a respect for the dignity of men and women without regard to race, creed or color." [158] Later that same day, Truman spoke in Cleveland and reminded his audience that he had urged the special session of Congress to pass legislation to protect the "basic rights of citizenship and human liberty." But, asserted Truman, the Republican party, which had been paying lip service to this kind of legislation for years, never could quite manage to act upon it when the "showdown" came.[159]

Climaxing Truman's drive to win the Negro vote was a speech he delivered in Harlem on October 29 (though the decision to speak there was made at the last minute). The first president ever to talk in Harlem, Truman was warmly welcomed by some 65,000 people who heard his remarks and saw him receive the first Franklin Delano Roosevelt Memorial Brotherhood Medal from the Reverend Dr. C. A. Johnson.[160] Addressing this assemblage on the first anniversary of the day he had been presented with the report of his civil rights committee, Truman discussed the meaning and significance of *To Secure These Rights*. After praising the

157. *Public Papers of the Presidents: Harry S. Truman, 1948*, p. 852.

158. Ibid., p. 854.

159. Ibid., p. 868.

160. *New York Times*, Oct. 30, 1948, p. 6.

work and the recommendations of the committee, Truman proceeded to outline his administration's record on civil rights:

> After the Civil Rights Committee submitted its report, I asked Congress to do ten of the things recommended by the committee.
> You know what they did about that.
> So I went ahead and did what the President can do, unaided by Congress.
> I issued two executive orders.
> One of them established the President's Committee on Equality of Treatment and Opportunity in the Armed Services.
> The other covered regulations governing fair employment practices within the federal establishment.
> In addition to that, the Department of Justice went into the Supreme Court and aided in getting a decision oulawing restrictive covenants.
> Several states and municipalities have taken action on the recommendations of the Civil Rights Committee, and I hope more will follow after them.
> Today the democratic way of life is being challenged all over the world. Democracy's answer to the challenge of totalitarianism is its promise of equal rights and equal opportunity for all mankind.
> The fulfillment of this promise is among the highest purposes of government.
> Our determination to attain the goal of equal rights and equal opportunity must be resolute and unwavering.
> For my part, I intend to keep moving toward this goal with every ounce of strength and determination I have.[161]

Apparently, the Truman record on civil rights did not impress key opinion-molders within the Negro community for, ironically, Truman failed to receive the editorial en-

---

161. *Public Papers of the Presidents: Harry S. Truman, 1948*, pp. 923–25.

dorsement of any major black newspaper except the *Chicago Defender*; the rest supported Dewey. For example, the *Pittsburgh Courier,* the most widely circulated Negro newspaper, declared on October 30: "Put Governor Thomas E. Dewey in the White House where he can do for all Negroes of the nation what he has done for the Negroes of New York state." [162] Whether Negroes who read such newspapers as the *Courier,* the *Baltimore Afro-American,* and the *New York Amsterdam News* had been influenced by their editorial stand would soon be determined on election day, November 2, 1948.

The results of that election staggered millions of Americans, including most Republicans, many Democrats, and practically all political pollsters. Truman achieved a certain political immortality because of his spectacular victory, which on the basis of hindsight was not quite so remarkable.[163] Although Truman had been harassed on both flanks by political defectors and challenged in the center by the leader of a formidable political organization, he successfully routed his enemies by battling on behalf of Franklin Roosevelt's New Deal coalition, which in 1948 was still a potent political force in the United States. In the words of Clark Clifford, an architect of the 1948 campaign: "We had to be bold. If we had kept on plugging away in moderate terms, we might have reached mid-field when the gun went off, so we had to throw long passes, anything to stir up labor, and to get the mass votes of the great cities of the Middle West, New England and the East." [164]

---

162. Cecilia Van Auken, "The Negro Press in the 1948 Presidential Election," *Journalism Quarterly* XXVI (1949), 431–35.

163. Lubell, *The Future of American Politics,* p. 190. An exciting description and analysis of the 1948 campaign can be found in Ross, *The Loneliest Campaign,* pp. 163–271.

164. *New York Times,* Nov. 4, 1948, p. 8.

Among the factors which contributed to Truman's 1948 victory was the widespread prosperity that the country was experiencing. Many voters, urban and rural alike, felt that if Dewey won the presidency, a depression would surely follow.[165] Truman exploited this issue during the campaign, and with it rallied to his banner millions of voters, especially from the middle and lower classes, who lived in the great cities and rural hinterlands of America. Included in the urban group were many black Americans, who discovered in Truman a spokesman for both their political and economic interests. For these reasons, almost two-thirds of the Negroes who voted in 1948 cast their ballots for him.

According to a post-election survey conducted by the NAACP, 69 percent of all Negro voters in twenty-seven major cities and communities across the country had voted for Truman. In fact, in some of these Negro districts, he received greater support than did Franklin Roosevelt in any of his elections.[166] And it was fortunate for Truman that Negroes found him to be such an attractive candidate, because if a sizable number of black voters had opted for Dewey or Wallace in any two of the three key states of California, Illinois, and Ohio, Dewey would have won the White House.[167]

To illustrate the crucial character of the Negro vote in these three states, it is necessary to examine the election returns in some detail. Truman carried California by 17,865 votes; in one black district of Los Angeles he received

---

165. For an analysis of the urban vote, see Lee, *Taft-Hartley*, pp. 143–52; for an analysis of the farm vote, see Matusow, *Farm Policies and Politics in the Truman Years*, pp. 185–89. A reexamination of the farm vote is undertaken by Ross, *The Loneliest Campaign*, pp. 256–60.

166. Henry Lee Moon, "What Chance for Civil Rights," *Crisis* LVI (1949), 42–45.

167. Arnold Aronson and Samuel Spiegler, "Does the Republican Party Want the Negro Vote?", *Crisis* LXVIII (1949), 365.

30,742 votes as compared with Dewey's 7,146 and Wallace's 4,092. Truman won Illinois by only 33,612; yet Chicago's Negroes provided him with a plurality almost four times the margin by which he carried the state. The election in Ohio was particularly close: Truman squeezed out a 7,107-vote victory. Again, as in California and Illinois, his winning margin was provided by blacks, this time from Cleveland and Akron, who gave him a 65,000-vote plurality over Dewey. Truman also did extremely well in Negro districts located in states he lost to Dewey. In New York's Harlem he polled 108,643 votes to Dewey's 34,076 and Wallace's 28,903. In New Jersey and Pennsylvania he carried black wards by 2-to-1, 3-to-1, and sometimes by 4-to-1 margins.[168]

Dewey generally ignored Negro voters, a policy decision which did not help him on election day. In short, "while Truman made capital of his civil rights proposals, Dewey kept silent about his civil rights accomplishments." [169] Dewey further damaged his standing with most Negroes by actively soliciting southern votes. The latter maneuver was especially self-defeating because few Southern Democrats voted for him, and most northern Negroes, offended by his ostensible disregard of their interests—especially economic —sided with Truman. On the other hand, it seems clear that Dewey carried Delaware, Indiana, and Maryland with the help of Negro voters. Dewey won Indiana by a margin of

---

168. *New York Times*, Nov. 30, 1948, p. 22. Congresswoman Helen Gahagan Douglas confirmed the importance of the black vote in California. She suggested in a letter to Walter White, written after the election, that "whenever there was a block of minority votes in the state they went almost solidly for the President. I am convinced that the President's Civil Rights Program was one of the most important factors in the successful outcome of the election" (Helen Gahagan Douglas to Walter White, December 3, 1948, Douglas File, Box 419, NAACP Papers, L.C.).

169. Aronson and Spiegler, "Does the Republican Party Want the Negro Vote?", p. 365.

13,246 votes, and the 16,467 votes he received from Hoosier Negroes allowed him to carry the state.[170] But in no state did Dewey and the Republican party receive a majority of the black vote in the 1948 election.

Henry Wallace's apparent surge of the spring and the early summer faded completely by November 2, 1948. The existence of widespread prosperity, the total lack of support in the farm belt, the inability to rebut the "Communist front" charge, the partial preemption of the Progressive party's domestic program by Truman, the Stalinist coup d'état in Prague—all these factors help to account for the rapid decline in Wallace's fortunes. Yet the 2.3 percent of the national vote which Wallace received was enough to deprive Truman of the electoral votes of several states. In New York, for example, Wallace picked up 509,559 votes, making it possible for Dewey to take the Empire State by a 60,951-vote margin. And the same story was repeated in Michigan and Maryland.[171]

Although Wallace prevented a Truman victory in New York, Michigan, and Maryland, he ironically contributed mightily to Truman's ultimate success. Long before the actual campaign began, Truman and his advisers—most notably, Clark Clifford—saw Wallace as such a serious threat that they devised a strategy to undercut his appeal with those voting blocs whose support was deemed vital to the hopes of the Democratic party. And not the least among them was the Negro bloc.

During the campaign Wallace solicited Negro support, but failed to obtain more than 10 percent of that vote, a factor which counted heavily in Truman's favor, especially

170. *Norfolk Journal and Guide*, May 10, 1952, p. 5.

171. Karl Schmidt, *Henry Wallace: Quixotic Crusader* (Syracuse, N.Y.: Syracuse University Press, 1960), pp. 232–51.

in the states of California, Illinois, and Ohio.[172] Most Negroes refused to forsake the Democratic party, thinking
that if they did, Truman's chances of winning would be
severely reduced. They believed that a vote for a third-party
candidate would benefit only Dewey, who, in their opinion,
was the least attractive candidate. Thus, Wallace was given
short shrift by the vast majority of voting Negroes, who
supported Truman because they were sharing in the country's prosperity and because the Dixiecrat revolt had convinced them that he was sincere in the advocacy of his civil
rights program.[173]

The Dixiecrats, too, had been convinced of the sincerity
of Truman's commitment, so much so that they organized a
political party for the purpose of depriving him of the
electoral votes he needed to win, thus allowing the House of
Representatives to decide the outcome. Their hopes were
frustrated by the fact that they carried only four southern
states: South Carolina, Alabama, Mississippi, and Louisiana. The relatively poor showing of the Thurmond-Wright
ticket (which received just 12,000 more votes than the
Wallace-Taylor combination) can be attributed to several
factors: (1) a reasonably good Democratic party discipline
that reinforced the ingrained voting habits of a substantial
number of southerners; (2) fear on the part of Southern
Democrats that if Truman won, he would punish the bolters
in and out of Congress by denying them their party position
and patronage privileges; (3) distrust of Dixiecrat motives,
that is, a suspicion that the States' Rights party was really
a vehicle for economic conservatism, which (at least in
1948), many southern whites, the beneficiaries of the New

---

172. Moon, "What Chance for Civil Rights," pp. 242–45.
173. MacDougal, *Gideon's Army*, III, 678–80; *Norfolk Journal and
Guide*, Nov. 27, 1948, p. 8.

Deal, rejected; (4) a growing southern liberalism as evidenced in newspapers, magazines, and the lessening of hard-core racism, especially in the border states and the upper South, where blacks were beginning to vote in increasing numbers.[174]

The results of the 1948 election demonstrated that the politics of civil rights had become institutionalized on the national level. Negroes had at last crossed the threshold of influence, making it possible for them to "win a place at the table where Madisonian realists played the game of interest politics in the traditional American way: those who have are heard." [175] In other words, black political strength in the states with the largest electoral votes was now sufficiently great to determine the outcome of a national election in the event that that election was closely contested. As Henry Moon, voting analyst for the NAACP, suggested even before the 1948 election, Negroes, because of their strategic position, were in a position to become a "balance of power" force in national politics.[176] This development, of course, might require them to swing back and forth between the parties to obtain maximum political leverage. In 1948, however, the loyalty of Negroes to the Democratic party produced the same results. How significant or decisive that black vote would be in the context of a Republican landslide was another question.

Subsequent to the election, civil rights remained a major domestic political issue. At a press conference on November

174. Emile Ader, "Why the Dixiecrats Failed," *Journal of Politics* XV (1953), 356–69.

175. William C. Berman, "The Civil Rights and Civil Liberties Policies of the Truman Administration," in *The Truman Era As a Research Period*, ed. Richard Kirkendall (Columbia: University of Missouri Press, 1967), p. 193.

176. Moon, *Balance of Power.*

16, President Truman was asked whether he was going to
send another civil rights message to Congress. He answered: "Yes, it will be in the Message on the State of the
Union, and will follow the Democratic platform. It will take
in the proposals agreed on in the Democratic platform." [177]
Alabama's Senator John Sparkman, in an attempt to blunt
Truman's expected legislative efforts, suggested on November 24 that a joint congressional committee be created to
study the social and economic problems of various minorities.[178] (The *New York Times* condemned this proposal as
"another Southern delaying action," which would only du-
plicate the work of the President's Civil Rights
Committee.) [179] On November 25 administration leaders intimated that in the forthcoming session of Congress an
attempt would be made to modify Senate Rule Twenty-two
in order to make possible the passage of civil rights legislation.[180] Such legislation would receive the president's active
support, reported Walter White following his November 28
meeting with Truman at the White House.[181]

---

177. *Public Papers of the Presidents: Harry S. Truman, 1948*, p.
974.

178. *New York Times*, Nov. 25, 1948, p. 1; *Norfolk Journal and
Guide*, Dec. 4, 1948, pp. 1–2.

179. *New York Times*, Nov. 26, 1948, p. 22.

180. Ibid., Nov. 27, 1948, pp. 1, 63.

181. NAACP press release, December 2, 1948, NAACP Papers, L.C.
Notwithstanding Truman's professed desire to carry the battle for
civil rights legislation to the Congress, his administration was pursu-
ing a racist policy in the burgeoning field of internal security. This
practice was discussed by Walter White in a letter he wrote to the
president on November 26, just two days before their scheduled
meeting at the White House. White stated: "The NAACP is greatly
concerned about an increasing tendency of the part of government
agencies to associate activity on interracial matters with disloyalty.
Thus various investigating agents of the government have been asking
white persons whether they associate with colored people. Colored
people have been asked whether they entertained white people in their

On December 24, 1948, the *New York Times* disclosed that the Republicans were hoping to embarrass the Democrats by pushing for civil rights legislation at the beginning of the new session of Congress.[182] Specifically, Senate Republicans planned to seek a slight change in the Senate rules so as to curtail the southern filibuster. Whether their proposals would dovetail with the plans of the Democratic liberals, who wanted to end debate by a simple majority vote, was not yet clear.

As the New Year approached, President Truman could look back at the fading year with a sense of satisfaction. He had been elected president of the United States because of the support given him by labor, farmers, and the various racial and religious minorities. But that support now obligated him to present to the Congress a program including the major reforms he espoused during the campaign. The question facing Truman as the new Eighty-first Congress prepared to convene, with a solid Democratic majority, was whether it would be more sympathetic to civil rights legislation than its immediate predecessor had been.

---

homes. In addition, there is considerable evidence before us that many colored government employees, who are now being charged with disloyalty, have such accusations brought against them because they have actively opposed segregation and discrimination in their places of employment or in their communities" (see OF 252K, HSTL).

182. P. 18.

Chapter 4

**THE CONGRESS, THE COALITION,
AND THE FEDERAL EXECUTIVE**

On the eve of the first session of the Eighty-first Congress, it seemed that President Truman was in a good position to achieve his legislative program. The Republicans had been defeated in the November election, and the conservative congressional coalition appeared to be on the defensive. But the Democrats, even with substantial majorities in both houses, needed good organization and direction. Liberals assumed that Truman would provide exemplary executive leadership while, concurrently, his congressional lieutenants would lead their legions with skill and imagination.

Here, however, was the rub. There was little evidence in

Truman's presidential career that he had mastered or could master the art and technique of manipulation and persuasion needed to compel his former associates to do his bidding on matters affecting domestic legislation.[1] Furthermore, administration spokesmen in Congress, other than House Speaker Sam Rayburn, were not exceptionally qualified to steer complex and controversial legislation through the congressional maze. For example, the new Senate majority leader was Senator Scott Lucas, "a downstate Illinois Democrat whose postures were liberal, but whose visceral instincts often tended to be conservative—particularly on matters concerning civil rights."[2] Lucas had fought against the tough civil rights plank at the 1948 Democratic national convention, a fact which undoubtedly helped to make his appointment as majority leader acceptable to Georgia's Richard Russell, an acknowledged leader of the de facto conservative coalition.[3] The Senate Democratic whip was Francis Myers of Pennsylvania, who was renowned neither for his leadership abilities nor for his unswerving devotion to civil rights. Myers, like Lucas, had supported the administration position on civil rights at the 1948 convention and had helped draft the mild civil rights plank which Truman wanted in the platform.[4]

In the House the quality of leadership was better in terms of general legislative effectiveness. Sam Rayburn, its Speaker, was a gifted parliamentarian and a party manager of considerable astuteness and ability. Like Truman, with

---

1. A critical analysis of Truman's leadership qualities can be found in Athan Theoharis, "The Truman Presidency," a paper read at the August 29, 1967, meeting of the Pacific Coast Historical Association.

2. Roland Evans and Robert Novak, *Lyndon B. Johnson: The Exercise of Power* (New York: New American Library, 1966), p. 40.

3. Ibid.

4. *Democracy at Work*, p. 167.

whom he maintained a close friendship, Rayburn was an organization man, who spoke for the centrist faction within the Democratic party. But also like his southern counterparts in the Senate, Rayburn had no use for civil rights legislation, a point he made clear many times before and during the 1948 campaign.[5] His assistant, John McCormack of Massachusetts, the House majority leader, served him with loyalty and respect. And Rayburn, aware that civil rights was a standing threat to the cohesiveness of the party, acknowledged and praised McCormack's skill in engineering compromises on this matter.[6]

As the Democratic congressional leadership girded itself for the battles to come, Congress convened on January 3, 1949. On that first day of the new session, Speaker Sam Rayburn and Rules Committee Chairman Adolph Sabath, a liberal Democrat, successfully spearheaded a drive to weaken the power of the Rules Committee, the graveyard of liberal legislation. Under their direction the House voted 275 (225 Democrats, 49 Republicans, and 1 independent) to 143 (112 Republicans and 31 Southern Democrats) to allow committee chairmen to introduce committee-cleared legislation directly to the House floor when their bills had been blocked by the Rules Committee for twenty-one or more days.[7] The new rule also empowered the Speaker to recognize at his discretion those committee chairmen who were seeking to circumvent the trap of the Rules Committee.

---

5. Richard Bolling, *House Out of Order* (New York: E. P. Dutton, 1965), p. 74.

6. As chairman of the platform committee of the Democratic national convention, McCormack arranged compromises on civil rights planks in 1944, 1952, and 1956 (ibid.).

7. *Congressional Record*, 81st Cong., 1st Sess., 1949, Vol. XCV, Part 1, pp. 10–11. Evidently Rayburn was not happy with the adoption of the twenty-one-day rule in later Congresses; see Bolling, *House Out of Order*, p. 207.

Thus, the administration found the means of bringing its program to the House floor, where at least a vote could be obtained on key legislation.

Following this important procedural victory, President Truman went to the Congress on January 5 to deliver his State of the Union address. Calling for the enactment of a "Fair Deal" for the American people, Truman once more requested that Congress consider his civil rights program. He said:

> The driving force behind our progress is our faith in our domestic institutions. That faith is embodied in the promise of equal rights and equal opportunities which the founders of our Republic proclaimed to their countrymen and to the whole world.
>
> The fulfillment of this promise is among the highest purposes of government. The civil rights proposals I made to the 80th Congress, I now repeat to the 81st. They should be enacted in order that the Federal Government may assume the leadership and discharge the obligations placed upon it by the Constitution.
>
> I stand squarely behind those proposals.[8]

The response to his message was predictably mixed. Walter White saw "a practicing as well as a talking about democracy." [9] Representative Eugene Cox of Georgia remarked: "It looks as though we are going the way England went, and without the restraint and caution the Britons exercised. An approval of the civil rights program will mean a creation of the greatest social disturbance the country has ever known." [10] New York Representative Emanuel Celler, chairman of the House Judiciary Committee, said

---

8. *Public Papers of the Presidents: Harry S. Truman, 1949* (Washington: United States Government Printing Office, 1964), p. 6.

9. *New York Times,* Jan. 6, 1949, p. 6.

10. Ibid.

that his committee would try to act on the civil rights program "within the first 100 days of the session." [11]

Though the president had cleared a major procedural hurdle in the House, he still faced what appeared to be an insuperable obstacle in the Senate, that is, a Senate filibuster. Unless the filibuster rule was liberalized, the South would surely block passage of all civil rights legislation. To avoid a prolonged and perhaps costly fight, Arkansas Senator John McClellen suggested that Truman abandon his demand for an FEPC in order to facilitate a workable compromise on the other features of his civil rights program.[12]

While Southern Democrats awaited further developments, leaders of both parties in the Senate were formulating plans which could have a significant bearing on the success or failure of any civil rights program in the Eighty-first Congress. Democratic Senator Carl Hayden of Arizona, the chairman of the Senate Rules and Administration Committee—which was in no way comparable in power or function to the House Rules Committee—and Nebraska's Senator Kenneth Wherry, the Senate minority leader, decided to sponsor jointly Senate Resolution Fifteen, authorizing the modification of Senate Rule Twenty-two so as to give the Senate greater power to limit filibusters.[13] They felt the existing rule was inadequate because it failed to provide the Senate with the means of limiting filibusters directed at motions. In other words, any number of Senators could forestall action on a particular bill by merely filibustering a motion to take up the measure, thereby subjecting the Senate to a delaying tactic for which there was no remedy. The

---

11. Ibid.

12. *American Jewish Yearbook, 1949* (Philadelphia: Jewish Publication Society of America, 1950), p. 101.

13. *Congressional Record*, 81st Cong., 1st Sess., 1949, Vol. XCV, Part 1, p. 59.

Hayden-Wherry proposal was designed to provide the Senate with a parliamentary rule allowing it to terminate debate on both a motion and a measure if two-thirds of those present and voting in the chamber were willing to invoke cloture.[14] It was possible that Resolution Fifteen could pass the Senate if a coalition of Republicans and northern Democrats could coalesce long enough to overpower southern opposition; otherwise, the fight for civil rights legislation would end even before a specific program had been introduced.

As Hayden and Wherry sought support for their resolution, President Truman made it clear that he was not prepared to let the civil rights issue slide into political oblivion, a point he emphasized on January 12 at a White House meeting with Herbert Bayard Swope, Robert Patterson, and Morris Ernst, members of a National Citizens Council on Civil Rights.[15] Truman informed them that he was going to do something "right away" to translate his civil rights program into legislation. The administration, he announced, was already drafting bills to support and implement the recommendations contained in his February 2, 1948, message to Congress.[16]

If Truman submitted actual legislation to Congress, it would have certainly produced a struggle in both houses. But that struggle would have been in vain unless or until the Senate liberalized Rule Twenty-two. Oddly enough, Senate Democratic liberals refused to be drawn into the debate on this question as hearings on Resolution Fifteen were initiated in the Senate Rules Committee on January 24. Their silence was so conspicuous that on January 25 Walter White sent a telegram of protest to Truman:

---

14. For the text of this resolution, see ibid.
15. *New York Times*, Jan. 13, 1949, p. 13.
16. *Pittsburgh Courier*, Jan. 22, 1949, pp. 1, 4.

We are gravely disturbed by strange apathy and silence of Democrats during hearings on amendment of Senate Rules. Not one Democrat has as yet fought for or even spoken out to end filibusters. We are perturbed. We trust our perturbation is premature, despite evidence to the contrary.[17]

White, representing the NAACP, wanted Democratic liberals to address the Senate Rules Committee on behalf of an amendment to Rule Twenty-two allowing debate to be terminated by a simple majority of a quorum, that is, by 25 out of 49 votes, rather than by the two-thirds requirement of those present and voting as specified in the Hayden-Wherry resolution and Rule Twenty-two. A resolution calling for simple majority cloture had been introduced by Senator Myers and was before the Rules Committee, but there was only token support for it in the Senate.[18] On the other hand, Republicans, such as Leverett Saltonstall of Massachusetts, William Knowland of California, Irving Ives of New York, and Homer Ferguson of Michigan, sponsored Senate Resolution Thirteen (which was identical to the Hayden-Wherry resolution) because they thought it stood the best chance of winning acceptance from the South.[19]

The hopes of these Republicans were dashed, for the South refused to accept the slightest change in the existing filibuster rule. How far the South was prepared to resist any compromise was indicated by Senators Richard Russell

---

17. Telegram to the President from Walter White, January 25, 1949, Truman Papers, OF 1827, HSTL.

18. *Congressional Record*, 81st Cong., 1st Sess., 1949, Vol. XCV, Part 1, pp. 58–59. Myers later changed his position in support of a constitutional majority, the same stand that Lucas took; ibid., p. 1584. For evidence that there was only slight support for Myers's original position, see *New York Times*, January 26, 1949, p. 6.

19. Congressional Record, 81st Cong., 1st Sess., 1949, Vol. XCV, Part 1, p. 58; also see *New York Times*, Jan. 26, 1949, p. 6.

of Georgia and Spessard Holland of Florida in testimony they gave to the Senate Rules Committee on January 31. Senator Russell declared that he "hoped those in charge of Mr. Truman's general legislative recommendations in the Senate would stop and consider all the implications of trying to bring up the rule amendment at this time." If the administration leaders persisted in their efforts to change Rule Twenty-two, the South would fight with all of its time-honored weapons, warned Russell.[20] Senator Holland revealed to the Rules Committee the contents of a letter he had written to Majority Leader Lucas about this issue. Pleading with Lucas to introduce those measures such as public power, reciprocal trade, "on which there is substantial unanimty among Democrats," Holland warned him that any other approach would bring on "an early and prolonged fight and would greatly postpone action on many important measures." [21]

Lucas and Myers, the Democratic leaders, knew what a filibuster would do to the rest of Truman's legislative program; hence, they intended to prevent or postpone one in order to get action, first, on the Taft-Hartley repealer, then being hurriedly considered by the Senate Labor and Public Welfare Committee. Apparently organized labor, one of the major interest groups to whom President Truman was beholden, wanted the Taft-Hartley Act repealed before any other legislation was considered; and this probably explains why the Rules Committee hearings on the Hayden-Wherry resolution were delayed until January 24.[22] Republican members of the Rules Committee wanted to commence hear-

---

20. U.S. Senate, Committee on Rules and Administration, *Hearings before the Committee on Rules and Administration,* 81st Congress, 1st Session, on S. Res. 11, 12, 13, 15, 19; pp. 176–88.

21. Ibid., pp. 170–76.

22. *Norfolk Journal and Guide,* Feb. 12, 1949, p. 8; and Sept. 24, 1949, p. 8.

ings on January 14, but their efforts had been rebuffed by the Democratic leadership.[23] Even after the conclusion of seven days of hearings Rules Committee Democrats refused to permit a vote authorizing the introduction of Resolution Fifteen on the floor of the Senate; such a move, they recognized, would spark a filibuster tying the Senate in procedural knots.[24]

The Republicans, conversely, hoped to capitalize on the controversy by dividing the Democrats and, at the same time, by blocking moves to repeal the Taft-Hartley Act. They pressed, therefore, for immediate action on Resolution Fifteen. On February 3 Senator William Knowland introduced a resolution calling on the Senate to relieve the Rules Committee of any further responsibility for the Hayden-Wherry resolution on grounds of unjustified procrastination.[25] On February 7, as the Senate was about to vote on the Knowland resolution, Lucas and Myers explained that it would be imprudent to take a matter from a standing committee of the Senate unless there was a legitimate reason for doing so. It was their opinion that this case did not require any particular need for "haste." [26] Republican Senator Wayne Morse of Oregon was irritated with such delaying tactics and charged that the Democrats "are trying to keep civil rights in the background because they know it will split their party wide open." [27] The Senate rejected the Knowland proposal by a vote of 56 to 31, after 7 Republicans joined 49 Democrats to defeat it.[28]

---

23. *Congressional Record,* 81st Cong., 1st Sess., 1949, Vol. XCV, Part 1, p. 860.

24. Ibid., p. 861.

25. Ibid., p. 793.

26. Ibid., p. 865.

27. Ibid., p. 864.

28. Ibid., p. 865; for an analysis of this vote, see *Norfolk Journal and Guide,* Feb. 12, 1949, pp. 1–2.

On February 9 the Senate Rules Committee voted 10 to 3 to recommend the passage of the Hayden-Wherry resolution.[29] After it was submitted to the floor on February 17, Lucas could no longer defer action. His problem was now to find enough votes to carry it in the face of organized southern opposition. As the showdown approached—by common consent the issue was to be introduced on February 28—Senator Humphrey of Minnesota pointed to Lucas's difficulties in a letter he had published in the *New York Times* on February 22: "The political problem we face is whether or not the Republicans and the Democrats who say they are for civil rights and say they are for curbing the filibuster will really stand up and be counted when a roll call is made." [30]

On the morning of February 28, Senator Lucas discussed the filibuster issue with the president, who, it was reported, wanted to meet this problem "head on." [31] That afternoon, while speaking on the Senate floor, Lucas moved that the Rules Resolution—the Hayden-Wherry proposal—become the Senate's next item of business.[32] His motion, as was expected, immediately sparked a southern filibuster, which George Galloway, a longtime student of congressional politics, considered to be "perhaps the bitterest in Senate memory." [33]

While Southern Democrats mobilized their forces to resist any change in Rule Twenty-two, administration spokesmen in the Senate planned to outflank them by submitting a

---

29. *Congressional Record*, 81st Cong., 1st Sess., 1949, Vol. XCV, Part 18, Daily Digest, p. 47.

30. P. 22.

31. *New York Times*, Mar. 1, 1949, p. 1.

32. *Congressional Record*, 81st Cong., 1st Sess., 1949, Vol. XCV, Part 2, p. 1584.

33. George B. Galloway, *The Legislative Process in Congress* (New York: Thomas Y. Crowell, 1953), pp. 561–69.

cloture petition to Alben Barkley, the president of the Senate.[34] If Barkley ruled that this petition was valid, his decision would then have to be upheld by a voting majority of the Senate, since the existing rule did not provide for the application of cloture on filibusters directed against a motion. In the event a majority decided to sustain the ruling, Lucas then would be in a position to take a cloture vote to limit the southern filibuster. If two-thirds of all senators present at the time of the vote endorsed cloture, then the Hayden-Wherry resolution could be introduced as a measure, thereby giving the South another opportunity to launch a filibuster, and thus making it necessary for Lucas to obtain cloture once more in order to bring the measure to a vote. The procedural pitfalls were numerous, but unless they were all negotiated, Truman's civil rights program would never clear the upper chamber.

As Lucas prepared to make his move, he had to take into consideration the attitude of the Senate Republicans. Some Republicans were reluctant to endorse the contemplated Barkley ruling because they felt that such action would serve to repudiate one of their most respected colleagues, Michigan's Senator Arthur Vandenberg.[35] Acting as president pro tempore of the Senate on August 2, 1948, Vandenberg had ruled that a motion to consider a proposed anti-poll tax bill was not a "pending measure" and hence not subject to a cloture vote.[36] But despite his earlier stand Vandenberg counseled Senate Republicans on March 2 to vote on the issue as their consciences dictated, suggesting that he would not be offended if they supported Barkley.[37]

Vandenberg may have inspired liberals to believe that

---

34. *New York Times*, Mar. 1, 1949, p. 1.

35. Ibid., Mar. 3, 1949, p. 1.

36. *Congressional Record*, 80th Cong., 2d Sess., 1949, Vol. XCIV, Part 8, pp. 9603–4.

37. *New York Times*, Mar. 3, 1949, pp. 22.

additional Republican support could be mustered for the all-important vote. But whatever hopes they had were quashed from an unexpected source: at a White House press conference on March 3, President Truman endorsed a change in Rule Twenty-two that would have permitted a majority of a senatorial quorum—that is, 25 votes out of 49—to invoke cloture, thus making his public position exactly the same as that of the NAACP and the Americans for Democratic Action.[38] Whether through accident or design, Truman at once undermined the position of northern Democrats, who were making a determined bid to win Republican support for a moderate change in Rule Twenty-two; and he further stiffened the resistance of the South to any thought of compromise. As Republican Senator Robert A. Taft later suggested:

The effort to take up the Hayden-Wherry Resolution . . . was greatly handicapped by the President's declaration in favor of cloture by a majority of a quorum. This made the position of the southern senators still more unyielding because the adoption of the Hayden-Wherry resolution would have provided cloture to support a later effort to change further the rules to meet the President's demands for fifty per cent cloture.[39]

The South was now jubilant, for, according to Arkansas's Senator J. William Fulbright, Truman's impolitic utterance meant that "we have gained a substantial number of

38. *Public Papers of the Presidents: Harry S. Truman 1949*, pp. 158–59. Marquis Childs observed in the March 9, 1949, edition of the *Washington Post* that Truman's stand on cloture cost him the support of a number of southern moderates who might have made it possible for him to obtain passage of at least 60 percent of his civil rights program.

39. *Congressional Record*, 81st Cong., 1st Sess., 1949, Vol. XCV, Part 2, p. 2664.

votes." [40] Senator Russell declared: "The President has now justified every statement that we have made that all this campaign was but a step toward simple majority cloture. I saw in the beginning that they were opening a Pandora's box. It is now clearly opened." [41]

Subsequent to the brouhaha created by Truman's remarks, Senator Wherry announced that he would not sign the cloture petition that Lucas had been circulating.[42] Although Senator Wherry proved to be recalcitrant, Senators Taft and Knowland, along with 14 other Republicans and 17 Democrats, did sign the petition, which Lucas then submitted to Vice-President Barkley on March 10, 1949.[43]

The day of decision had finally arrived. Immediately after Barkley received the petition for the purpose of initiating a procedural move to end the debate on the motion to take up Senate Resolution Fifteen, Senator Russell raised a point of order, contending, as he did on August 2, 1948, that according to Senate Rule Twenty-two, cloture might only be invoked when a "pending measure," not a motion, was before the Senate. Vice-President Barkley overruled Russell's point of order because, in Barkley's judgment, "a motion to proceed to the consideration of a bill is an absolutely indispensible process in the enactment of legislation." Barkley also declared that "without a motion to proceed to the consideration of a bill or resolution, the Senate cannot consider it, and therefore a motion to proceed is . . . a necessary part of the process taken by Congress or any other legislative body in order that a bill may finally become a law." As

---

40. Ibid., p. 1886.

41. *New York Times*, Mar. 4, 1949, p. 1.

42. Ibid., p. 7.

43. *Congressional Record*, 81st Cong., 1st Sess., 1949, Vol. XCV, Part 2, p. 2166.

soon as Barkley made his unprecedented ruling, Russell appealed the chair's decision to the entire Senate.[44]

The Senate prepared to resolve the issue of the Barkley ruling on March 11. But before the vote was taken, Senator Vandenberg addressed his fellow senators about the matter at hand. Stating that he personally favored the Hayden-Wherry resolution, Vandenberg, nonetheless, declared his opposition to the Barkley ruling because it was "an affront to due legislative process." It was Vandenberg's opinion that the Senate would have to reject Barkley's decision in order to preserve the integrity of the Senate. After a lengthy debate the Senate voted 46 to 41 to overturn Barkley's rule; 23 Republicans joined 23 Democrats (mostly from the South and the Mountain States) to give Dixie a very important procedural victory.[45] According to Walter White, Vandenberg's speech had considerably influenced the final alignment on the question: "Mr. Vandenberg has cost us from five to seven votes. He has given an aura of respectability to those who wanted an excuse to vote to upset Mr. Barkley." [46]

---

44. Ibid., pp. 2174–75.

45. Ibid., pp. 2228–29. Several years later, Roy Wilkins was to suggest that this vote had been "the most crucial vote on civil rights in the past ten years." It was also his view that among the Republicans "who should have been expected to sustain the chair, but who voted to overrule were; Bricker (Ohio); Capehart and Jenner (Ind.); Donnell and Kem (Mo.); Hickenlooper (Iowa); Reed and Schoppel (Kansas); Vandenberg (Mich.); and Thye (Minn.)." Of the Democrats, Wilkins felt they had mustered all the "persons they could have reasonably have expected to muster except three, Hayden and McFarland of Arizona, and McCarran of Nevada." See Roy Wilkins to Archibald Carey Jr., November 10, 1952, Republican National Committee Folder, Box 444, NAACP Papers, L.C.

46. See Minutes of the NAACP Executive Board, March 14, 1949, Box A-12, NAACP Papers, L.C. The NAACP Board also sharply attacked the results of the March 11 vote and called on President Truman and Senate Democrats "to break the filibuster by holding the Senate in continuous session regardless of how long the Dixiecrats may be able to hold out" (ibid.).

Not to be overlooked was the part President Truman played in the unfolding of this political drama. Suggested the *New York Times:*

> It is scarcely disputable, we believe, that Mr. Truman himself contributed to the causes of this defeat. His offhand statement that he favored the imposition of cloture by a vote of a bare majority of the Senate, rather than by the two-thirds vote for which his own Senators were working, was another of those impromptu and somewhat imperious remarks which have cost the President heavily on occasion. This particular remark came at the least fortunate moment in the whole discussion, alarmed the moderates, stiffened the die-hards.[47]

Nor did the *Times* ignore Republican complicity in the Senate's rejection of the Barkley ruling:

> No mistakes of judgment of attitude on the President's part, however, justify in our opinion the part played in this affair by a majority of Republican Senators. At Philadelphia last June the Republican party, in a bid for votes, pledged itself to abolish the poll tax, adopt an anti-lynching law and guarantee equal opportunity to employment, regardless of race. . . . They will have a hard time squaring this action (union with the South) with the brave promises made last year at Philadelphia.[48]

The Senate's rejection of the Barkley ruling did not end the southern filibuster; the Lucas motion to take up the Hayden-Wherry resolution still remained on the Senate calendar as the first order of business facing the Senate. Thus, the expectant renewal of the southern "talkathon" led, on March 13 and 14, to backstage efforts toward a compromise settlement. Those participating in its early stages included

---

47. Mar. 16, 1949, p. 26.
48. Ibid.

Senators Lucas, Wherry, Russell, and Hayden.[49] Lucas's involvement marked a sudden switch in his tactics; rather than continue the battle to overcome the filibuster, he now wanted an accommodation with the southerners to end the floor debate on Resolution Fifteen. In fact, as was later brought out in a floor colloquy involving Senators Knowland and Russell on March 17, Lucas had said at the time he was involved in the compromise discussions: "Gentlemen, as far as a change in rules is concerned, you can write your own ticket." [50] He was even prepared, Russell later averred, to go so far as to permit a change in Rule Twenty-two requiring a supporting vote of two-thirds or even three-fourths of the *entire* Senate to sustain cloture; and, if necessary, to include a provision in the agreement stating that "cloture would not even be applicable to a motion to change the rules, or a resolution to change the rules." [51]

Lucas's willingness to abandon the field to the enemies of civil rights legislation reflected his dismay over what was happening elsewhere to the Truman legislative program. Other legislation piling up behind the stalled Resolution Fifteen, included: a bill extending rent control, due to expire on March 31 unless the Senate acted beforehand; a bill continuing the European Recovery Program, facing termination on April 3 if the Congress failed to act in the interim; the Taft-Hartley repealer now in the final phase of clearance by the Senate Labor Committee; and an armed forces reorganization bill then blocked in Senator Russell's Armed Services Committee until the "heat was off" on civil rights.[52]

---

49. *Congressional Record*, 81st Cong., 1st Sess., 1949, Vol. XCV, Part 2, p. 2673.

50. Ibid.

51. Ibid.

52. *New York Times*, Mar. 15, 1949; and *Norfolk Journal and Guide*, Mar. 12, 1949, p. 16.

It was in this context, then, that the Southern Democratic and Republican coalition was able to seize the initiative and hammer out an amendment to the Hayden-Wherry resolution that was designed to make the southern position impregnable to attack not only for the rest of the session but for future sessions as well. That amendment, drafted by Wherry, Hayden, and Russell, was similar to Resolution Fifteen in only one respect: it provided the Senate with a mechanism to halt filibusters directed at motions as well as measures. Other features found in the amendment, but not in the original resolution, raised the voting requirement for cloture from two-thirds of those present and voting in the Senate chamber—the existing requirement—to two-thirds of the entire body or sixty-four senators. The amendment also stipulated that cloture could not be invoked to halt filibusters directed against future motions to change Rule Twenty-two.[53]

While final discussions were taking place pursuant to the "compromise" settlement, Senator Lucas announced to the press on March 14 that he thought it would be a good idea to drop the civil rights issue for a while. It was time, observed Lucas, for the Senate to move on to other business. For that reason, he declared his intention of adjourning the Senate in order to remove his motion from the top of the Senate calendar.[54] In other words, an adjournment, as distinct from a recess, would make it possible not only to end the filibuster but also to deny the conservative coalition the chance to deal with the issue within the framework of the Hayden-Wherry resolution. (By March 14 Lucas had apparently backed away from any further participation in the continuing discussions regarding a possible compromise, for fear that his involvement could prove to be embarrassing both for the

---

53. *Congressional Record,* 81st Cong., 1st Sess., 1949, Vol. XCV, Part 2, pp. 2509–10.

54. *New York Times,* Mar. 15, 1949.

White House and the national Democratic party.) Also on March 14 Lucas expressed his desire for an adjournment but did not press the matter because, by his own admission, the votes were not available to sustain such a request.[55]

On March 15 the conservative coalition showed its hand, and administration forces quickly realized that they had been outplayed. The southern filibuster was discontinued that day in order to allow the Hayden-Wherry resolution to come to a vote. By a 78 to 0 margin the Senate voted to make that much-debated resolution the immediate order of business facing the Senate. After that vote was taken, Senator Wherry introduced a petition signed by 52 senators, including 12 non-Southern Democrats, calling on the Senate to approve the Wherry amendment to the original resolution.[56]

The formal introduction of the Hayden-Wherry resolution precipitated an intense Senate debate on a number of issues ranging from the nature and purpose of the Southern Democratic-Republican coalition to the future of civil rights and race relations in America.[57] Senator Lucas made it clear that if the Senate adopted this amendment, it would be the equivalent to a "near funeral service for civil rights." He thought the issue should be dropped and that arrangements be made with President Truman to have a special session of Congress meet to deal exclusively with civil rights.[58] Joining the debate, Senator Wayne Morse attacked his fellow Republicans for having formed a coalition with Southern Democrats, whose policies and politics, in his opinion, did not have the support of the majority of the American

---

55. *Congressional Record*, 81st Cong., 1st Sess., 1949, Vol. XCV, Part 2, p. 2420.

56. Ibid., pp. 2462–2510.

57. Ibid., pp. 2509, 2571–2613, 2719–20.

58. Ibid., p. 2561.

people.[59] Freshman Senator Hubert Humphrey of Minnesota declared that "this is only the first blow to the Truman program and the Fair Deal," and predicted that if "this alliance can be formed and made to stick, we shall have a great deal of trouble." [60] Illinois Democrat Paul Douglas, in his maiden speech on the Senate floor, noted that of the 30 Democrats who joined the Republicans in signing the petition on behalf of the Wherry amendment, 20 were from the South, 4 from the border states and 6 from the area of the Rockies; of the 22 Republicans, who signed it, only 5 were from states east of the Alleghenies. In other words, this coalition's control of the Senate was formed at the expense of those states having more people and resources.[61]

Supporters of the Wherry amendment, such as Senator Carl Hayden of Arizona, claimed that its adoption would provide "for the first time in 140 years an assured means of ending a filibuster." [62] In a strong defense of the amendment bearing his name, Senator Wherry claimed that its passage would actually make it easier to obtain cloture because the Senate would have clarified the ambiguity which existed on the question of whether cloture applied to a motion as well as a measure.[63]

The deal which had been consummated in the cloakrooms of the Senate was now about to be approved by the Senate as a whole. On March 17, before voting on Wherry's amendment to the Hayden-Wherry resolution, the Senate rejected 57 to 29 Republican Senator Raymond Baldwin's amendment calling for the continuation of the present two-thirds voting requirement. Also voted down even more decisively

---

59. Ibid., p. 2595.
60. Ibid., p. 2612.
61. Ibid., pp. 2665–66.
62. Ibid., pp. 2570–71.
63. Ibid., p. 2588.

was Senator Morse's amendment permitting cloture to be invoked by a majority of a quorum—the position President Truman had supported. The Wherry amendment itself was approved by a vote of 63 to 23, with only 8 Republicans and 15 Democrats opposing it.[64] Thus was the will of the Senate expressed on this procedural matter; but in reality the vote meant that the Truman administration's civil rights program had been scuttled.

Referring to the events of March 17, the *New York Times* observed: "Last November Governors Thurmond and Wright, running on a States Rights ticket, received about 2½% of the votes cast for the President. . . . In the matter of federal action on civil rights we will continue to be ruled from Birmingham." [65] More to the point in terms of what actually happened in the Senate were the remarks of Senator Matthew Neely, a Democrat from West Virginia. He charged that the Republican-Dixiecrat combination, which had blocked moves to liberalize the Senate rules, also sought the defeat of efforts to repeal the Taft-Hartley law. "The vote on the Taft-Hartley repeal is," he suggested, "the payoff the Republicans will exact for the assistance G. O. P. Senators gave the Dixiecrats in the civil rights fight." [66]

More than civil rights had been affected by the March 17 vote; Truman's entire legislative program had been jeopardized by the coalition's victory. During a press conference held at his vacation White House in Key West on March 18, Truman made mention of the recent controversy over rules in the spirit of a man who had been chastened by defeat:

----

64. Ibid., pp. 2720–24. The opposition to the amendment was registered by liberals of both parties. Moderate and reactionary elements of the Senate supported it overwhelmingly.

65. *New York Times*, Mar. 18, 1949, p. 24.

66. *Pittsburgh Courier*, July 2, 1949, p. 3.

Q: Mr. President, Senator Morse of Oregon in this morning's paper has said that the Senate Democrats and Republicans agreed on not passing but one civil rights bill —that is, a new poll tax bill. Would you care to comment on that?

A: No comment. He is in the Congress and I am not. I only advise the Congress on what I think is good for the country. Then they agree as they see fit. We have three independent prongs to the Government of the United States. . . . And neither of the others ought to interfere with the duties of the other two.[67]

At another press conference a week later, Truman indicated that he was still hopeful of getting a civil rights program through Congress.[68] How he would achieve such a feat Truman did not say.

Despite his defeat in the Senate, the president submitted civil rights legislation to Congress. On March 3 Representative Mary Norton introduced the administration's anti–poll tax bill, H.R. 3199. Senator McGrath presented the administration's entire civil rights program to the Senate on April 28, consisting of S. 1725, an omnibus civil rights bill; S. 1726, an anti-lynching bill; S. 1727, an anti–poll tax bill; and S. 1728, an FEPC bill. Representative Adam Clayton Powell submitted the administration's FEPC bill, H.R. 4453, to the House on April 29. To complete the congressional introduction of the administration's civil rights program, Representative Emanuel Celler of New York dropped the omnibus civil rights bill, H.R. 4682, and anti-lynching bill, H.R. 4683, into the House hopper on May 16.[69]

The omnibus bill authorized a civil rights commission in

---

67. *Public Papers of the Presidents: Harry S. Truman, 1949*, p. 169.

68. Ibid., p. 182.

69. See Clark Clifford's Civil Rights File, HSTL.

the executive branch; created a civil rights division in the Department of Justice, to be headed by an assistant attorney general; provided for a joint congressional committee on civil rights; strengthened existing civil rights statutes; further protected the right of suffrage; and prohibited discrimination and segregation in interstate transportation.[70]

The anti–poll tax bill would abolish the poll tax as a prerequisite for voting in federal elections. The anti-lynching bill provided stiff maximum punishment amounting to twenty years imprisonment and/or a $10,000 fine for any member of a lynch mob and "any person who, whether or not a member of a lynch mob, instigates, incites, organizes, aids, abets, or commits a lynching by any means whatsoever." In addition, it authorized punishment amounting to five years imprisonment and/or a $5,000 fine for peace officers "who neglect or willfully fail to make diligent efforts to apprehend and hold in custody members of a lynch mob." [71]

The FEPC bill stated that the "right to employment without discrimination is declared to be a right of all persons within the jurisdiction of the United States and the protection of the right of the individual to be free from discrimination is declared to be national policy." [72] The bill authorized the president to appoint a seven-member commission to implement that policy. The commission would have the power to issue cease-and-desist orders in order to prevent unlawful employment policies—defined as a refusal to hire, discharge of, or discrimination against, an individual because of race, religion, color, national origin or ancestry—by firms with fifty or more employees, recruitment agencies,

---

70. Ibid.
71. See Stephen J. Spingarn File, HSTL.
72. Ibid.

and labor unions. Cease-and-desist orders would only be issued after they had been sanctioned by the courts, and any party affected by a final order from the commission would have the right of judicial review in the circuit courts.[73]

By submitting actual civil rights legislation, Truman established a historical precedent, but this action did not immunize his administration from criticism by the NAACP. On May 26, 1949, the NAACP informed Senator Lucas—who earlier announced that the administration had decided to abandon efforts to pass civil rights legislation during the first session—that millions of Negroes were "shocked by the failure of the Democratic Party to abide by its party platform." Making specific reference to the debacle of March 17, the NAACP declared that "the faint-heartedness and outright defection of some liberal Democrats was not anticipated." And because of what had happened, the NAACP now urged the president to call a special session of Congress to deal exclusively with the issue of civil rights.[74]

This incipient Negro disenchantment with the Democratic party was carried directly to the White House itself by Roy Wilkins, who wrote David Niles, a White House aide, on June 20 that "there has been a considerable change in the mood of the colored since January 1." Wilkins himself did not hold Truman responsible for what had happened; rather, he blamed congressional leaders of both parties for the failure of Congress to act in this field.[75] Wilkins's public willingness to absolve Truman of any blame for the events of the spring did not carry over to the NAACP. Holding its annual convention in Los Angeles in mid-July, 1949, the NAACP passed the following resolution:

---

73. Ibid.

74. NAACP press release, May 26, 1949, NAACP Papers, L.C.

75. To David Niles from Roy Wilkins, June 20, 1949, President's Personal File 293, HSTL.

It is our firm conviction that the 81st Congress of the United States presently in session has betrayed the mandate given it by the American people in the last election in the field of civil liberties. President Truman and the Congress must share responsibility for this betrayal. Both failed to pursue with vigor, persistency and strength a course of action which would have put into law the comprehensive civil liberties program which the President promised the American people.[76]

One of the leaders of the southern bloc who opposed the legislation that Wilkins and the NAACP wanted was Senator Richard Russell, who favored an accommodation with Truman as long as appropriate terms could be arranged. A compromise might be reached, felt Russell, if Truman accepted as a starting point for further negotiations Arkansas Congressman Brooks Hays's civil rights program, consisting of a voluntary FEPC (that is, one without enforcement powers), a constitutional amendment calling for the abolition of the poll tax, and an anti-lynching bill giving considerably more power to the states than the Truman bill proposed.[77] Meeting with Russell at the White House in mid-July, Truman informed him that the Hays plan was unacceptable. The South thus failed to persuade Truman to weaken his civil rights program.[78]

Evidently the president's position on FEPC proved to be the major stumbling block to any compromise with the South. Even before he had talked with Russell, Truman had learned from Clark Clifford that representatives of the NAACP, the ADA, the AFL, and the CIO, with whom he had spoken on June 2, wanted the administration to give FEPC

---

76. Resolutions Folder for the 40th Annual Convention, Box 387, NAACP Papers, L.C.

77. Hays, *A Southern Moderate Speaks*, pp. 25–52.

78. *Washington Post*, July 13, 1949.

the highest legislative priority.[79] This was done with the consent of Senator Lucas, who promised on July 7 to place it at the top of the civil rights agenda in the Senate.[80] It may have been a tactical error on the part of both Negro and white liberal organizations and labor unions, as well as on the part of the administration, to have insisted on FEPC at the expense of the Hays plan, especially since there was little likelihood of getting anything more out of Congress after the March 17 vote. In any event, Truman could not afford to ignore such liberal advice; but, at the same time, he knew that his continuing endorsement of FEPC made little difference legislatively, so his relationship with the South did not necessarily have to deteriorate any further. On August 30 he asked Congressman Sabath to include FEPC on a list of "must" legislation for the first session of the Eighty-first Congress, but Sabath could not assure Truman that the House would act on this particular bill, even though it had cleared the House Education and Labor Committee on August 2.[81]

If the situation was unpromising in the House, it was bleak in the Senate, not only because of the March 17 vote but because Senator Patrick McCarran, chairman of the Senate Judiciary Committee, had appointed Mississippi's Senator James Eastland—a Thurmond supporter in 1948 —to head the Judiciary subcommittee on civil rights.[82] As chairman of this subcommittee, he could pigeonhole all of

79. "American Rights for American Citizens," NAACP Annual Report, 1949, p. 15. NAACP Papers, L.C.

80. Ibid.

81. *New York Times*, Aug. 31, 1949, p. 46; the committee's recommendations can be found in U.S. House of Representatives, *Report from Committee on Education and Labor to accompany H.R. 4453, August 2, 1949* (Washington: Government Printing Office, 1949).

82. *Pittsburgh Courier*, Sept. 24, 1949, pp. 1, 4.

Truman's civil rights program with the exception of FEPC and the anti–poll tax bill. Mississippi's other senator, John Stennis, headed a Rules Committee subcommittee that was responsible for anti–poll tax legislation.[83] It now appeared that Mississippi was now in legislative control of all civil rights legislation—excepting FEPC—in the United States Senate.

Eastland's promotion suggests that the national Democratic party had given up completely any intention it may have had to purge those congressional Democrats who had bolted the party to support Strom Thurmond in 1948. Alexander Heard observes that "the Dixiecrats were given regular committee assignments as Democrats, including chairmanships and any other sanctions imposed were considerably short of a purge." [84] Eastland's success in the Senate, for example, had been matched earlier in the House by the appointment of another Thurmond supporter, Congressman William Colmer of Mississippi, to the important House Rules Committee. Although President Truman had approved the ouster of five Dixiecrat members of the Democratic National Committee and was prepared to deprive active Dixiecrats of patronage, his failure to press congressional leaders to take action against bolters like Eastland and Colmer was evidence of his reluctance to engage in organizational conflict.[85]

That civil rights had reached something of a dead end in the Senate was confirmed by Senator Lucas on October 3, when he declared that "it seems doubtful that a prolonged discussion of any civil rights bill at this session would be helpful." [86] Because of this legislative impasse, he won Tru-

---

83. *Norfolk Journal and Guide*, Sept. 3, 1949.
84. Heard, *A Two Party South?*, p. 24.
85. See *Norfolk Journal and Guide*, Sept. 3, 1949, p. 3.
86. Ibid., Oct. 15, 1949, p. 11.

man's permission to postpone action on civil rights until the start of the next session, when a concerted effort would be made to pass the FEPC bill which had been reported out of the Labor and Public Welfare Committee without recommendation on September 23. According to Lucas, various civil rights organizations favored the postponement "because they were aware that there would be a better chance for success in the next session than in the tail end of this one." [87]

The administration's decision to promote FEPC rather than other civil rights legislation angered the Republican minority leader, Senator Wherry, who charged that Lucas and his associates had selected "the one civil rights bill that they know will be the hardest to pass. They hope it will fail, and they hope they can go to the country in the campaign of 1950 to claim that it was the Republicans who blocked it." [88] It was Wherry's contention that if the administration was prepared to fight for anti-lynching or anti–poll tax legislation, there was a good chance to halt a filibuster with the new rule. He insisted that the priority given to FEPC by Lucas would prevent action on legislation "which has the best chance of passage." [89] Senator Humphrey agreed with Wherry's analysis; hence he urged that the Democratic leadership call up anti–poll tax and anti-lynching legislation

---

87. Democratic National Committee Folder, Box 444, NAACP Papers, L.C. About the matter of the postponement, Thurgood Marshall reported to Roy Wilkins that Congressman Adam Clayton Powell learned that, subsequent to the announcement of the postponement, "Cox of Georgia and Colmar [sic] of Mississippi brought the Social Security Bill out of Committee so that it appears that the deal was to bring other legislation out in front of civil rights" (Memorandum to Roy Wilkins from Thurgood Marshall, October 5, 1949, Civil Rights Bills File, 1951, NAACP Papers, L.C.).

88. New York Times, Oct. 4, 1949, p. 7.

89. Norfolk Journal and Guide, Nov. 19, 1949, p. 2.

before FEPC. "If we can get these bills through," he said, "we should be able to get a FEP legislation enacted." Lucas ignored these requests, and thus anti-lynching legislation, which had been on the Senate calendar since June 17, was not introduced on the floor during the first session. On the other hand, the FEPC bill was placed on the Senate calendar on October 17, preparatory to a renewed struggle in the second session beginning in January.[90]

The impasse in the Senate seemingly failed to daunt President Truman, who reaffirmed his commitment to the cause of civil rights while delivering several speeches in mid-November, 1949. Addressing a luncheon on the National Conference of Christians and Jews on November 11, the president remarked:

> I have asked that our Federal Government take an active part in this effort to achieve greater justice. I have called for legislation to protect the rights of all its citizens, to assure their equal participation in national life, and to reduce discrimination based upon prejudice. In view of the fundamental faith of this country and the clear language of our Constitution, I do not see how we can do otherwise than adopt such legislation.[91]

On November 15 the president spoke at the annual meeting of the National Council of Negro Women. Included in his prepared statement was the declaration that "we are awakened as never before to the true meaning of equality—equality in the economic world. We are going to continue to advance in our program of bringing equal rights and equal opportunities to all citizens." [92] A more realistic appraisal of

---

90. Ibid., Nov. 5, 1949, p. 2.

91. *Public Papers of the Presidents: Harry S. Truman, 1949*, p. 562.

92. Ibid., p. 566.

the situation was made by Alabama's Senator John Spark-man. He did not think Congress would pass FEPC because it "would have an even greater impact in Northern industrial centers than in the South. For that reason, you are going to find many members of Congress voting against it along with the Southerners." [93]

While the administration experienced frustration in its dealings with Congress, it took steps on the executive level to combat discrimination and to advance the cause of black aspirations. Responding to pressure exerted by Negro news-papers, President Truman on October 15, 1949, nominated a Negro, William R. Hastie, the governor of the Virgin Islands and formerly dean of the Howard University Law School, for a position on the Third Circuit Court of Appeals.[94] Truman's selection of Hastie marked at the time the highest position on the federal judiciary to which a Negro had been appointed.

The administration also made other moves in its battle against discrimination. White House aide Stephen Spingarn, who drafted much of Truman's civil rights legislation, recommended in a memorandum to Clark Clifford that the Justice Department incorporate into its 1950 budget a request for fifteen additional lawyers and adequate clerical assistance for its civil rights section, which in 1949 had an authorized strength of only seven lawyers, one less than in 1948, the year of Truman's civil rights message. Not only were the lawyers needed but, as Spingarn suggested, their addition "would be further assurance that the administration meant business in the civil rights field and would offset the legislative defeats in this field which we are likely to

93. *Norfolk Journal and Guide*, Nov. 19, 1949, p. 2.

94. The Negro press had been requesting such an appointment through the summer of 1949; see *Norfolk Journal and Guide*, Aug. 20, 1949, p. 10.

receive in 1950." [95] When Clifford failed to answer the memorandum, Spingarn turned to Charles Murphy, Truman's assistant special counsel, for support. Murphy felt that Spingarn's proposal was sound, so on November 28 he contacted Attorney General J. Howard McGrath, a recent appointee, about the matter. The Justice Department quickly enlarged its budget to include appropriations for the understaffed civil rights section.[96] Because of the imagination of Spingarn and the favorable responses of Murphy and McGrath, the Justice Department prepared to strengthen its legal arm at a time when civil rights litigation was becoming the most effective method of challenging and changing some of the discriminatory social patterns in American life.

Another example of the administration's initiative in the civil rights field could be found in the area of housing. On December 2, 1949, Solicitor General Philip Perlman declared in New York that "the Federal Housing Authority is amending its rules so as to refuse to aid the financing of any property the occupancy or use of which is restricted on the basis of race, creed, or color." [97] The next day Franklin D. Richards, the Federal Housing Authority commissioner, stated that very few of the nation's dwellings would be affected by the policy change announced by Perlman. "It will be the exceptional case," explained Richards, "where property cannot receive federal mortgage aid." [98] In other words, the Perlman announcement did not affect property on which agreements already existed "to prohibit sale or rental to, or occupancy by, colored persons or other racial or

---

95. Memorandum to Clark Clifford from Stephen J. Spingarn, November 22, 1949, Stephen J. Spingarn File, HSTL.

96. Stephen J. Spingarn File, HSTL.

97. *New York Times*, Dec. 3, 1949, p. 1.

98. *Norfolk Journal and Guide*, Dec. 10, 1949, pp. 1–2.

religious minority groups." On December 12, 1949, the Federal Housing Authority made it known that after February 15, 1950, it "would no longer insure mortgages on homes whose deeds were to contain restrictive covenants." [99] This release confirmed the fact that all covenants existing prior to February 15, 1950, would remain unaffected by the new rules laid down by the Federal Housing Administration.

Although the president may have hoped that administrative measures would become a substitute for legislative success, he could not ignore the political facet of the civil rights struggle, or else his political image in important northern states would be tarnished. Hence, as the new congressional session approached, Truman once more prepared to engage in another fruitless battle with Congress, if only to prevent the Republicans from exploiting the civil rights issue for their own benefit. Consequently, when the president went to Congress to deliver his fifth State of the Union address on January 4, 1950, he said:

> I again urge the Congress to enact the civil rights proposals I made in February 1948. These are proposals for the enactment of Federal statutes which will protect all our people in the exercise of their democratic rights. . . .
> Some of these proposals have been before the Congress for a long time. Those who oppose them, as well as those who favor them, should recognize that it is the duty of the elected representatives of the people to let these proposals come to a vote.[100]

On January 9 the administration submitted to Congress its budget message containing the suggestion that "a perma-

---

99. *New York Times*, Dec. 16, 1949, p. 1.

100. *Public Papers of the Presidents: Harry S. Truman, 1950* (Washington: United States Government Printing Office, 1965), pp. 9–10.

nent Fair Employment Practices Commission should be established. To keep minority groups economically submerged is not only unjust and discriminatory, but also prevents the best use of available manpower." [101] The administration requested that Congress provide the proposed agency with a million dollars for operating expenses during fiscal year 1951.[102]

The major problem facing the administration, especially in the Senate, was finding the means of bringing FEPC to a vote. For the purpose of assisting the administration in this endeavor, over 4,000 delegates of the National Emergency Civil Rights Mobilization, which the NAACP had been organizing since November, 1949, came to Washington in mid-January, 1950. On January 16 Senator Lucas told the delegates, who represented organizations like the NAACP and the American Civil Liberties Union, that the administration would push for the passage of FEPC, even though there was little chance that it would be enacted into law.[103] The following day a number of the delegates met with President Truman, who told them "that every effort is being made to get a vote on these measures in the Senate. The leader of the majority and the Vice President assured me that they will eventually get a vote if it takes all summer." He then advised the group to continue to pressure Congress, since "that is possibly the only way we can get action." [104] Truman himself, however, was reluctant to invest much executive capital in a legislative enterprise that could bankrupt the rest of his program.

---

101. Ibid., p. 94.
102. Ibid., p. 98.
103. *New York Times*, Jan. 17, 1950, p. 8.
104. *Public Papers of the Presidents: Harry S. Truman, 1950,* pp. 115, 128.

As far as civil rights legislation was concerned, the situation was indeed desperate. The administration's chances of carrying the Senate had been scuttled when it lost the filibuster fight. In the House, FEPC legislation had been approved by the House Education and Labor Committee by a vote of 14 to 11 on August 2, 1949; but, to the chagrin of its supporters, the bill fell into the clutches of the House Rules Committee, which failed to clear it for floor action.[105] If the FEPC bill was to be rescued from the Rules Committee, the partisans of that bill would have to turn to the twenty-one-day rule for procedural relief, making it possible for the Speaker to call to the House floor those committee-approved measures which had been retained by the Rules Committee for at least twenty-one days. But Congressman Eugene Cox, a member of the Rules Committee and a determined foe of civil rights legislation, recognized that House liberals would utilize the twenty-one-day rule in order to bypass his committee. Consequently, he sought to repeal the rule, but his efforts were rebuffed by the House on January 20, 1950, by a vote of 236 to 183.[106]

The focus of the House was now on Speaker Rayburn, himself unsympathetic to FEPC legislation. Aware of Rayburn's antipathy, Harlem Congressman Adam Clayton Powell, a sponsor of the administration's FEPC bill in the House, sent a telegram to President Truman on January 19, 1950, urging him to put pressure on Rayburn to recognize Congressman John Lesinski, chairman of the House Education and Labor Committee, which had already approved the FEPC bill. As Powell said in his telegram, ". . . It is felt that unless this is done by you—he will not be recognized by the

---

105. *Congressional Quarterly Almanac* VI (1950) (Washington: Congressional Quarterly News Features, 1951), 375–80.

106. *New York Times*, Jan. 21, 1950, p. 8.

Speaker." And if Truman refused, asserted Powell, "it can only mean in the eyes of the American people that you are not for civil rights as much as you have proclaimed." [107]

On January 23, 1950, Speaker Rayburn, the master of his domain, refused to recognize Congressman Lesinski, who sought to introduce the FEPC bill on to the House floor via the twenty-one-day rule.[108] At his February 2 press conference Truman was queried as to whether he had instructed Rayburn to recognize Representative Lesinski. Said the President: "No I did not ask him to recognize anybody. I asked him to consider the passage of FEPC in both Houses. I did not ask him to recognize anybody. That is the business of the Speaker. He has been in charge of that, and nobody can tell him whom to recognize." [109] That was one side of the issue; Arthur Krock illuminated a different facet: "Very seldom do informed observers agree with Representative Marcantonio [New York], yet a good many did when he remarked: 'It is obvious to everyone that everybody wants civil rights as a campaign issue but not as a law and that goes for Harry Truman, the Democratic party and the Republican party.' " [110]

Rayburn's hostility notwithstanding, House liberals made one last attempt to introduce FEPC; they sought to force a showdown by a device known as Calendar Wednesday—a parliamentary rule which obligated the Speaker to call alphabetically the standing committees of the House on

---

107. Telegram to the President from Adam Clayton Powell, January 19, 1950, Truman Papers, OF 1827, HSTL.

108. *Congressional Record*, 81st Cong., 2d Sess., 1950, Vol. XCV, Part 2, p. 722.

109. *Public Papers of the Presidents: Harry S. Truman, 1950*, p. 143.

110. *New York Times*, Jan. 26, 1950, p. 26.

successive Wednesdays in order to give them a chance to present legislation. On February 22 the House Education and Labor Committee was called, giving Representative Lesinski, its chairman, his opportunity to introduce the FEPC bill. The House immediately transformed itself into a committee of the whole to consider it.[111] After fifteen hours of wrangling, Republican Representative Samuel K. McConnell of Pennsylvania managed to introduce a substitute amendment calling for the creation of an FEPC without enforcement powers. The House approved his amendment by a vote of 222 to 178, as 104 Republicans joined 118 Democrats to override liberal opposition.[112] Thus the House passed an FEPC bill that Truman neither wanted nor, in good conscience, could accept. "The whole affair," wrote the *New York Times,* "has become a mockery of responsible legislative practice; the prospective filibuster awaiting FEPC in the Senate only adds to the hollowness of the entire procedure." [113]

As the *Times* noted, the House passage of FEPC, even with the crippling McConnell amendment, at least would have the effect of keeping the issue temporarily alive so far as the Senate was concerned. Because of the House action, FEPC had now become, in the words of Roy Wilkins, "the hottest thing on the Senate calendar," and he added, "it plagues the administration at every turn." In fact, the House, contended Wilkins, "has put the administration on more of a hot spot than it would have been if the House had not acted at all." But ever the realist, Wilkins knew that "in pragmatic politics all this means that the supporters of FEPC will have

111. See *Congressional Quarterly Almanac,* VI (1950), 375–80.

112. *Congressional Record,* 81st Cong., 2d Sess., 1950, Vol. XCV, Part 2, pp. 2253–54.

113. Feb. 24, 1950, p. 24.

records on *both* Representatives *and* Senators when the election comes around next November." [114]

The Negro press was indignant over what had happened in Congress. The *Chicago Defender,* the only major Negro newspaper to support Truman in 1948, published a front-page editorial entitled "Promises versus Performances": "As we enter the 1950 election campaign, the Democrats, both locally and nationally, should do a little soul searching. The action promised by the Democrats in 1948 caught the imagination of the people. Now, two years later, we have more promises and few accomplishments." [115]

Although the *Defender*'s bitterness was justified, the administration was seeking relief through litigation. On April 3 and 4, 1950, Attorney General J. Howard McGrath and Solicitor General Philip Perlman appeared before the Supreme Court to argue on behalf of Elmer Henderson, whose case challenging the legality of discrimination and segregation in interstate transportation was now being adjudicated. [116] Earlier, and without President Truman's fore-knowledge, the Justice Department had submitted *amicus curiae* briefs to the Court not only in support of Henderson but G. W. McLaurin and Herman Sweatt as well. Their cases questioned the legality of discrimination and segregation in the field of higher education. [117] The Henderson brief,

---

114. Roy Wilkins to Addie L. Weber, April 24, 1950, McConnell Bill File, Box 408, NAACP Papers, L.C.

115. Mar. 10, 1950.

116. *Pittsburgh Courier,* Apr. 8, 1950, pp. 1, 5. Philip Elman, who was mostly responsible for drafting this brief for the government, wrote Thurgood Marshall that "while I am not too confident that the Supreme Court will go as far as we have (not in this case, at least), I think we have taken a long step in the right direction" (Philip Elman to Thurgood Marshall, October 19, 1949, Department of Justice Folder, Box 405, NAACP Papers, L.C.).

117. Konvitz, *Expanding Liberties,* pp. 247–51.

submitted by the Justice Department on October 5, 1949, was particularly noteworthy because in it the government advanced, for the first time, the argument that

> so long as the doctrine of the Plessy case stands, a barrier erected not by the Constitution but by the courts will continue to work a denial of rights and privileges and immunities antagonistic to the freedoms and liberties on which our institutions and our form of government are founded. "Separate but equal" is a constitutional anachronism which no longer deserves a place in our law. . . . It is neither reasonable or right that colored citizens of the United States should be subjected to the humiliation of being segregated by law, on the pretense that they are being treated as equals.[118]

While the Court considered these cases, politics as usual dominated the Congress and the White House. On April 11 President Truman, after conferring with Vice-President Barkley and Senator Lucas, decided to postpone Senate action on a committee-cleared FEPC bill in order to obtain a quick Senate vote on Marshall Plan appropriations.[119] Roy Wilkins quickly assailed this decision, but at a White House press conference on April 13 the president defended it as a necessity, while promising, somewhat enigmatically, that FEPC would be carried to a "logical conclusion." [120]

---

118. Brief of the United States in *Henderson* v. *United States*, pp. 65–66.

119. *New York Times*, Apr. 12, 1950, p. 18.

120. *Public Papers of the Presidents: Harry S. Truman, 1950*, p. 253. On this point the comment of Richard Longaker seems relevant: "It seems to have been a common legislative technique to give only half-hearted support to civil rights legislation, such as FEPC legislation, in return for Southern cooperation in the passage of foreign policy or welfare measures" (Richard P. Longaker, *The Presidency and Individual Liberties* [Ithaca, N.Y.: Cornell University Press, 1961], p. 41).

In line with Truman's promise, Lucas presented to the Senate on May 5 a motion calling for the introduction of the FEPC bill. Southern Democrats immediately began to filibuster even though they knew, as did everyone else, that the entire affair was nothing more than a ritualistic exercise.[121] On May 19 the Senate terminated these proceedings when it voted to reject Lucas's cloture petition: 52 senators, consisting of 19 Democrats and 33 Republicans, supported cloture; 32 senators, including 26 Democrats and 6 Republicans, rejected it.[122] Following this vote, Lucas and the Republican leadership quarreled over which party had been responsible for the petition's defeat.[123] Given the poor Democratic showing—only 36.5 percent of the Senate Democratic membership voted for cloture—it would seem that the Republicans had the better of the argument. Later, Republican Senator Robert Taft, speaking off the Senate floor, noted that neither Truman nor the Democratic National Committee had brought pressure to bear on the nine absentee Democrats whose votes might have helped Lucas obtain the necessary 64 votes.[124]

While President Truman watched his legislative program slowly disappear into a congressional quagmire, he was not without a victory or two in the civil rights field. On May 22 the President's Committee on Equality of Treatment and

---

121. Ruchames, *Race, Jobs, and Politics*, p. 208.

122. *Congressional Record*, 81st Cong., 2d Sess., 1950, Vol. XCV, Part 6, pp. 7299–7300. Of the twenty-six Democrats voting against cloture, five were outside the South: Hayden and McFarland of Arizona; Kerr of Oklahoma; McCarran of Nevada; and Johnson of Colorado (ibid.).

123. Ibid., p. 7301.

124. *New York Times*, May 20, 1950, p. 8. It was Wilkins's opinion that the Dixiecrats did not defeat cloture; it was defeated "by the non-Southern 'nay' votes plus the absentees" (Roy Wilkins to Walter White, May 23, 1950, FEPC Folder, Box 408, NAACP Papers, L.C.).

Opportunity in the Armed Forces, the Fahy Committee, submitted to Truman its report affirming the fact that segregation had been formally abolished in the armed forces. The report, *Freedom to Serve*, spelled out in detail how the Pentagon, especially the Army, was finally persuaded that equality of opportunity would produce a "better Army, Navy and Air Force." [125] But what the report did not reveal was that notwithstanding the efforts of the Fahy Committee, a creation of the 1948 election campaign, the United States Army had been prepared to resist indefinitely attempts to achieve desegregation. In short, only President Truman's active intervention made possible a resolution of this administrative imbroglio, thereby insuring compliance with Executive Order 9981.[126] By strongly backing the committee he had appointed, Truman demonstrated his desire to fight for racial progress in an area where his administration could act without upsetting the precarious Democratic party balance in the Congress and the nation. Action replaced rhetoric, as politics and morality merged to produce justice.

Although the Committee's goal of total desegregation had not yet been achieved in many Army units scattered around the globe, Truman expressed satisfaction with the progress that had been made:

It is, therefore, with a great deal of confidence that I learn from the Committee that the present programs of the three Services are designed to accomplish the objectives of the President; and that as these programs are carried out, there will be, within the reasonably near future, equality of treatment and opportunity for all per-

125. *Freedom to Serve*, p. 66.

126. Dalfiume, *Desegregation of the U.S. Armed Forces*, pp. 197–200.

sons in the Armed Services, with a consequent improvement in military efficiency.

I attach the highest importance to the Committee's assignment. In the Committee's own words, equality of treatment and opportunity in the Armed Services is right, it is just, and will strengthen the nation.[127]

In addition to praising the work of the committee, the president also included in his acceptance statement a reference to the FEPC struggle in the Senate:

This report is submitted as the United States Senate is considering a motion to take up a FEPC bill. The work of the President's Committee . . . shows what can be accomplished by a Commission in this admittedly difficult field. I hope the Senate will take this Report into consideration as it debates the merits of FEPC, and that, as I urged in my State of the Union Message in January, it will permit this important measure to come to a vote.[128]

Administrative initiative, as evidenced by the work of the Fahy Committee, represented one method of circumventing the legislative bog that was Congress; another viable alternative might be found in the courts. On June 6, 1950, the Supreme Court announced its decisions in the cases of *McLaurin* v. *Oklahoma, Sweatt* v. *Painter,* and *Henderson*

---

127. *Public Papers of the Presidents: Harry S. Truman, 1950*, p. 431. It is important to note, however, that "the Fahy Committee won Army Secretary Gordon Gray's agreement to open up progressively more specialist jobs to Negroes in all army units, and to remove the Army's quota on Negro inductions, though Gray obtained President Truman's secret written agreement to go back to a quota if the Army received a disproportionate number of Negroes" (see Lee Nichols, *Breakthrough on the Color Front* [New York: Random House, 1954], p. 108).

128. *Public Papers of the Presidents: Harry S. Truman, 1950*, p. 431.

v. *The United States*.[129] With Justice Tom C. Clark disquali-
fying himself, the other eight justices unanimously agreed
that the civil rights of the Negroes, whose cases they re-
viewed, had been violated. Although the justices refused to
decide these cases within a broad constitutional context, as
had been requested by the Justice Department, the position
they advanced was sufficient to suggest that the Supreme
Court was well disposed to reexamine race relations law
more systematically than any other time in the twentieth
century. The *Pittsburgh Courier* subsequently commented:
"The United States Department of Justice deserves much
credit, also, for the part it played in insisting that discrimination means segregation, and that segregation is
illegal." [130]

As the Supreme Court moved into a new era in race
relations law, the Congress remained as intractable as ever.
The administration's last attempt to secure a Senate vote on
civil rights was set for July 12, when Senator Lucas planned
to submit another cloture petition on behalf of FEPC.[131] To
prepare for this vote, Stephen Spingarn and Charles Murphy drafted a memorandum which they submitted to President Truman on July 3 recommending that every effort be
made to get a maximum vote in favor of the second cloture
petition.[132] According to a July 5 memorandum that Spin-

---

129. *McLaurin* v. *Oklahoma State Regents*, 339 U.S. 637 (1950);
Sweatt v. *Painter*, 339 U.S. 629 (1950); *Henderson* v. *United States*,
339 U.S. 816 (1950). Apparently, the decision in the last-named suit
did not produce immediate results in favor of Elmer Henderson. He
was compelled to return to the federal courts again after it became
clear that the Interstate Commerce Commission was ignoring the will
of the court. For additional details pertaining to this case, see *Norfolk
Journal and Guide*, Apr. 5, 1952, p. 3.

130. June 17, 1950, p. 14.

131. Stephen J. Spingarn File, HSTL.

132. Memorandum to the President from Charles Murphy and
Stephen J. Spingarn, July 3, 1950, Stephen J. Spingarn File, HSTL.

garn wrote for his FEPC file: "The President told us to go ahead on this matter. Charlie is to call Senator Lucas and Bill Boyle and arrange for us to get together with them to coordinate our work." [133] This was the first time Truman had actively committed himself to support such a proposal in Congress; he was mindful of the coming congressional elections and America's new responsibilities in Korea. Thus having received Truman's permission, William Boyle, chairman of the Democratic National Committee, sent telegrams and letters on July 8 to party officials throughout the country asking them for their support.

> . . . I call upon each party official to cooperate to the fullest extent to make certain of full attendance in the United States Senate in support of the President and the platform of the Democratic party in this important vote. . . . While the amended rule makes it more difficult to prevent unlimited debate, success can be obtained if all Democrats who supported the President on this vital issue are present and voting, and if the Republicans cooperate. . . .[134]

The Senate vote, taken on July 12, fell 9 short of the total needed for cloture. This time, 55 Senators—22 Democrats and 33 Republicans—supported cloture; 33 Senators—27 Democrats (including 6 non-Southern) and 6 Republicans —opposed it.[135] Truman's active intercession made little difference in the final outcome; his civil rights program was now interred in the legislative graveyard of the Eighty-first Congress.

Although FEPC had failed to pass Congress, the Korean War kept the issue alive as far as Negro leaders were

133. Stephen J. Spingarn File, HSTL.

134. *New York Times*, July 9, 1950, p. 37.

135. *Congressional Record*, 81st Cong., 2d Sess., 1950, Vol. XCV, Part 8, pp. 9981–82.

concerned. On July 16, 1950, A. Philip Randolph, cochairman of the National Committee for a Permanent FEPC, wired Truman requesting that he issue an executive order similar to 8802 "as an integral factor in the mobilization of manpower against North Korean Communist aggression." [136] On September 8, 1950, the Urban League urged the President to cope with the manpower problem in a democratic manner.[137] On September 10 Randolph again spoke out in favor of an emergency FEPC on grounds of "enlightened self-interest" and "moral necessity." [138] In Congress, New York Senator Herbert Lehman also urged Truman to issue an executive order, similar to the one recommended by Randolph.[139] Since the president was too involved with foreign affairs and was no longer subject to pressure from civil rights organizations, he ignored these requests. Suddenly, it seemed, civil rights was no longer the urgent political issue it had been. The postwar liberal tide was now receding, carrying with it the frustrated hopes of millions of American Negroes.

The 1950 congressional election confirmed the fact that the Fair Deal was spent as a political force, for in that year a number of northern Democrats suffered crushing defeats; for example, both Senators Lucas and Myers—Truman's floor leaders in the Senate—were retired by the voters.[140] The Democrats retained control of Congress, but their majorities were considerably reduced, in the House from 261 to 234, and in the Senate from 53 to 49.[141] If the Eighty-first

---

136. *American Jewish Yearbook, 1952* (Philadelphia: Jewish Publication Society, 1953), p. 95.
137. *New York Times*, Sept. 9, 1950, p. 15.
138. Ibid., Sept. 11, 1950, p. 15.
139. Ibid., Oct. 16, 1950, p. 8.
140. Evans and Novak, *Lyndon B. Johnson*, p. 41.
141. *New York Times*, November 9, 1950, p. 1.

Congress had buried civil rights legislation, the Eighty-second would not even think the issue worthy of consideration. Especially noteworthy in that regard were the post-election comments of Congressman Porter Hardy of Virginia, who pointed out that in the Eighty-second Congress Southern Democrats would hold a majority of Democratic seats in the House and would lack only one Democratic seat of holding a majority in the Senate. As Congressman Hardy suggested, "That speaks for itself as far as civil rights legislation is concerned." [142]

Although many voters had been bewitched by Senator Joseph McCarthy's manifold distortions and bothered by the enigmatic nature of the Korean War, black Americans were more concerned with employment problems and racial discrimination. Hence, they were not interested in the issues which the Republicans advanced in 1950. Negroes endorsed Democratic candidates, as is shown by an analysis of votes in black wards in ten widely scattered cities, including New York, Philadelphia, Chicago, and Los Angeles.[143] Only in Baltimore did Negroes reject the Democratic candidate, incumbent Senator Millard Tydings, because they found his racist views simply unacceptable.[144]

Negroes had good reasons to remain with the Democratic party in 1950. Not only were they still benefiting from the post–World War II economic boom (though to a much lesser

142. *Norfolk Journal and Guide*, November 25, 1950, p. 2. Or in the words of Clarence Mitchell, the Washington representative of the NAACP's national office: "So far as numbers are concerned, our position in the 82nd Congress will not be greatly different from what it was in the 81st" (Memorandum to Walter White from Clarence Mitchell, November 9, 1950, Congressmen and Senators Folder, Box 419, NAACP Papers, L.C.).

143. Lubell, *The Future of American Politics*, p. 165.

144. *Negro Yearbook, 1952* (New York: Wm. H. Wise, 1952), p. 301.

extent than most whites), but they were also aware that President Truman had helped to make possible the desegration of the armed forces and that his administration had challenged Jim Crow jurisprudence. Thanks, then, to the Truman administration, American Negroes had achieved slight progress in their quest for racial justice; but that progress was still too limited and fragmentary. Practically all areas of American life remained blighted by a pattern of culture which had no place in a democratic society.

Chapter 5

PRESIDENTIAL POLITICS OF
CIVIL RIGHTS: 1952

When the Eighty-second Congress convened on January 3, 1951, it was clear that any civil rights program advanced by President Truman would soon find itself in legislative limbo. Arizona's Senator Ernest McFarland, the new Democratic majority leader, and Lyndon Johnson of Texas, the new majority whip, were opposed to FEPC and to any major liberalization of Rule Twenty-two.[1] Furthermore, the Sen-

---

1. Evans and Novak, *Lyndon B. Johnson,* pp. 39, 43. At the forty-first annual meeting of the NAACP, a resolution was passed attacking and deploring the elevation of McFarland and Johnson to

ate Democratic Policy Committee, which helped to determine legislative priorities, was controlled by Richard Russell of Georgia. The situation in the House was equally
bleak, for on January 3, 1951, the lower chamber rescinded
the twenty-one-day rule (thereby enhancing the power of
the conservative Rules Committee) and voted to return to
the rules which governed the House during the days of the
Eightieth Congress.[2]

On January 8, 1951, President Truman delivered to Congress his State of the Union address, which dealt largely
with problems created by the Korean War. He downgraded
domestic issues and mentioned civil rights in a manner
calculated to restore party harmony in a period of international crisis, saying: "We must remember that the fundamentals of our strength rest upon the freedoms of the people. We must continue our efforts to achieve the full
relization of our democratic ideals. . . . We must assure
equal rights and equal opportunities to all our citizens." [3] A
week later Truman included in his budget message a recommendation that Congress pass FEPC legislation to prevent
discrimination "during a period of defense mobilization." [4]
The 1951 budget message, however, contained no specific
allotment for the proposed agency's operating expenses.
Civil rights leaders, like A. Philip Randolph, realizing that
FEPC was a legislative dead letter, demanded that the president issue an executive order to compensate for the lack of
congressional action. To placate his critics, Truman an-

---

leadership positions in the Senate; see NAACP press release, January
4, 1951, Government General File, Box 1951, NAACP Papers, L.C.

2. *Congressional Record*, 82d Cong., 1st Sess., 1951, Vol. XCVII,
Part 1, p. 17.

3. *Public Papers of the Presidents: Harry S. Truman, 1951* (Washington: United States Government Printing Office, 1965), p. 12.

4. Ibid., p. 80.

nounced at a White House press conference on January 18, that he was considering new legal moves to cope with the employment situation created by the Korean War.[5] Truman's emphasis on the need for legality was predicated on the fact that Senator Russell had written into the 1945 Independent Offices Appropriation Act, and all subsequent acts, a clause that specifically prohibited the president from using any emergency funds placed at his disposal by Congress to finance the operation of an FEPC.[6] For this reason, apparently, the White House ignored the Labor Department's December, 1950, draft of an executive order authorizing the establishment of an FEPC similar in design and operation to President Franklin Roosevelt's wartime agency.[7]

Nevertheless, President Truman could not pursue a policy of total inaction on this question since he was aware that the black vote could be as crucial in the 1952 election as it had been in 1948. Hence, on February 2, 1951, taking his first tentative step in the direction of establishing some kind of machinery to fight discrimination in industries handling defense contracts, he issued Executive Order 10210, which declared that "there shall be no discrimination against any person on the ground of race, creed, color, or national origin, and all contracts hereunder shall contain a pro-

---

5. Ibid., p. 112.

6. This amendment was attached to Public Law 358, sec. 213, 78th Congress, 2d Session. On the other hand, there were those critics who argued that the Supplemental Appropriations Act of 1951, which the Eighty-first Congress approved as Public Law 843 on September 27, 1950, gave the president sufficient authority to issue that order; see Will Maslow to Arnold Aronson, March 12, 1951, FEPC File, Box 1951, NAACP Papers, L.C.

7. Philleo Nash Files, Box 17, HSTL. There is some evidence in the NAACP Papers suggesting that this particular order had been drafted with the help of the National Council for a Permanent FEPC; see FEPC File, Box 1951, NAACP Papers, L.C.

vision that the contractor and any subcontractor there-
under shall not so discriminate." [8] Despite its imposing language, Executive Order 10210 was essentially meaningless
because it lacked an enforcement clause. President Truman,
in other words, would not create an FEPC unless or until
Congress displayed a willingness to finance it.

In a meeting with President Truman at the White House
on February 28, Walter White and other Negro spokesmen
made it clear that Executive Order 10210 did not go far
enough and that they wanted stronger executive action.
Consequently, they presented to him a six-point program
that included a recommendation for an FEPC with an enforcement mechanism. [9] Presumably, Truman promised
them something, because on March 20 Walter White wired
him in Key West: "Let us know when Executive Order for
FEPC will be signed by you." [10] On April 4 White and Randolph wrote the president asking when they could expect
him to act; he did not answer their letter. [11] Truman had no
intention of going beyond Executive Order 10210, as such a
move would have precipitated a bitter row with Congress.

---

8. Executive Order 10210, in 16 F.R. 1049.

9. A copy of their demands can be found in the FEPC File, Box
1951, NAACP Papers, L.C. With respect to that meeting, one of those
who attended, Elmer Henderson, director of the American Council on
Human Rights, observed that "the President was very cordial in his
reception and listened attentively to all that was said . . . [but] it
was very evident that the President was under considerable pressure
by those not in sympathy with the civil rights program. I am convinced that the conference alone was not sufficient to cause any of the
points we raised to be acted upon" (Conference on Negro Leaders
Folder, FEPC File, Box 1951, NAACP Papers, L.C.).

10. A copy of the telegram is in the FEPC File, Box 1951, NAACP
Papers, L.C.

11. Truman Executive Order Folder, Box 1951, NAACP Papers,
L.C.

(In order to head off any possible future action by Truman, the House earlier had rejected on March 13, 1951, a bill allowing for the emergency reorganization of federal agencies, partly because of southern fears that the President would use this new authority to create an FEPC.) [12]

Truman's refusal to issue the order White and Randolph wanted added impetus to the growing Negro disenchantment with him and his administration. Also contributing to the development of this mood was Truman's appointments of Millard F. Caldell, former governor of Florida as federal civil defense administrator, and Robert Ramspeck, former congressman from Georgia, as chairman of the United States Civil Service Commission. Both men were, in the view of Walter White, "outspoken and unabashed white supremacists." [13]

Now convinced that the evidence showed "an alarming administration trend toward appeasement of credited Dixiecrats and other reactionaries," the NAACP organized a conference to meet in Washington on May 22–23, 1951, "in order to formulate a program of action on behalf of civil rights in this emergency." [14] Speaking to representatives of thirty-one national organizations participating in the conference, White said: "Truman, we all know, is hogtied by his opposition among his own party and Republicans. But sympathy for his plight must not blind us to the fact that his cessation of active support for civil rights legislation

---

12. *Congressional Record*, 82d Congress, 1st Sess., 1951, Vol. XCVII, Part 2, p. 2174.

13. Walter White to John Wilson, April 19, 1951, Box 1951, NAACP Papers, L.C.

14. Ibid. See also Memorandum to Walter White from Henry L. Moon, April 30, 1951, Civil Rights Conference File, Box 1951, NAACP Papers, L.C.

and his appointment of men like Caldwell and Ramspeck can be interpreted only as surrender on this issue." [15]

In addition to the speechmaking, the conference sought to rally flagging congressional support for civil rights legislation. During a meeting with Senator Kenneth Wherry, the Republican floor leader, a delegation from the conference obtained his promise to press for a Senate Rules Committee consideration of a Senate resolution which had been introduced by Senator Herbert Lehman and others on March 22, 1951 to liberalize Rule Twenty-two.[16] Wherry kept his word and brought back the news to the delegation, while it was consulting with Senator McFarland, the majority leader, that the Rules Committee had agreed "to again take up the issue of changing the Senate rule on cloture." [17] This action convinced Walter White that "the civil rights issue is not dead but instead is going to be an important factor in the 1952 elections." [18]

Subsequent to this two-day meeting in Washington, pressure began to build up once more for President Truman to issue an executive order creating a federal FEPC. Governors of seven states, including Ohio, Michigan, and Minnesota, designated June 25, 1951—the tenth anniversary of Presi-

---

15. Civil Rights Conference File, Box 1951, NAACP Papers, L.C. White was more critical of Truman in a letter he sent to Venice T. Spraggs: "There were a few who thought we ought to have gone to the White House. But we deliberately and conspicuously avoided asking for another conference to hear Mr. Truman tell us that 'I am still for civil rights.' The time has come for him to do something about civil rights instead of telling us how he feels personally" (Walter White to Venice T. Spraggs, May 31, 1951, Civil Rights Conference File, Box 1951, NAACP Papers, L.C.).

16. NAACP press release, May 24, 1951, Civil Rights Mobilization Folder, Box 1951, NAACP Papers, L.C.

17. Ibid.

18. Walter White to Venice T. Spraggs, May 31, 1951, Civil Rights Conference File, Box 1951, NAACP Papers, L.C.

dent Roosevelt's Executive Order 8802—as Fair Employment Day. Mayors of New York, Cleveland, and other cities asked Truman to issue a new executive order, as did leaders of sixteen national organizations, such as Patrick Murphy Malin of the American Civil Liberties Union and William Green of the American Federation of Labor. And on June 25, 1951, as if to highlight the symbolic significance of the day, Mrs. Eleanor Roosevelt, Walter White, and A. Philip Randolph participated in a flower-placing ceremony at the gravesite of Franklin Roosevelt in Hyde Park.[19] On the same day Senator Hubert Humphrey and eight colleagues, including Senator Wayne Morse, introduced an FEPC bill which more closely resembled the 1949 administration bill than the measure submitted earlier in the session by Republican Senator Irving Ives.[20] There was little chance, however, that either bill would reach the floor, since Senator McFarland, the majority leader, later stated that he would not permit floor action on any FEPC legislation.[21]

Earlier, Senator McFarland revealed that moves by party leaders, including President Truman, were under way in the spring of 1951 to heal the North-South breach in the Democratic party preparatory to the 1952 campaign. Consequently, Truman restored to the Mississippi congressional delegation its patronage privileges, and, furthermore, held many conferences with individual senators at the White House.[22] (It is possible that these maneuvers had been stimulated by Guy Gabrielson, the chairman of the Republican National Committee, who, along with Senator Karl Mundt of South Dakota, was publicly calling in 1951 for a formal-

---

19. See July 16, 1951, Newsletter of the National Council for a Permanent FEPC, FEPC File, Box 1951, NAACP Papers, L.C.

20. *New York Times*, June 26, 1951, p. 22.

21. *Norfolk Journal and Guide*, Jan. 12, 1952, p. 14.

22. Ibid., Mar. 31, 1951, p. 1.

ized grouping of Republicans and Southern Democrats into a single party structure prior to the 1952 election. The purpose of such a merger, it was rumored, would facilitate the selection of a Taft-Byrd or Eisenhower-Russell ticket.) [23]

But despite Truman's efforts to mollify the South, Dixie was still restless. And according to Arthur Krock, the threat of an internal party rupture was potentially greater and more serious in 1952 than it had been in 1948, because the leadership of the southern movement to prevent Truman's renomination in 1952 now included such powerful and important figures as Senator Harry Byrd of Virginia and Governor James F. Byrnes of South Carolina.[24] Byrd made his position clear in a rancorous speech he delivered in Selma, Alabama, on November 1, 1951. After assailing Truman and calling for the restoration of the two-thirds rule at the 1952 convention and the repeal of the "Humphrey civil rights resolution," Byrd counseled fellow southerners to come together and decide upon a course of action in the event the party refused to oblige the South.[25] But while Senator Byrd fulminated against the White House, Senator Clinton Anderson of New Mexico, a respected member of the Senate Democratic establishment, predicted that a party compromise on civil rights for 1952 was a "good possibility." [26] And in line with that policy, Frank E. McKinney, the newly installed head of the Democratic National Committee, extended an olive branch to Dixie.[27]

---

23. *Baltimore Afro-American*, Mar. 24, 1951. Senator Mundt thought this coalition was essential "not only for the Republican party and our two party system but also for the most effective fight possible against communism in America" (*New York World Telegram and Sun*, Aug. 11, 1951).

24. *New York Times*, Oct. 14, 1951.

25. *Norfolk Journal and Guide*, Nov. 10, 1951, p. 1.

26. Ibid., Nov. 24, 1951, p. 1.

27. Ibid., Nov. 10, 1951, p. 1.

But the olive branch concealed a thorn. The White House was not in a position to ignore completely those black voters who helped to make possible Truman's victory in 1948. But while administration supporters and friends sought to bridge the differences between the major factions of the party, President Truman maneuvered to keep his base of support as wide as possible, a tactic dictated by the fact that his own popularity was at an all-time low because of the frustrations generated by the Korean War. To this end on November 2, 1951, Truman vetoed H.R. 5411, which contained a provision requiring integrated schools situated on federal property to conform "to the laws of the states in which such installations are located." In his veto message Truman declared:

> This proposal, if enacted into law, would constitute a backward step in the efforts of the Federal Government to extend equal rights and opportunities to all our people. During the past few years, we have made rapid progress toward equal treatment and opportunity in these activities of the Federal Government where we have a direct responsibility to follow national rather than local interpretations of non-discrimination.
>
> Two outstanding examples are the Federal Civil Service and our armed forces, where important advances have been made toward equalizing treatment and opportunity. . . .
>
> We have assumed a role of world leadership in seeking to unite people of great cultural and racial diversity for the purpose of resisting aggression, protecting their mutual security and advancing their own economic and political development. We should not impair our moral position by enacting a law that requires a discrimination based on race. Step by step we are discarding old discriminations; we must not adopt new ones.[28]

28. Truman Papers, Bill File 107, HSTL. Evidently, the United States Army, at least in one instance, violated the spirit of this veto message. For evidence see the *Norfolk Journal and Guide*, Sept. 13, 1952, p. 14.

Praising the Truman veto, the *Pittsburgh Courier* wrote: "By this forthright statement the President has made new friends who expect America to justify its moral leadership by practicing what it preaches around the world." [29]

But because of the civil rights deadlock in Congress, the accomplishments Truman cited in his veto message had been achieved by executive action; in this manner progress had been made in the period from 1948 to 1950. The Korean War, however, changed the domestic political climate from one of liberalism to one of reaction and made it more difficult for the administration to keep pace with its earlier moves.

Yet, ironically, the Korean War was responsible for several new developments. It provided General Matthew Ridgeway, commander of American troops in Korea, with the opportunity to integrate black troops into white units.[30] The war also forced President Truman to move beyond his earlier executive order regarding discrimination in defense-subsidized industries. Thus, on December 3, 1951, he issued Executive Order 10308 establishing a Government Contract Compliance Committee "to examine and study the rules, procedures, and practices of the contracting agencies of the Government as they relate to obtaining compliance with Government contract provisions prohibiting discrimination . . . [and] to determine in what respects such rules, procedures and practices may be strengthened and improved." [31]

---

29. Nov. 17, 1951, p. 16.

30. *United States Civil Rights Commission Report 3, Employment,* p. 47. See also Dalfiume, *Desegregation of the U.S. Armed Forces,* pp. 204–10.

31. White and Randolph, having learned beforehand that the proposed order provided for "virtually no enforcement powers or machinery," tried without success to prevent the release of the order in order to make suggestions to insure its effectiveness; see Telegram to Harry Truman from Walter White and A. Philip Randolph, November 30, 1951, Executive Order Folder, Box 1951, NAACP Papers, L.C.

(That eleven-man committee, including six representatives from the public at large and five from various governmental agencies, was later headed by Dwight Palmer, chairman of the board of the General Cable Corporation.) The creation of this committee, declared President Truman, was "one more step in the program I have undertaken to use the powers conferred on the Executive by the Constitution and the statutes to eliminate the practice of discrimination in connection with activities of the Federal Government." [32]

Although the *New York Times* stated that here was "a new FEPC," [33] the GCCC was no such thing, a point emphasized by Philleo Nash, a White House administrative assistant, at a press conference the day the order was released. As Nash suggested, the GCCC could only advise the President how he might best obtain compliance with governmental requirements prohibiting discrimination in the execution of contracts between the government and private firms. [34]

The issuance of the order may have had a beneficial effect on the country's foreign relations. Dr. Channing Tobias, a member of the United States delegation to the 1951 United Nations General Assembly meeting in Paris, wrote President Truman on December 12, 1951: "I think that I should say to you that the publication of the Executive Order in the Paris edition of the H. T. [*Herald Tribune*] has had a very good effect on our Delegation and the delegations that are

32. *Public Papers of the Presidents: Harry S. Truman, 1951*, pp. 640–41. This committee transmitted its report, *Equal Economic Opportunity*, to the president on January 16, 1953; see *Equal Economic Opportunity* (Washington: United States Government Printing Office, 1953); also see the letter of January 19, 1953, which President Truman wrote to President-elect Dwight D. Eisenhower concerning the recommendations and proposals found in *Equal Economic Opportunity: Public Papers of the Presidents: Harry S. Truman, 1952–1953* (Washington: United States Government Printing Office, 1966), p. 1216.

33. Dec. 4, 1951, p. 32.

34. Ibid., p. 26.

friendly to us." [35] On the other hand, Negro leaders expressed disappointment with Truman's order. Clarence Mitchell, the Washington representative of the NAACP's national office, pointed to the fact that the order contained no enforcement mechanism.[36] The *Pittsburgh Courier* declared that "even though we are not satisfied with this half-a-loaf committee, we must admit that it is better than nothing at all." [37]

Southern Democrats quickly sensed the political implications behind the release of this order. Georgia's Senator Walter George observed that Truman "may be preparing to run for President again." [38] Louisiana Representative F. H. Herbert remarked that "Mr. Truman is again thinking in terms of politics." [39] But then so was the South. Dixie Democrats, anticipating a fierce struggle over civil rights in 1952, were hoping to nominate Senator Richard Russell as the party's presidential candidate; otherwise, their support would go to General Dwight Eisenhower, if he were available and running either as a Democrat or Republican.

During the first days of 1952 civil rights was again emerging as a potent political issue. President Truman made a specific reference to civil rights in his seventh State of the Union address, which he delivered to Congress on January 9, 1952. He asserted:

> As we build our strength to defend freedom in the world, we ourselves must extend the benefits of freedom

---

35. Channing Tobias to Harry Truman, December 12, 1951, Truman Papers, 526B, HSTL.

36. FEPC File, Box 1951, NAACP Papers, L.C.

37. Dec. 15, 1951, p. 18.

38. *New York Times*, Dec. 4, 1951, p. 26. Senator J. William Fulbright of Arkansas suggested that Truman's order was a "diversionary movement to take the public spotlight off the tax collection scandals" (*Pittsburgh Courier*, Dec. 8, 1951, p. 5).

39. *New York Times*, Dec. 4, 1951, p. 26.

more widely among all our own people. We need to take action toward the wider enjoyment of civil rights. Freedom is the birthright of every American.

The Executive Branch has been making real progress toward full treatment and equality in the armed forces, in the civil service, and in private firms working for the Government. Further advances require action by the Congress, and I hope that means will be provided to give the members of the House and Senate a chance to vote on them.[40]

With this statement Truman formally placed the civil rights question on the 1952 political agenda; but much to the relief of the South, his remarks, according to the *New York Times*, were cast in such a way as to avoid creating "new ire." [41] Avoidance of conflict was also the goal of the Senate Democratic leadership. For example, Senators McFarland and Johnson apparently had no intention of letting a Rules Committee resolution modifying cloture requirements from two-thirds of the entire Senate to two-thirds of those present and voting reach the Senate floor.[42] (That resolution passed the Rules Committee on January 29, 1952, after several months of hearings, discussion, and deliberation.) [43]

To keep the civil rights issue alive, the NAACP organized a civil rights mobilization for a two-day meeting in Washington in mid-February, at which time representatives of fifty-

---

40. *Public Papers of the Presidents: Harry S. Truman, 1952–1953*, p. 16.

41. Jan. 10, 1952, p. 19.

42. *Norfolk Journal and Guide*, Jan. 12, 1952, p. 14. See also U.S. Senate, *Hearings before the Committee on Rules and Administration, 82nd Congress, 1st Session, on S. Res. 41, S. Res. 52, S. Res. 105, S. Res. 203.* (Washington: Government Printing Office, 1951). The testimony of Walter White can be found on pp. 34–46; and that of Senator Russell, pp. 250–67.

43. *Congressional Record*, 82d Congress, 2d Sess., 1952, Vol. XCVIII, Part 13, Daily Digest, p. 101.

two national organizations heard speeches from Senators Humphrey, Lehman, Ives, and Benton.[44] President Truman was invited to speak, but, according to Matthew Connelly, his appointments secretary, it was not possible "to commit the President at this time." [45] The minutes of the mobilization later recorded that "President Truman, for some inexplicable reason, found himself too busy to greet the eight hundred and fifty key persons who had come at their own expense to Washington in support of the civil rights program which played a decisive role in his reelection in 1948." [46]

Perhaps the reason Truman refused to attend had something to do with the fact that he was pondering his political future: he had to decide whether or not to seek another term, at a time when both the Korean War and McCarthyism had greatly eroded the support and good will he had built up thanks to his dramatic victory in 1948. Certainly Negroes wanted Truman to remain another four years in the White House, as was made clear on March 8, when twenty-one Negro leaders urged him to run for reelection.[47] On March 29, however, Truman announced that he would not seek the office of the presidency again.[48] His earlier loss to Tennessee's Senator Estes Kefauver in the New Hampshire Democratic primary probably spurred him into that decision; Truman surely realized that his candidacy could have irrevocably split the party. After all, the South in

---

44. Civil Rights Mobilization 1952, Box 1952, NAACP Papers, L.C.

45. See Roy Wilkins to Philleo Nash, January 18, 1952; Matthew Connelly to Roy Wilkins, January 25, 1952; Civil Rights Mobilization Speakers and Speeches File, Box 1952, NAACP Papers, L.C.

46. Minutes of the Civil Rights Mobilization, Civil Rights Mobilization File, Box 1952, NAACP Papers, L.C.

47. *New York Times*, Mar. 9, 1952, p. 58.

48. *Public Papers of the Presidents: Harry S. Truman, 1952–1953*, p. 225.

1952 would simply not tolerate him as many Southern Democrats had in 1948, as evidenced by the growing opposition of such leading figures as Senator Byrd. Thus, being a good party man—that is, a centrist whose commitments to the well-being of the organization transcended personal desire—Truman probably weighed the alternatives to his retirement and found them wanting; hence he decided to pass the scepter to somebody whose views he found congenial and whose chances for election were perhaps better than his own.

The news of Truman's withdrawal evoked a mixed response of praise and disappointment from the Negro community. Walter White remarked:

No segment of the voters was more startled by President Truman's abdication from the presidential race than the Negro. Although he has appeared to soft-pedal the civil rights issue during recent months, no occupant of the White House since the nation was born has taken so frontal or consistent a stand against racial and religious discrimination as has Mr. Truman.[49]

The *Norfolk Journal and Guide* titled its editorial discussing Truman's announcement "Something Vital Was Lost When Truman Withdrew." The editorial itself commented that "Mr. Truman stood for . . . the simple human rights that brought this nation into being, and for which the peoples of Asia, Africa, and South America and all the islands of the seas are getting ready to fight." [50]

After March 29 the political spotlight shifted to other Democrats who could make a suitable standard-bearer. Illinois Governor Adlai E. Stevenson soon found himself the center of attention because, in the words of James Reston,

49. NAACP press release, April 3, 1952, NAACP Papers, L.C.
50. Apr. 5, 1952, pp. 1–2.

New York Times columnist, he was "the man most likely to hold together the liberal-labor-Southern coalition that Franklin D. Roosevelt built into the most successful American political combination of modern times." [51] Yet Stevenson's views on FEPC could prove to be something of a liability in the North and West. Believing that the states ought to initiate action to abolish discrimination in employment, he opposed a "compulsory" FEPC bill; but he could justify federal intervention if the states shirked their responsibility. [52] Stevenson's views were such that he received a prompt endorsement from South Carolina's Governor James F. Byrnes, who had been a Truman foe since 1948. [53] Unfortunately, though, for President Truman, who had been encouraging Stevenson's candidacy for the reason Reston mentioned, the Illinois governor declined to make himself available for the nomination and made it clear in late April that his only political goal was to remain governor of Illinois for another four-year term.

Stevenson's decision came at a time when Senators Estes Kefauver of Tennessee and Richard Russell of Georgia were actively campaigning for the party's presidential nomination. Kefauver had gained national prominence in 1951 through his televised investigation into the world of organized crime. Although that investigation brought Kefauver into the public limelight, it alienated President Truman, who would not forgive him for having called attention to the connection between crime and some big city Democratic machines. On the matter of civil rights, Kefauver as a senator had voted for the Barkley ruling; had supported the Wherry amendment; had opposed cloture on the FEPC bill;

---

51. *New York Times*, Mar. 31, 1952, pp. 1, 9.
52. Ibid.
53. Ibid.

and had endorsed a voluntary "FEPC" and federal anti-lynching legislation in the absence of state legislation.[54] In the
words of Senator Paul Douglas of Illinois, who came out in
favor of Kefauver after the Stevenson statement of late
April, Kefauver "is the best available candidate. . . . He
has shown a readiness to meet the sentiments of the country
more than half way. . . . He is not a southerner, he is an
American." [55]

If Senator Kefauver was an unusually liberal southerner,
Senator Russell, the other southern candidate, was Dixie's
grand strategist in the Senate. Able and articulate, Russell
was the choice of his fellow southerners for the nomination.
In an interview with the *Pittsburgh Courier* in April, 1952,
Russell restated his opposition to anti–poll tax and anti-
lynching legislation, and his rejection of a compulsory FEPC.
He said: "My only serious difference with the Truman policies is compulsory FEPC. I am honest and practical in my
differences while many of the civil rights advocates are
emotionally shallow and insincere." [56]

On May 6 Kefauver and Russell collided in the Florida
primary for that state's twenty-four convention votes. During the campaign Russell declared that if he received the
presidential nomination of the party, he would disavow any
civil rights plank authorizing the creation of a "compulsory" FEPC. Conversely, Kefauver told the Florida voters
that he supported a voluntary FEPC, but would be "morally
bound" to support the party platform even if it featured a
"compulsory" FEPC.[57] Although Russell won nineteen of
Florida's twenty-four convention votes, Kefauver still ran
extremely well in the cities and, with the help of Negro

---

54. *Congressional Quarterly*, December 16, 1955, p. 1284.
55. *Norfolk Journal and Guide*, Apr. 26, 1952, pp. 1–2.
56. Apr. 26, 1952, pp. 1, 4.
57. *New York Times*, Apr. 28, 1952, p. 1.

votes, managed to pick up five convention votes of his own.[58]

The results of the Florida primary deepened the difficulties of the Democratic party. Russell was clearly unacceptable to northern liberals, and Kefauver was already rejected by the big city bosses and the president. Thus, the split over civil rights, which President Truman had accentuated in 1948, was still very much in evidence in the spring of 1952. Senator Humphrey, an outspoken liberal, declared that if the party backtracked on its 1948 platform pledges, it would be removed from office. He insisted that the Democratic party did not deserve to endure if it equivocated on the issue of civil rights.[59] On the other hand, Senator Allen Ellender of Louisiana said that the South could not and would not accept a civil rights platform similar to the one contained in the 1948 platform. If the liberals had their way again, it was Ellender's opinion that the South had no choice but to present its own candidate for the presidency in 1952.[60]

President Truman, too, was busily articulating his civil rights views. Speaking to the convention of the Americans for Democratic Action in Washington on May 17, the president declared that it was necessary for the Democratic party to nominate a liberal candidate and to draft a liberal platform. There was a good reason for such a position, suggested Truman: "I have been in politics for over forty years, I know what I am talking about and I believe I know something about the business. One thing I am sure of: never, never throw away a winning program." Referring to civil rights, the President said that the party had to stand

---

58. Ibid., May 7, 1952, p. 1; also see *Norfolk Journal and Guide*, May 10, 1952, p. 14.

59. *Norfolk Journal and Guide*, Apr. 5, 1952, p. 12.

60. Ibid., June 7, 1952, p. 6.

firm on its 1948 pledges; as far as he was concerned, there was no room for compromise.[61]

While these rhetorical exchanges were taking place, men whose commitments were more organizational than ideological were attempting to find a middle position to which most Democrats could repair. To this end Frank McKinney, the Democratic national chairman, selected John W. McCormack, the House majority leader, to head the platform committee responsible for drafting the 1952 civil rights plank. Also included on this committee were former senator Francis Myers, the chairman of the 1948 platform committee; Alabama Senator John Sparkman; Representative Brooks Hays of Arkansas, the author of the 1949 compromise civil rights package; and Negro Congressman William Dawson, the vice-chairman of the Democratic National Committee, who reportedly favored platform conciliation to prevent a party rupture, while placing more faith in the party's nominee than in its platform. Conspicuously absent from this committee was Senator Humphrey; he had been excluded by the party leaders, who hoped to prevent a repetition of 1948 by keeping him as isolated as possible.[62]

Word that a compromise on the civil rights plank was brewing was reported by Robert Spivack in the *New York Post*. Spivack suggested that party leaders were hoping to "tone down the 1948 plank on civil rights" by eliminating specific references to FEPC and other civil rights measures.[63] This news alarmed Walter White, who was already of the opinion that "none of the avowed candidates for the presidency has an acceptable record on the vital issues of civil

---

61. *Public Papers of the Presidents: Harry S. Truman, 1952–1953*, pp. 341–47.

62. *Norfolk Journal and Guide*, May 24, 1952, p. 7.

63. May 15, 1952.

rights." [64] Writing to Chairman McKinney on May 16, White informed him that twenty Negro organizations had met in New York on May 9 to draft their demands for the 1952 campaign, which included, among other points, the modification or burial of Rule Twenty-two, voting rights legislation, and "welfare state aid in areas of housing, health, and education." White also noted that if the talk of a party compromise was correct, then "there will be widespread repercussions among Negroes and other liberal voters against yielding to those who would perpetuate second-class citizenship for Negroes and other minorities." [65]

In his reply to White's letter, McKinney defended those Democrats selected to serve on the drafting committee and suggested, in reference to Spivack's article, that he could not accept responsibility for the interpretation that "others may place on my words." [66] Not consoled by McKinney's comments, White informed him that "the majority of the committee have records either of hostility or apathy towards civil rights. This is causing great perturbation not only among Negro voters but many other Americans who are concerned with this fundamental question." [67]

Other moves in the direction of compromise were also undertaken on Capitol Hill. Senator McFarland was in contact with the representatives of the NAACP in early May in

---

64. The quote is from a speech White delivered on April 19, 1952, to an NAACP meeting in Atlanta; Box 444, NAACP Papers, L.C.

65. Walter White to Frank McKinney, May 16, 1952, Democratic National Committee Folder, Box 444, NAACP Papers, L.C. A copy of the pamphlet *What the Negro Wants*, containing the demands of the NAACP and other Negro organizations, can be found in Box 444, NAACP Papers, L.C.

66. Frank McKinney to Walter White, May 27, 1952, Democratic National Committee Folder, Box 444, NAACP Papers, L.C.

67. Walter White to Frank McKinney, May 29, 1952, Democratic National Committee Folder, Box 444, NAACP Papers, L.C.

an effort to find some common ground between that organization and Senator Russell, who realized that his lack of a foothold in the liberal camp would probably cost him the nomination.[68] Evidently the NAACP was offered an anti-lynching bill in return for its cooperation.[69] But the negotiations collapsed, it seems, because the party's Senate leadership refused to consider for floor action a Rules Committee resolution limiting debate by two-thirds of those present and voting.[70]

Thus as June, 1952, approached, the Democratic party had not yet found a candidate around whom most Democrats could rally. Of the declared candidates the most liberal was Averell Harriman, the Mutual Security Agency administrator, who appeared in the guise of a crusading Fair Dealer, embracing without equivocation the administration's civil rights program, including an FEPC with enforcement powers.[71] Nevertheless, Harriman failed to receive the backing of President Truman, probably because Harriman's advanced liberal views threatened to produce party division and turmoil. What centrist-oriented Democrats like Truman sought, in the words of Allan Sindler, "was . . . a leader in the authentic tradition of the New Deal and Fair Deal who could both unify the party and appeal broadly to the voting citizenry." [72]

The Republicans also had their problems, for they were sharply divided between the supporters of General Dwight

---

68. *Norfolk Journal and Guide*, May 24, 1952, p. 7.

69. Ibid., May 10, 1952, p. 5; Aug. 12, 1952, pp. 1, 4.

70. Ibid., May 24, 1952, p. 14.

71. Ibid., June 28, 1952, p. 13.

72. Allan P. Sindler, "The Unsolid South: A Challenge to the Democratic National Party," in *The Uses of Power: 7 Cases in American Politics,* ed. Alan F. Westin (New York: Harcourt & Brace, 1962), p. 232.

D. Eisenhower and a large bloc endorsing the presidential aspirations of Senator Robert Taft of Ohio. In Eisenhower, Taft met a contender of unquestioned popularity, even though his views on domestic issues were not well defined. To remedy that situation, Eisenhower, after resigning from the Army, held a wide-ranging press conference in Abilene, Kansas, his boyhood home, on June 5, 1952. During the conference Eisenhower was queried about such matters as FEPC. He replied:

> I do not believe that we can cure all of the evils in men's hearts by law and when you get to compulsory action of certain specific phases of this thing I really believe we can do more than to make it a Federally compulsory thing. And this is said with the utmost sympathy for anyone who feels himself to be a member of a group that has been depressed or unfairly treated.[73]

In other words, Eisenhower was opposed to federal FEPC legislation, a position which would endear him to moderates and conservatives around the country, particularly in the South, where he was contesting Senator Taft for delegates to the Republican national convention.

Eisenhower was questioned also about his views regarding racial segregation in the armed forces. He answered by saying that "I have been one of those who has tried to eliminate segregation in the armed services. We can no longer afford to hold on to the anachronistic principles of race segregation in the armed service organizations." [74] He added that additional progress ought to be made as rapidly as possible. In actuality, Eisenhower had argued differently in testimony he gave on April 2, 1948, to the Senate Armed Services Committee, then considering universal military

---

73. *New York Times,* June 6, 1952, p. 1.
74. *Norfolk Journal and Guide,* June 14, 1952, p. 2.

training legislation. He said at that time that he was prepared to go no further than to permit the integration of Negro platoons into white companies. Complete integration, he warned, would mean that Negroes would lose opportunities for promotion to the higher non-commissioned positions.[75]

Senator Taft, the other leading Republican contender, had a position which civil rights advocates could construe as far more enlightened and well defined than that of General Eisenhower. Taft, for example, favored the abolition of compulsory segregation in the use of public facilities or public accommodations; the establishment of home rule for Washington, D.C.; the enactment of anti–poll tax and anti-lynching legislation; the application of cloture by a two-thirds vote of those present and voting (Eisenhower did not know whether he approved this change); and the elimination of segregation in the public schools of Washington, D.C.[76] On the volatile issue of FEPC, Taft opposed all legislation that included a "compulsory" enforcement mechanism, but he was willing to go along with a voluntary plan, which, apparently, was still too advanced for the general.[77]

After Eisenhower and Taft revealed their positions on FEPC, the National Negro Press Association reported:

With the two leading Republican candidates against compulsory FEPC legislation, some members of Congress were of the view that there is no need for the Democratic National Committee to run the risk of another Dixiecrat walkout by adopting a strong civil rights plank, but the

---

75. U.S. Senate, *Hearings . . . on Universal Military Training* (Washington: United States Government Printing Office, 1948), pp. 995–96.

76. *Pittsburgh Courier*, Apr. 26, 1952, p. 12; July 5, 1952, p. 13; and *Norfolk Journal and Guide*, July 5, 1952, p. 18.

77. *Pittsburgh Courier*, Apr. 26, 1952, p. 18.

thing to do is to go back to the mild plank of 1944. Others said to keep the 1948 plank but drop from it commendation of President Truman for his fight for civil rights legislation.[78]

And the *New York Times* disseminated the news that Senator Humphrey was prepared to stand on the 1948 civil rights plank without extending it.[79]

At this point President Truman went on the attack. Speaking to a commencement audience of 15,000 at Howard University on June 13, Truman not only defended his civil rights record but explicitly challenged the position General Eisenhower had taken on the subject. He said:

> There has been a great working of the American conscience. All over the land there has been a growing recognition that injustice must go, and that the way of equal opportunity is better for all of us.
> The civil rights report and the civil rights program give voice and expression to this great change of sentiment. They are the necessary instruments of progress. They are the trumpet blast outside the Walls of Jericho —the crumbling walls of prejudice.

After citing the improvement made in the fields of education, housing, and employment, Truman added:

> Some of the greatest progress of all has been made in the armed services. Service in the armed forces of our country is both a duty and a right of citizenship. Every man or woman who enters one of our services is certainly entitled to equal treatment and equal opportunity.
> There has been a great deal of talk about the need for segregation in the armed services. Some of our greatest generals have said that our forces had to have segregated

---

78. *Norfolk Journal and Guide*, June 14, 1952, p. 2.
79. June 6, 1952, p. 1.

units. But our experience has proved that this was nonsense.

Near the end of his speech Truman declared that the resources of the federal government had to be committed in the battle for civil rights if progress was to be made:

I am not one of those who feel that we can leave these matters up to the states alone, or that we can rely solely on the efforts of men of good will. Our Federal Government must live up to the ideals professed in our Declaration of Independence and the duties imposed upon it by our Constitution. The full force and power of the Federal Government must stand behind the protection of rights guaranteed by our Federal Constitution.[80]

President Truman's Howard University speech, politically motivated and partisan in tone, suggests that Truman had apparently decided to make an all-out rhetorical effort to hold the black vote for the Democratic party in 1952. Another indication of his decision is that on June 23 he wired the Forty-third Annual Conference of the NAACP, meeting in Oklahoma City, that "the ten-point program I sent to Congress in 1948 is still my civil rights program for the American people." [81]

While Truman was mending his political fences, the Senate was preparing to adjourn. Shortly before this happened, the Senate Labor and Public Welfare Committee approved on June 24 a compromise FEPC bill which had been jointly drafted by Senator Humphrey and Republican Senator Irving Ives of New York for the purpose of providing both

---

80. *Public Papers of the Presidents: Harry S. Truman, 1952–1953*, pp. 420–24. For editorial praise of this speech, see *Pittsburgh Courier*, June 28, 1952, p. 6.

81. Truman Papers, President's Personal File 393, HSTL.

political conventions with a model FEPC plank.[82] Although the Humphrey-Ives bill was not nearly as strong as the earlier Truman bill (the compulsory feature having been removed), the chances were not good that either convention would be prepared to support it. Both parties intended to keep the lid on the civil rights cauldron.

The Republican convention opened in Chicago in early July. Though civil rights was not a major issue at that convention, the issue was still conspicuous enough to cause concern among the Republicans managing General Eisenhower's drive for the nomination. The problem first arose when Harold C. Burton and another Negro member of the New York delegation—which Governor Thomas Dewey had organized solidly behind General Eisenhower—announced in Chicago that they were shifting their votes from General Eisenhower to Senator Taft because it was their belief that Taft was more responsive to, and understanding of, Negro aspirations.[83] Governor Dewey and others apparently exerted considerable pressure to bring them back into line, for a few days later, Burton let it be known that he was once more supporting Eisenhower for the nomination.[84]

Meanwhile, the Republican Resolution Committee, headed by Senator Eugene Milligan of Colorado, was drafting a civil rights plank which represented a considerable retreat from the one the 1948 convention had approved.[85] The 1952 platform, including the much-weakened civil

---

82. *New York Times*, June 25, 1952, p. 12. See also U.S. Senate, *Report of Committee on Labor and Public Welfare to accompany S.3368, 1952*. Republican Senators Robert Taft and Richard Nixon refused to support the majority position and reserved the right to file individual views at a later date; see p. 15 of the *Report*.

83. *Norfolk Journal and Guide*, July 12, 1952, p. 12.

84. *New York Times*, July 9, 1952, pp. 1, 18.

85. *Norfolk Journal and Guide*, July 12, 1952, p. 12. Senators Nixon and Ives were also members of the Milligan committee.

rights plank, was scheduled to be read to the convention on July 10. Just before Senator Milligan made his report, the forty black delegates to the convention caucused among themselves and decided to introduce for floor consideration a minority-sponsored resolution which included a compulsory FEPC and a Republican pledge to seek a change in Senate Rule Twenty-two allowing a majority to impose cloture.[86] Burton, who had been prepared to lead the fight for the 1948 plank, was delegated the responsibility by his fellow Negroes to submit their tough resolution to the convention.

Burton subsequently consulted with New York Congressman Jacob Javits, Senator Irving Ives (who promised him his support for the substitute measure), and Governor Alfred E. Driscoll of New Jersey.[87] Driscoll advised him not to introduce this resolution because, in Driscoll's opinion, it had no chance of winning and "there were more effective ways of accomplishing the results" the Negroes wanted.[88] Following his conversation with Driscoll, Burton proceeded to inform the convention that he and his fellow Negroes approved the Milligan report. Although Burton was speaking only for himself and not other Negro delegates (who did not approve of the Milligan report), his false and misleading statement made it possible for the Republican convention to skirt what could have been a damaging floor fight.[89] Thus the report that Milligan presented became the 1952 Republican platform.

The party's civil rights plank underscored the fact that its 1948 committment to federal action had been superceded by a renewed emphasis on state initiative, a shift designed

---

86. Ibid., p. 1.
87. Ibid.
88. *Pittsburgh Courier*, July 19, 1952, p. 1.
89. Ibid.

to help Republican efforts in the South. The plank read as follows:

> We condemn bigots who inject class, racial and religious prejudice into public and political matters. Bigotry is un-American and a danger to the Republic.
>
> We deplore the duplicity and insincerity of the party in power in racial and religious matters. Although they have been in office as a majority party for many years they have not kept nor do they intend to keep their promises.
>
> The Republican Party will not mislead, exploit or attempt to confuse minority groups for political purposes. All American citizens are entitled to full, impartial enforcement of federal laws relating to their civil rights.
>
> We believe that it is the primary responsibility of each state to order and control its own domestic institutions, and this power, reserved to the states, is essential to the maintenance of our Federal Republic. However, we believe that the federal government should take supplemental action within its Constitutional jurisdiction to oppose discrimination against race, religion or national origin.
>
> We will prove our good faith by:
>
> Appointing qualified persons, without distinction of race, religion or national origin, to responsible positions in the government.
>
> Federal action toward the elimination of lynching.
>
> Federal action toward the elimination of poll taxes as a prerequisite to voting.
>
> Appropriate action to end segregation in the District of Columbia.
>
> Enacting federal legislation to further just and equitable treatment in the area of discriminatory employment practices. Federal action should not duplicate state efforts to end such practices; should not set up another huge bureaucracy.[90]

---

90. Porter and Johnson, *National Party Platforms: 1840–1964*, p. 504.

After approving the platform, the convention nominated General Eisenhower for the presidency and California Senator Richard M. Nixon for the vice-presidency. The convention then adjourned to await the results of the Democratic convention, which was scheduled to meet in Chicago during the third week in July.

As the Democratic party faithful streamed into Chicago, they were faced with the prospect of another fierce floor fight on civil rights. Democratic party liberals, many of whom supported the presidential candidacy of either Averell Harriman or Senator Estes Kefauver, were determined to retain the 1948 civil rights plank or, possibly, to go beyond it. Senator Humphrey declared that he put "country above the party" in his civil rights stand and also contended that if the Democratic party abandoned its "winning position," it would not only commit political suicide but would revert to its spineless condition of the 1920's.[91] The chairman of Americans for Democratic Action, the former attorney general Francis Biddle, said that if the platform committee reported out a plank weaker than that of 1948, a floor fight would surely ensue. He claimed 654 floor votes for a plank at least as strong as 1948.[92] New York Senator Herbert Lehman, a member of the Platform Committee on Civil Rights, announced support for "a strong and forward-looking platform which will be outspoken and unequivocal on the great issues of our time, including but not confined to civil rights." [93] Lehman intended to fight specifically for a resolution he and Connecticut Senator William Benton had introduced in the Senate calling for a major liberalization of Rule Twenty-two.[94] Evidently Lehman's

---

91. *Norfolk Journal and Guide*, July 26, 1952, p. 2.
92. Ibid.
93. *New York Times*, July 17, 1952, p. 1.
94. Ibid., July 18, 1952, p. 8.

views were shared by other members of the Platform Committee, including Senator Warren Magnuson of Washington and Rhode Island Senator Theodore Francis Green.[95]

On July 18 Walter White addressed the Platform Committee on behalf of fifty-four civil rights organizations. He strongly endorsed a nine-point civil rights program that included a compulsory FEPC, anti-lynching legislation, and a modification of Rule Twenty-two along the lines of the Lehman-Benton resolution.[96] Elmer Henderson, director of the American Council on Human Rights, informed the committee that, in his view, the Republican plank, though disappointing, had some appealing elements in it, such as the call for the elimination of Jim Crow from Washington, D.C. Henderson also said that if the Democrats retreated from their 1948 plank "a number of people will not vote for the Democratic ticket in November." [97]

After having heard the recommendations of various groups and individuals, the Platform Committee settled down to write the party's 1952 civil rights plank, in which interest, according to the *New York Times,* also "stretched far beyond the hearing room . . . [and] appeared to be all over Chicago." [98] And because of the efforts of Senator John Sparkman of Alabama and Negro Congressman William Dawson of Chicago, the Platform Committee was able to reach agreement on the language and substance of the civil rights plank.[99] On the evening of July 23, John McCormack, the chairman of the 1952 Platform Committee, presented

---

95. *Norfolk Journal and Guide,* July 26, 1952, p. 12.

96. A copy of White's testimony can be found in the Democratic National Committee Folder, Box 444, NAACP Papers, L.C.

97. *Norfolk Journal and Guide,* July 26, 1952, p. 12.

98. July 19, 1952, p. 6.

99. For an illuminating discussion of how this plank was finally pieced together, see Hays, *A Southern Moderate Speaks,* pp. 70–80.

his committee's draft to the convention for its consideration. The civil rights plank read as follows:

IMPROVING CONGRESSIONAL PROCEDURES

In order that the will of the American people may be expressed upon all legislative proposals, we urge that action be taken at the beginning of the Eighty-third Congress to improve Congressional procedures so that majority rule prevails and decisions can be made after reasonable debate without being blocked by a minority in either house.

CIVIL RIGHTS

The Democratic Party is committed to support and advance the individual rights and liberties of all Americans.

Our country is founded on the proposition that all men are created equal. This means that all citizens are equal before the law and should enjoy equal political rights. They should have equal opportunity for education, for economic advancement, and for decent living conditions.

We will continue our efforts to eradicate discrimination based on race, religion or national origin.

We know this task requires action, not just in one section of the nation, but in all sections. It requires the cooperative efforts of individual citizens and action by state and local governments. It also requires federal action. The federal government must live up to the ideals of the Declaration of Independence and must exercise the powers vested in it by the Constitution.

We are proud of the progress that has been made in securing equality of treatment and opportunity in the nation's armed forces and the Civil Service and all areas under federal jurisdiction. The Department of Justice has taken an important part in successfully arguing in the courts for the elimination of many illegal discriminations, including those involving rights to own and use real estate, to engage in gainful occupations and to enroll in publicly supported higher educational institutions. We are determined that the federal government shall continue such policies.

At the same time, we favor federal legislation effectively to secure these rights to everyone: (1) the right to equal opportunity for employment; (2) the right to security of persons; (3) the right to full and equal participation in the nation's political life, free from arbitrary restraints. We also favor legislation to perfect existing federal civil rights statutes and to strengthen the administrative machinery for the protection of civil rights.[100]

In the words of a *New York Times* editorial, the 1952 plank seemed similar to 1948 but lacked the "fighting words that would have immediately caused another full-scale Southern bolt." [101]

Immediately after the reading of the platform, Speaker Sam Rayburn, the chairman of the 1952 Democratic national convention, ignoring the vocal objections of Governor Hugh White of Mississippi and Governor Herman Talmadge of Georgia, rammed the platform through by voice vote. Once the platform was approved, Rayburn allowed the Georgia and Mississippi delegations to record their opposition to it.[102]

For the most part the reaction to the civil rights plank was favorable. Senator Humphrey felt it was "stronger and more comprehensive than in 1948." "I am particularly pleased," he said, "with the section we have adopted on changing the Senate Rules." [103] Roy Wilkins, too, felt it was

---

100. Porter and Johnson, *National Party Platforms: 1840–1964*, p. 487.

101. July 25, 1952, p. 16.

102. Ibid., p. 12. For a balanced and perceptive analysis of the "loyalty" issue, which was far more volatile and troublesome a problem in 1952 than civil rights, see Allan Sindler, "The Unsolid South: A Challenge to the Democratic National Party," pp. 230–81.

103. *Norfolk Journal and Guide*, Aug. 2, 1952, p. 7. Humphrey may have prevailed upon Senator Lehman not to take the issue of the civil rights plank to the floor of the convention; see Hays, *A Southern Moderate Speaks*, pp. 73–79.

a definite improvement over the 1948 plank because of the adoption of the paragraph titled "Improving Congressional Procedures." [104] Solicitor General Philip Perlman, who was President Truman's special representative on the Platform Committee, remarked: "It is my plank, I ought to think a lot of it. It has cloture in it. It has everything in it for which we have been fighting." [105] Southerners thought they could live with this plank because, in the words of Senator Sparkman, "You can't find FEPC mentioned in it, and there is no word of compulsion." [106]

Although the platform passed in the spirit of harmony, and although it was generally well received by the delegates, there were a number of delegates who were piqued by what had happened. Congressman Adam Clayton Powell was particularly incensed with developments inside the Platform Committee. He said:

I am disappointed at the liberal bloc for not bringing out a minority report, which they had promised to do until the last minute, and to me it smells like a sell out. I think a deal was made that they (the liberals) would not bring a minority report and Sparkman would keep the Dixiecrats quiet.

Sparkman told me personally, Emanuel Celler told me personally, Senator Lehman told me personally that William Dawson's speech (in the platform committee) killed all the amendments which we brought forward by various members of the liberal bloc to strengthen civil rights sentiment. I was shocked when Lehman told me that he offered a substitute FEPC plank, and Dawson voted against it.[107]

---

104. *Norfolk Journal and Guide*, Aug. 2, 1952, p. 7.
105. Ibid.
106. *Pittsburgh Courier*, Aug. 16, 1952, p. 6.
107. *Norfolk Journal and Guide*, Aug. 2, 1952, p. 2. Congressman Powell also had a private reason for venting his spleen on Dawson. Ever since October, 1945, the Chicago-based Dawson was receiving

Congressman Dawson defended himself by attacking "disrupters." He insisted that

> our people must trust their leaders. The people must have confidence in me. The committee's job was to work out a good plank that would be effective and hold our great party together. My job was not to disrupt and split the party. That platform is a great achievement—the strongest civil rights plank we ever had. It was accepted unanimously by the convention. I am proud of what we accomplished.[108]

The unity for which Dawson was working was designed to enhance the presidential buildup of Illinois Governor Adlai E. Stevenson. Stevenson had become, at the last minute, a reluctant candidate for the presidential nomination. He was not, however, the favorite of most black delegates. They supported Averell Harriman because of his strongly expressed Fair Deal views, and Senator Kefauver was their choice for Harriman's running mate.[109]

Once Governor Stevenson had received the blessings of President Truman and other party moguls, his nomination was assured, and he easily secured on the third ballot what he had earlier in the year declined to seek. Stevenson was nominated because he was the only candidate who could

---

presidential patronage for Harlem that normally would have been given to Powell. The White House made this arrangement with Dawson after Powell had referred to Mrs. Bess Truman, the president's wife, as "the last lady of the land." Powell made this remark about Mrs. Truman because she refused to resign from the Daughters of the American Revolution after that organization had denied Powell's wife, pianist Hazel Scott, permission to perform in Constitution Hall in Washington, D.C. See *Norfolk Journal and Guide*, Sept. 6, 1952, p. 2.

108. *Pittsburgh Courier*, Aug. 2, 1952, p. 1.

109. *Norfolk Journal and Guide*, July 5, 1952, p. 18; July 26, 1952, p. 14.

unite both factions of the party: his welfare state orientation won him the support of the liberals; his moderate racial views did not alienate the South. In this respect he was the man in the middle, very much like Senator Truman at the 1944 Democratic national convention.

After Governor Stevenson's nomination was endorsed by the convention, party leaders, including President Truman, met in Chicago to select a vice-presidential candidate. They decided to strengthen the North-South axis of the party by tapping Alabama Senator John Sparkman for the nomination.[110] A loyal party worker and a welfare state liberal of sorts, Sparkman had played an important role in drafting the 1952 civil rights plank of the party.

Although Sparkman was acceptable to the party professionals, he was a persona non grata with most of the convention's Negro delegates and an unhappy choice for some liberals. In response to his nomination, sixty Negro delegates, led by Congressman Adam Clayton Powell, marched off the convention floor rather than vote for a candidate whose civil rights views they found abhorrent. Powell, in explaining and justifying this action, asserted that "they [can] cram a candidate down our throat but they cannot make us vote for him. I personally will not campaign for the national ticket." [111] Walter White, who had practically made the NAACP an informal affiliate of the national Democratic party, said: "It will be difficult if not impossible for the Democratic party to sell to Negro voters, as well as to many other civil rights advocates, any nominee whose voting record has been one of consistent opposition to the civil rights objectives of the Democratic party as stated in the 1948 platform and reaffirmed and extended in the platform

110. Truman, *Memoirs*, II, 497.
111. *New York Times*, July 27, 1952, p. 1.

adopted here only two days ago." [112] Senator Lehman remarked that Sparkman had to embrace the civil rights
plank of the Democratic party without any reservations. "If
he does not," said Lehman, "there is no question but that it
will weaken the ticket in New York." [113]

Black newspapers, too, were highly critical of Senator
Sparkman's nomination. "Sparkman Wrong Guy" read the
front page headline of the August 9, 1952, *Pittsburgh Courier*. Also displayed prominently on this front page was
Sparkman's civil rights voting record, which the *Courier*
characterized as "0–0." The August 9, 1952, *Norfolk Jour-

---

112. *Norfolk Journal and Guide*, Aug. 2, 1952, pp. 1–2. After the
convention, Clarence Mitchell interviewed Sparkman and discovered
that he fully supported the platform and that he felt the chances of
getting civil rights legislation through Congress had been improved
because the words "FEPC" and "filibuster" were not included in it.
Sparkman also said that, in the words of Mitchell, "a candidate for
Vice President must appeal to an electorate that is vastly different
from the electorate that a Senator must appeal to in Alabama." As
for addressing that enlarged constituency, Sparkman said, again in
the words of Mitchell, "that at this time he must weigh his statements
on civil rights carefully because there is still a possibility that some of
the Southern states will support Eisenhower by way of retaliation
against the civil rights plank" (Clarence Mitchell to Walter White,
August 1, 1952, Democratic National Committee File, Box 444,
NAACP Papers, L.C.).
    Also of interest are the comments dispatched to Walter White by a
well-known and respected southern liberal, Aubrey Williams: "I was
disturbed over reports that you felt you could not support the Stevenson-Sparkman ticket because of Sparkman's record on civil rights
legislation. I regret that record just as you do. But Sparkman is
better than that record. You and I know he would most probably not
be in the Senate today if he had voted the way you and I would have
liked him to vote. The real McCoy in the situation is that John is
hated by every Dixiecrat in Alabama. In fact, every Dixiecrat and
white supremacist . . . are all out for Eisenhower and are tearing at
Sparkman with everything they got" (Aubrey Williams to Walter
White, August 1, 1952, Democratic National Committee File, Box 444,
NAACP Papers, L.C.).
    113. *Norfolk Journal and Guide*, Aug. 2, 1952, pp. 1–2.

nal and Guide published a Sparkman statement which had been delivered in Mobile, Alabama, on April 17, 1950: "21 Southern Senators are banded together and pledged to use every parliamentary device possible to defeat civil rights legislation." [114] But in spite of this adverse publicity, the Democratic party could take solace in the fact that an August Associated Press survey of twelve southern states showed that the vast majority of over a million registered Negroes planned to vote the Democratic ticket in November. [115]

In the North the situation was somewhat different because there, Adam Clayton Powell continued, even after the Democratic convention, to attack Congressman Dawson and the Democratic ticket. On August 3, at a press conference in Harlem, Powell stated that Dawson was responsible for sabatoging the party's liberal civil rights plank. Then after declaring that Negro Americans "cannot swallow" the Stevenson-Sparkman and Eisenhower-Nixon tickets, Powell announced that he and other Harlem Negroes had accepted an invitation from Governor Stevenson to meet with him in Springfield, Illinois, in two weeks. [116]

Meanwhile, Governor Stevenson was doing little more to mitigate the blow the blacks had received because of the party's nomination of Sparkman. At a press conference on August 4, the Illinois governor, in response to a question on civil rights, made it abundantly clear that he did not favor "compulsory" FEPC legislation, nor did he sympathize with

---

114. P. 14.
115. *New York Times*, Aug. 11, 1952, p. 9. The NAACP had organized a campaign in April to register black voters in the South. Apparently this drive had met with some success; see Memorandum to Walter White from Henry L. Moon, August 20, 1952, Presidential Campaign File, Box 444, NAACP Papers, L.C.
116. *Norfolk Journal and Guide*, Aug. 9, 1952, pp. 1–2.

the proposal in the Democratic platform calling for a majority cloture. It was his impression that "it would be a very dangerous thing indeed to limit debate in a parliamentary body in a democracy." [117]

But almost overnight, it seems, Stevenson changed his position. On August 7, in the company of Averell Harriman, he conferred for almost two hours with Roy Wilkins of the NAACP and gave him assurances that he would support changes in Senate Rule Twenty-two making it easier to terminate filibusters and, furthermore, would support the Humphrey-Ives FEPC bill, which the Senate Labor and Public Welfare Committee had passed in the waning days of the Eighty-second Congress. Stevenson also expressed the belief that he could do business with the South on the matter of civil rights; and in order to get something done, he would be prepared to take a "half loaf or even a quarter loaf" to the "whole loaf" which the NAACP wanted. On the subject of Sparkman, Wilkins learned in an off-the-record comment from Stevenson that he "did not actually pick Sparkman, but he thought Sparkman was the best man for the job of maintaining a cooperative attitude on the part of the Senate and getting legislation through." Stevenson also confided to Wilkins, in the words of Wilkins, that "Sparkman was better in this regard than any of the others mentioned for the post." In his meeting with Wilkins, Stevenson did not say "he opposed Sparkman, but only that the story that he had picked him was not accurate." [118]

Obviously, something had happened between August 4 and August 7 to cause Stevenson to shift his position so abruptly. It can be assumed that his remarks to Wilkins were predicated on his sudden realization (induced perhaps

---

117. *New York Times*, Aug. 5, 1952, p. 12.

118. Roy Wilkins to Walter White, August 13, 1952, Democratic National Committee File, Box 444, NAACP Papers, L.C.

by the presence of Averell Harriman) of the importance of the Negro vote to the Democratic party in the face of the ominous challenge from General Eisenhower. Wilkins, of course, was delighted with Stevenson's conversion; he now felt that "Stevenson seems to be definitely our man in the sense that he believes, basically, in the objectives we seek. . . . He is with us on the *substance;* he may part with us occasionally on *tactics.*" [119]

Several weeks later, on August 26, 1952, Wilkins met with General Eisenhower in New York to discuss the matter of civil rights. Once more the general made it clear that "he could not support" the enactment by Congress of what he called "compulsory FEPC legislation." On the matter of filibusters, Eisenhower stated his opposition to them, but "he could not promise to do anything about changing the Senate Rules." On a more positive note, Eisenhower declared that he was in favor of ending segregation in the District of Columbia and that, if elected, "he will eliminate discrimination wherever it exists in Federal employment under his control." [120]

Following his interview with the Republican candidate, Wilkins concluded:

General Eisenhower is friendly and gracious. He appears honest and sincere in his declared opposition to discrimination, but he speaks always in general terms. He sees nothing inconsistent, apparently, in his opposition to a Federal FEPC and the sponsorship of such a bill by leading Republican Senators, including Senator Ives of the key state of New York. Eisenhower wants merely to survey

119. Ibid.
120. Memorandum to the Board of Directors from Roy Wilkins, September 8, 1952, Democratic National Committee File, Box 444, NAACP Papers, L.C.

discrimination in employment, not exact a law to correct the condition.[121]

While General Eisenhower remained firm in his position, Governor Stevenson, after having made his commitment to Wilkins, now had to convince voters of New York State that his credentials were impeccably liberal. Addressing the New York Democratic party state convention on August 28, Stevenson made public the position he had earlier disclosed to Wilkins.[122] That Stevenson speech, plus the one he delivered the same day to the New York Liberal party convention, impressed twenty-six black spokesmen, who, led by Powell, met with Stevenson a day later. At that time Powell announced that he was entirely satisfied with Stevenson's civil rights stand and "would be going all out for him now." [123] And less than two weeks later, the NAACP declared that "the most forthright position taken by any of the Presidential and Vice Presidential candidates of the two major parties has been that of Governor Adlai E. Stevenson. We commend the clarity and courage of his pronouncements." [124]

While Stevenson was consolidating his position with Negro voters, he was losing ground in the South. There, in mid-September a *New York Times* survey revealed that the question of civil rights and states rights was the major question on the minds of most voters.[125] And in light of Stevenson's New York speeches, South Carolina Governor James F. Byrnes announced on September 18 that he would

121. Ibid.

122. *Major Campaign Speeches of Adlai E. Stevenson, 1952* (New York: Random House, 1953), pp. 23–29.

123. *Norfolk Journal and Guide*, Sept. 6, 1952, p. 2.

124. NAACP press release, September 11, 1952, NAACP Papers, L.C.

125. Ibid., September 14, 1952.

support General Eisenhower for the presidency.[126] By joining Governor Robert F. Kennon of Louisiana, who had already bolted the Democratic party, Byrnes's disaffection was augmenting Republican party chances in the South, once the bastion of the Democracy.

Hoping to establish himself as a candidate worthy of southern support, Stevenson spoke in Richmond, Virginia, on September 20. After having endorsed the Democratic party's civil rights plank, he said: "I should justly earn your contempt if I talked one way in the South and another elsewhere." [127] Stevenson reaffirmed his commitment to civil rights with a speech in New Orleans on October 10.[128]

General Eisenhower, Stevenson's opponent, also went South in the quest for votes. As reported in the October 1 *Charleston News and Courier,* Eisenhower, in the company of Governor James F. Byrnes of South Carolina, had been greeted a day earlier by an estimated 50,000 faithful supporters in Columbia, South Carolina. The news story continued: "Then the University of South Carolina band on the other side of the steps broke into Dixie. Ike had said he was one who could stand when the band played Dixie. He and Byrnes clapped through most of it." [129] Speaking in Wheeling, West Virginia, on October 1, Eisenhower declared that he favored an end to segregation in Washington, D.C., in the armed forces, and any remaining restrictions on the basic American right to vote. He added:

We seek in America a true equality of opportunity for all men. I have no patience with the idea of second class

---

126. Ibid., September 19, 1952.
127. *Major Campaign Speeches of Adlai E. Stevenson, 1952,* pp. 149–56.
128. Ibid., pp. 235–44.
129. P. 1.

citizenship. For many years the administration has been pointing to a promised land where no Americans could be subjected to the indignities of discrimination. But their promised land has always proved to be a political mirage.

In his campaign swing through Virginia and North Carolina, the General made no references to the civil rights issue.[130]

As the tempo of the campaign began to pick up at the beginning of October, the Democratic high command was becoming increasingly aware that it was in trouble not only in the South but, for different reasons, in the North as well. This point was made amply clear in a message Walter White transmitted to Wilson Wyatt, Stevenson's campaign manager.[131] Included in that message was a copy of a memorandum White had just received from Henry L. Moon, the director of public relations of the NAACP. Moon informed White of the poor impression that Senator Sparkman was making on northern voters, who "were generally supporters of the Roosevelt and Truman administrations and want to

---

130. *Norfolk Journal and Guide*, Oct. 4, 1952, p. 2. A documented indictment of the racist tactics employed by Eisenhower supporters in the South during the campaign was presented by Walter White to Lessing J. Rosenwald. Wrote White: "On the Monday night before election leaflets were showered from airplanes on Southern cities containing some of the most vicious racist propaganda against the Negro we have seen since the days of Bilbo. Governor Sherman Adams wrote me on behalf of General Eisenhower saying of course he did not approve such tactics, but marked the letter personal and confidential. When I repeatedly sought permission to make clear General Eisenhower's rejection of such tactics, Governor Adams sent me a batch of General Eisenhower's speeches already made, saying they should be sufficient answer" (Walter White to Lessing J. Rosenwald, November 7, 1952, Box 444, NAACP Papers, L.C.).

131. Walter White to Wilson Wyatt, September 30, 1952, Democratic National Committee File, Box 444, NAACP Papers, L.C.

vote for Stevenson." It was Moon's opinion, based on con-versations he recently had with friends and members of the NAACP, that Sparkman's utterances on civil rights subse-quent to the Democratic national convention were greatly damaging the prospects of holding in line "civil rights advo-cates" whose support the Democrats had to have if "they hope to win the election." [132] Given Moon's bleak report, "What do you suggest be done?", White asked Wyatt.[133]

This, then, was the context in which the Democrats, led by President Truman and Governor Stevenson, now decided to make a concerted effort to hold the Negro vote in the North in order to compensate for the possible loss of some southern states.[134] Truman himself carried the burden of the campaign for that vote. On October 11, at the request of Stevenson's campaign managers, he made a major address on civil rights to Negroes in Harlem.[135] In his speech Tru-man attacked the Republicans as the opponents of civil rights legislation, described the (Republican) McConnell FEPC amendment "as a toothless substitute for FEPC," and pointed to the Wherry Amendment as another example of Republican obstructionism. Truman followed this descrip-tion with a discussion of the various measures he had initi-ated on the executive level: the abolition of segregation in the armed forces; the creation of a Fair Employment

---

132. Memorandum to Walter White from Henry L. Moon, Septem-ber 29, 1952, Democratic National Committee File, Box 444, NAACP Papers, L.C.

133. Walter White to Wilson Wyatt, September 30, 1952, Demo-cratic National Committee File, Box 444, NAACP Papers, L.C.

134. *Norfolk Journal and Guide*, Oct. 11, 1952, p. 1. Congressman William Dawson now implored White to work hard on behalf of the black vote; see William Dawson to Walter White, October 9, 1952, Democratic National Committee File, Box 444, NAACP Papers, L.C.

135. Phillips, *The Truman Presidency*, p. 426.

Board; and the administration-sponsored briefs in the various court cases which affected Negro rights.[136]

At this point Truman warned his audience "to expect a return to the dark days of the depression" if the Republicans won. After raising the specter of "Hooverism," he proceeded to attack Eisenhower's civil rights position. The president declared:

> The Republican candidate . . . is the front man for the party that adopted the Wherry rule in the Senate . . . and a watered-down version in the House. His is the party that beat a retreat this year in the civil rights platform. That's the lousiest plank you ever read on the subject.
>
> And while the Republican candidate was in uniform, he told the Armed Services Committee of the Senate that a certain amount of segregation is necessary in the Army. You and I know that is morally wrong. And what is more, it's even militarily wrong. Our troops are demonstrating, every day, that Americans can stand side by side—regardless of color—and fight better because of it. . . .
>
> I am afraid, my friends, that the Republican candidate does not offer you much hope so far as civil rights are concerned.

Truman concluded his speech by mentioning that Adlai Stevenson had fought hard for a state FEPC, even though the Republican-controlled Illinois Senate was opposed to it, and had desegregated the Illinois National Guard.[137]

Apparently Eisenhower was stung by President Truman's remarks about his 1948 stand on desegregation of the armed forces. In a speech on October 17 in Newark, Eisenhower attacked Truman for having voted as a senator in 1942 against waiving state poll tax requirements for mem-

---

136. *Public Papers of the Presidents: Harry S. Truman, 1952–1953*, pp. 798–99.

137. Ibid., p. 800–801.

bers of the armed forces. Eisenhower, in that same speech, made it clear that he supported FEPC in forty-eight states and would use his influence, if elected President, to get every state to pass FEPC laws.[138] In other words, he still opposed federal FEPC legislation.

The next day, speaking in Brooklyn, President Truman responded to the Eisenhower speech with a sharp blast of his own. He asked:

> Has the general come forward with a single, new constructive program? Has his leadership done a single thing to change the policies of the Republican party?
> Take civil rights for example.
> Here is an issue on which new leadership might try to bring the Republican party back to its great—but almost forgotten—tradition of freedom and human rights. But nothing like that has happened. The Republican candidate has just uttered crass equivocations designed to win the votes—and the contributions—of the Dixiecrat millionaires. He is still opposed to using the powers of the Federal Government for an effective FEPC law.[139]

On October 21 the president continued his assault on Eisenhower's civil rights position, with speeches in Newark and Philadelphia. In Newark he heaped scorn on Eisenhower's FEPC–states rights position.[140] And in Philadelphia, Truman suggested that Eisenhower "is in favor of civil rights but he's against enforcement by the government," a position which Truman felt would not end race discrimination in jobs.[141] Clearly, he was now campaigning as hard, if not harder, for black votes as he did in 1948.

---

138. *Norfolk Journal and Guide*, Oct. 25, 1952, p. 1.
139. *Public Papers of the Presidents: Harry S. Truman, 1952–1953*, p. 887.
140. Ibid., p. 897.
141. Ibid., p. 909.

Truman's barrage must have worried General Eisenhower's managers, because the Republican candidate went to Harlem on October 24 in quest of Negro votes. Speaking to a crowd of about 5,000 people, Eisenhower vowed to fight segregation in Washington, D.C. He then accused President Truman and the Democratic party of making false promises to Negro voters for the past seven years. After assuring his audience that there would be no depression if he took office, Eisenhower added:

> So I cannot come before you with the competition of promises, but I do come before you with a pledge. If you want to put this crusade at the helm of your government; if you want to substitute 22 caliber men who are trying to hold 45 caliber jobs with the finest men and women that we can draw from all sections of this country from every walk of life—and let me say plainly, based upon merit and without respect to color or creed; if you want to have a government of that kind, then you belong in this crusade.[142]

Governor Stevenson arrived in Harlem on October 27 and received an enthusiastic greeting from over 100,000 people. He spoke for ten minutes, but refused to dwell on civil rights, since, as he told his audience, his position was well known. Nevertheless, he did declare that "if I promised you everything, I would deserve your contempt." After pointing to the "cruel difficulties" involved in achieving his program, Stevenson praised Senator Sparkman as a candidate "who would work to the limit of his abilities" in order to fulfill the Democratic party program." [143]

In the last days before the election President Truman carried the civil rights issue to the Negro voters of Chicago

---

142. *New York Times,* October 22, 1952, pp. 20–21.
143. Ibid., October 28, 1952, pp. 1–2.

and Detroit, where he once more attacked Eisenhower, his party, and his program. On October 29 Truman told 35,000 blacks on Chicago's South Side that Senator John Sparkman of Alabama, Governor Stevenson's running mate, had helped to write the 1952 Democratic civil rights plank, and that Sparkman had pledged to support it. In describing that platform Truman said:

> [It] is the strongest civil rights stand ever taken by a major political party in this country. It favors effective Federal action on civil rights, including FEPC; and it urges a change in the rules of procedure in Congress so that a handful of men can't stand in the way when others want to vote.[144]

In another Chicago speech Truman charged that the leadership Eisenhower promised to exert in the civil rights struggle would also be provided by Dixiecrats like Governors Byrnes of South Carolina, Shivers of Texas, and Kennon of Louisiana. "And if you think that is a funny kind of leadership in the fight for civil rights," remarked Truman, "you are just a low down mudslinger—like I am." [145]

Truman closed out his campaign to keep Negroes in the Democratic fold with a speech in Detroit on October 30. Once more, he insisted that Senator Sparkman was a loyal Democrat and would work hard to carry out the Democratic platform; once more, he recommended the election of Governor Stevenson; and once more, he spoke of his own deep commitment to racial justice and human equality.[146]

What lay behind Truman's speechmaking efforts was his realization that the black vote could prove as decisive in

---

144. *Public Papers of the Presidents: Harry S. Truman, 1952–1953,* p. 987.

145. Ibid., p. 990.

146. Ibid., pp. 1006–7.

determining the outcome of the 1952 election as it had in 1948. Thus Truman worked diligently to convince Negroes that the Democratic party and Governor Stevenson were their true benefactors. Unable, however, to produce anything in 1952 as dramatic as Executive Order 9981, which had created the Fahy Committee in 1948, Truman had to resort to rhetoric as a way of reminding Negroes of his party's past accomplishments and its continuing good faith.

On the eve of the 1952 election, black Americans seemed safely in the Democratic camp. Few could agree with the position taken by the *Pittsburgh Courier:* "If a Republican is elected president and is accompanied by a Republican control of Congress, all of the important Congressional committees will be headed by Republicans, and all of them will be outside the South." [147] Most Negroes agreed with the observation of the *Norfolk Journal and Guide* that the presence of so many states-righters in General Eisenhower's crusade was reason enough to support the Illinois Governor.[148]

Neither the Democratic party's strong defense of its New Deal and Fair Deal heritage nor the attractive personality of Governor Adlai Stevenson was enough on election day to overcome the national frustrations caused by the stalemated Korean War, the savagery of McCarthyism, and the appeal of General Eisenhower.[149] All in all, the Democratic party was dealt its worst drubbing in any national election since the 1920's, as the Republicans captured both the White House and the Congress.

The black vote in 1952 was preponderantly Democratic, but, unfortunately for Stevenson, the overwhelming Eisen-

---

147. Oct. 25, 1952, p. 6.

148. Oct. 4, 1952, p. 15.

149. Allen J. Matusow, *Farm Policies and Politics in the Truman Years,* p. 250.

hower victory nullified its impact. Ironically, more Negroes voted for Stevenson in 1952 than for Truman in 1948; Stevenson received 73 percent of the Negro vote as compared with the approximately 66 percent given to Truman.[150] (It would appear that many blacks who voted for Henry Wallace in 1948 returned to the Democratic party in 1952, thereby accounting for the greater Stevenson percentage.) A 1952 NAACP survey of forty-five widely scattered cities across the country showed that Stevenson swept Negro wards in all of them.[151] Another survey indicated that Negro voters in Louisiana, South Carolina, Kentucky, Arkansas, and West Virginia kept those states in the Democratic column.[152] Thus, in 1952, black voters, both in the North and the South, appeared to be among the most loyal Democrats in the United States.

After the election battle was over, the president met with representatives of the National Newspaper Association who came to the White House on November 14 to present him with a plaque for his services to the cause of civil rights. At that ceremony the following statement was read to Truman:

> Out of your courageous efforts . . . has come among us: A new freedom from fear and intimidation. A new opportunity for millions of our fellow citizens to register and vote for the first time in fifty years. The first chance since the Revolution and the war of 1812 to become entirely integrated in the Army and Navy.[153]

President Truman responded by remarking that he was in "dead earnest" about the civil rights proposals he had made,

---

150. *Crisis* LIX (1952), 616.

151. Ibid.

152. Henry Lee Moon, "The Negro Vote in Presidential Election of 1956," *Journal of Negro Education*, August, 1957, pp. 219–30.

153. *Norfolk Journal and Guide*, Nov. 22, 1952, p. 2.

and that he would work for their adoption as long as he lived.[154]

The Justice Department, on its own initiative, backed up the president's words with action that was fraught with the highest significance. On December 2, 1952, after having waited until the election had passed so as to eschew the charge of playing partisan politics, the new attorney general, James P. McGranery, representing the United States government, submitted to the Supreme Court an *amicus curiae* brief supporting five cases litigated by Negro plaintiffs challenging the validity of the "separate but equal" doctrine in the field of education.[155] The administration brief raised the point that the issue of racial discrimination had to be viewed in the context "of the present world struggle between freedom and tyranny." It was the administration's judgment that "racial discrimination furnishes grist for the Communist propaganda mills and it raises doubts even among friendly nations as to the intensity of our devotion to the democratic faith." [156] To emphasize the seriousness of the situation, the brief quoted from a letter which Secretary of State Dean Acheson had written to the attorney general:

> The continuance of racial discrimination in the United States remains a source of constant embarrassment to this government in the day-to-day conduct of its foreign relations; and it jeopardizes the effective maintenance of our moral leadership of the free and democratic nations of the world.[157]

154. *Public Papers of the Presidents: Harry S. Truman, 1952–1953*, p. 1050.

155. Author's interview with Philip Elman, September 22, 1964.

156. Brief for the United States as *amicus curiae* in cases 8, 101, 191, 413, 448, Supreme Court of the United States, October Term, 1952, p. 6.

157. Ibid., p. 9.

Then referring specifically to the cases at hand, the government stated its position:

In the briefs submitted by the United States in *Henderson* vs. *United States,* 339 U.S. 816, and in *Sweatt* vs. *Painter,* 339 U.S. 629, and *McLaurin* vs. *Oklahoma State Regents,* 339 U.S. 637, the Government argued that racial segregation imposed or supported by law is *per se* unconstitutional. We renew that argument here. Without repeating in detail the grounds stated at length in those briefs, for the conclusion that the doctrine of "separate but equal" is wrong as a matter of constitutional law, history and policy, the United States again urges the Court, if it should reach the question, to re-examine and overrule that doctrine.

The Government submits that compulsory racial segregation is itself . . . unconstitutional discrimination. "Separate but equal" is a contradiction in terms. Schools or other public facilities where persons are segregated by law, solely on the basis of race or color, cannot in any circumstances be regarded as equal. . . .

Whatever the merits in 1896 of a judgment as to the wisdom or reasonableness of the rule of "separate but equal," it should now be discarded as a negation of rights secured by the Constitution.[158]

If the Court decided to overturn the "separate but equal" doctrine in the field of public education, the government suggested:

That . . . the Court should take into account the need, not only for prompt vindication of the constitutional rights violated, but also for an orderly and reasonable solution of the vexing problems which may arise in eliminating such segregation.

A reasonable period of time will obviously be required to permit formulation of new provisions of law governing

---

158. Ibid., pp. 17–26.

the administration of schools in areas affected by the Court's decision.

To the extent that there may exist popular opposition in some sections to abolition of racially-segregated school systems, we believe that a program for orderly and progressive transition would tend to lessen such antagonism. An appropriate tribunal to devise and supervise execution of such a program is a district court, which could fashion particular orders to meet particular needs.[159]

With this action the Justice Department broadened its efforts to shape a new judicial policy for what was fast becoming the most crucial domestic problem confronting the American people at mid-century.

As President Truman was preparing to leave office, he received on January 12, 1953, a letter from Roy Wilkins. After noting Truman's accomplishments in the field of civil rights, Wilkins concluded with the following observation: "Mr. President, you have been responsible through the pronouncements from your high office, for a new climate of opinion in this broad area of civil rights." [160] Truman replied to Wilkins's letter on January 14, 1953. Perhaps thinking of how history would judge his performance, he wrote:

It was good of you to write as you did. The progress in equal rights that has been made in the past seven years is a source of satisfaction to me and I am very glad to have your confirmation of what I feel is a substantial change. It is most gratifying to me to have you say that there is a new climate of opinion on civil rights. . . .[161]

159. Ibid., p. 28.

160. Wilkins to Truman, January 12, 1953, Truman Papers, OF 596, HSTL. A perceptive analysis of civil rights developments as they related to the Truman administration can be found in a letter Roy Wilkins sent to Archibald J. Carey Jr.; see Roy Wilkins to Archibald J. Carey Jr., November 10, 1952, Republican National Committee File, Box 444, NAACP Papers, L.C.

161. Truman to Wilkins, January 14, 1953, Truman Papers, OF 596, HSTL.

On January 15, 1953, President Truman delivered his farewell address to the American people. Referring to civil rights, he said:

We have made progress in spreading the blessings of American life to all of our people. There has been a tremendous awakening of the American conscience on the great issue of civil rights—equal economic opportunities, equal rights of citizenship and equal educational opportunities for all our people, whatever their race, religion or status of birth.[162]

There had indeed been an "awakening of the American conscience," for which President Truman could take considerable credit. His actions and policies, made necessary by political and moral demands, did much to shape and advance the civil rights struggle in America in the years he occupied the White House.

---

162. *Public Papers of the Presidents: Harry S. Truman, 1952–1953*, p. 1202.

CONCLUSION

The politics of civil rights became nationally prominent at approximately the time Harry Truman became president of the United States. Both challenged and threatened by this issue, President Truman responded to it in such a way as to obtain maximum political benefit for him and his party. Personal wariness and political canniness characterized his *modus operandi* in handling an issue which could have produced lasting division within the Democratic party.

President Truman had already worked his way through the civil rights maze in the years he served as a senator from Missouri. That is, he gave evidence in his senatorial years that he appreciated the power of the black vote in Kansas City and elsewhere/Like most of his fellow white Missourians, Truman opposed social equality; but he was also a political realist who acknowledged that the interests of his Negro constituents needed protection. Hence, as a senator he could support civil rights proposals, knowing that they would not clear the Senate and come back to haunt him in his home state/

This ambivalence, a respect for the traditional order combined with a recognition of political realities, Truman carried with him into the White House in April, 1945. Operating on a national level, where political hazards were so much greater, Truman employed the same tactics in dealing with the FEPC controversy that had worked so well in Missouri. He raised the art of civil rights advocacy to new heights while shying away from anything that resembled a substantive program, which could have alienated the South, the section that had supported him in the showdown fight with Henry Wallace at the 1944 Democratic national convention. Later, of course, the development of new and more subtle tactics led to the establishment of the President's Civil Rights Committee and the dispatching of the February 2, 1948, civil rights message to Congress, which, in turn, precipitated a furious southern reaction.

The evidence adduced in this study would suggest that President Truman's sponsorship and endorsement of a civil rights program from 1948 on was not synonomous with active support for its passage. He, his supporters, and his opponents in Congress were participants in a civil rights drama in which ritualized action characterized the role performances of the players from the White House down. Thus, southerners who took umbrage at President Truman's *legislative* commitment to civil rights mistook his rhetoric for the real thing. Surely, the leading House Democrat, Sam Rayburn, and even Senator Richard Russell, knew that Truman was not about to smash the Democratic party for the sake of a dubious congressional victory. It must be remembered that the men who controlled the national Democratic party were centrists, whose role was to preserve the party as a viable political organization, come what may, by making concessions to key interest groups only when necessary and by preventing potentially disruptive internal struggles from becoming embarrassingly manifest.

Truman's willingness to make such a concession to Negro voters led him to issue Executive Order 9981 creating the Fahy Committee. It should be noted, then, that this order was not simply an exercise in good will, but rather the product of political pressure applied by A. Philip Randolph, Walter White, and others at a time when a presidential incumbent needed all the support he could muster in states with the greatest votes in the electoral college. Like Executive Order 8802, which President Roosevelt had issued to create an FEPC, 9981 was further recognition of the growing political influence of northern Negroes and their white allies.

Ironically, then, an authoritarian military establishment, itself no model for theorists of the good society, was altered somewhat to accommodate the ethos of democratic man. Here was the beginning of a controlled experiment that was hardly applicable to civilian society at large, but which for Negroes represented a breakthrough of sorts and a challenge to the stereotypes of many whites who never thought of black Americans except in terms of servitude based upon assumptions of biological and cultural inferiority.

That racial breakthrough was undoubtedly President Truman's greatest civil rights achievement—and it illustrates the intelligent use of executive power to change, within admittedly narrow limits, a racist social structure. This emphasis on executive action, an extension of precedents developed by the Roosevelt administration, included the issuance of executive orders and the drafting of *amicus curiae* briefs which the Justice Department submitted to the Supreme Court, as in the important case of *Brown* v. *Board of Education*. Thus, President Truman recognized his responsibility to hold the country together. But centrist politician that he was, Truman moved only because he had no choice: Negro votes and the demands of the cold war, not simple humanitarianism—though there may have been some of that—produced whatever token gains Negroes were to make in the years Truman inhabited the White House.

In the 1940's the Truman administration, whose liberal rhetoric was well ahead of the country, at least did not have to worry about a political reality which developed in the mid-1960's: the wrath of the northern backlash. In the Truman years the economy was still able to provide jobs for most everyone, thereby reducing the psychological tensions and economic fears of lower-middle-class whites. Furthermore, memories of the depression tended to unite Negroes and whites in the North along class lines, preventing division solely along lines of race. Also, the black population in the northern cities was not as large in the Truman years as it was to become in the 1960's. For these reasons, then, Truman's stance in favor of civil rights did not jeopardize the northern urban Democratic party coalition.

If the Truman administration failed to resolve America's most tragic and dangerous domestic problem, it was not because of political indifference. The problem was too vast and too complex for even the most politically skilled and popular of presidents, which admittedly Harry Truman was not. Nevertheless, President Truman helped to move the issue of civil rights into the forefront of American life, where it has been ever since. His legacy was humane, his commitment to federal action sound. Because of him and a number of key figures within his administration, the politics of civil rights had become a primary issue of concern for the American people.

BIBLIOGRAPHY

Manuscript Sources

Alben Barkley Papers, University of Kentucky Library.
Oscar L. Chapman Papers, Harry S. Truman Library.
Clark L. Clifford Civil Rights Files, Harry S. Truman Library.
Charles Murphy Civil Rights File, Harry S. Truman Library.
Philleo Nash Files, Harry S. Truman Library.
National Association for the Advancement of Colored People Papers, Library of Congress.
Stephen J. Spingarn Civil Rights File, Harry S. Truman Library.
Adlai E. Stevenson Papers, Princeton University Library.

Harry S. Truman Papers from the Central Files of the White House, 1945–1953, Harry S. Truman Library.

Records of the President's Committee on Civil Rights, 1946–1947, Harry S. Truman Library.

Records of the President's Committee on Equality of Treatment and Opportunity in the Armed Forces, 1949–1950, Harry S. Truman Library.

Government Publications

All of the following publications were published at various dates by the Government Printing Office in Washington, D.C.:

Fair Employment Board, United States Civil Service Commission, *Fair Employment in the Federal Service*, 1952.

Fair Employment Practice Committee, *Final Report*, 1947.

Fair Employment Practice Committee, *First Report*, 1945.

The President's Committee on Civil Rights, *To Secure These Rights*, 1947.

The President's Committee on Equality of Treatment and Opportunity in the Armed Forces, *Freedom to Serve*, 1950.

The President's Committee on Government Contract Compliance, *Equal Employment Opportunity*, 1953.

The Public Papers of the Presidents: Harry S. Truman, 1945, 1961.

The Public Papers of the Presidents: Harry S. Truman, 1946, 1962.

The Public Papers of the Presidents: Harry S. Truman, 1947, 1962.

The Public Papers of the Presidents: Harry S. Truman, 1948, 1964.

The Public Papers of the Presidents: Harry S. Truman, 1949, 1964.

The Public Papers of the Presidents: Harry S. Truman, 1950, 1964.

The Public Papers of the Presidents: Harry S. Truman, 1951, 1965.

The Public Papers of the Presidents: Harry S. Truman, 1952–1953, 1966.

1959 Report of the United States Commission on Civil Rights, 1959.

1961 Report of the United States Commission on Civil Rights, 1961.

1963 Report of the United States Commission on Civil Rights, 1963.

United States Congressional Record, 75th Congress, 1st Session, through 82d Congress, 2d Session, 1938–52.

United States House of Representatives, Committee on Education and Labor, *Hearings before a Special Subcommittee, 81st Congress, 1st session on H.R. 4453 and companion bills, May 26, 1949.*

United States House of Representatives Committee on Education and Labor, *Report to Accompany H.R. 4453, August 2, 1949.*

United States Senate, Committee on Armed Services, *Hearings on Universal Military Training, 1948.*

United States Senate, Committee on Labor and Public Welfare, *National Act Against Discrimination in Employment, Report and Minority Views, 1950.*

United States Senate, Committee on Labor and Public Welfare, *Hearings on Labor and Labor-Management Relations, 82nd Congress, 2nd Session on S. 1732 and S. 551, April 7–May 6, 1952.*

United States Senate Committee on Labor and Public Welfare, *Report to Accompany S. 3368, 1952.*

United States Senate, Committee on Labor and Public Welfare, *Minority Views from the Committee on Labor and Public Welfare to Accompany S. 3368, July 3, 1952.*

United States Senate, Committee on Rules and Administration, *Hearings before the Committee on Rules and Administration, 81st Congress, 1st Session, on S. Res. 11, 12, 13, 15 and 19, 1949.*

United States Senate, Committee on Rules and Administration, *Report with Minority Views from the Committee on Rules and Administration to Accompany S. Res. 15, February 17, 1949.*

United States Senate, Committee on Rules and Administration, *Hearings before the Committee on Rules and Administration, 82nd Congress, 1st Session, on S. Res. 41, 52, 105, 203, 1951.*

Newspapers and Periodicals

Annals of the American Academy of Political and Social Science.
Arkansas Gazette.
Atlantic Monthly.
Baltimore Afro-American.
Charleston News and Courier.
Chicago Defender.
Crisis, 1945–53.
Journal of Negro Education.
Journal of Negro History.
Journal of Politics.
Journalism Quarterly.
Kansas City Call.
Monthly Journal of Race Relations, 1945–1948.
Nation.
New Republic.
New York Post.
New York Times, 1945–1953.
Norfolk Journal and Guide, 1944–1953.
PM.
Phylon.
Pittsburgh Courier, 1944–1953.
Public Opinion Quarterly.
St. Louis Star-Times.
University of Chicago Law Review.
Washington Post.

Interviews

Oscar Chapman, Washington, D.C., June 25, 1962.
Philip Elman, Washington, D.C., September 22, 1964.

George Elsey, Washington, D.C., June 28, 1962.
Oscar Ewing, Chapel Hill, North Carolina, June 27, 1962.
Clarence Mitchell, Washington, D.C., January 4, 1969.
Charles Murphy, Washington, D.C., September 23, 1964.
Philleo Nash, Washington, D.C., June 29, 1962.
A. Philip Randolph, New York, July 9, 1962.
Stephen J. Spingarn, Washington, D.C., June 23, 1962.
Harry S. Truman, Independence, Missouri, May 10, 1962.
Roy Wilkins, New York, August 10, 1962.
Wilson Wyatt, Louisville, Kentucky, February 8, 1967.

Unpublished Studies

Hamby, Alonzo. "Harry S. Truman and American Liberalism, 1945–1948." Ph.D. dissertation, University of Missouri, 1965.
―――. Comments delivered at a session of the American Historical Association meeting on December 29, 1966.
Kifer, Allen F. "The Negro Under the New Deal." Ph.D. dissertation, University of Wisconsin, 1961.
Theoharis, Athan. "The Truman Presidency." Paper delivered at the August 29, 1967, meeting of the Pacific Coast Branch of the American Historical Association.

SECONDARY SOURCES

Books

Abels, Jules. *Out of the Jaws of Victory.* New York: Henry Holt & Co., 1959.
Abrams, Charles. *Forbidden Neighbors.* New York: Harper & Bros., 1955.
Abrams, Richard, and Levine, Lawrence, eds. *The Shaping of Twentieth Century America.* Boston: Little, Brown & Co., 1965.
Allen, Robert S., and Shannon, William. *The Truman Merry-Go-Round.* New York: Vanguard Press, 1950.
American Jewish Yearbook, 1949. Philadelphia: Jewish Publication Society, 1950.

American Jewish Yearbook, 1951. Philadelphia: Jewish Publication Society, 1953.

Biddle, Francis. *In Brief Authority.* New York: Doubleday & Co., 1962.

Blaustein, Albert P., and Ferguson, Clarence C., Jr. *Desegregation and the Law.* New Brunswick, N.J.: Rutgers University Press, 1957.

Bolling, Richard. *House Out of Order.* New York: E. P. Dutton & Co., 1965.

Brock, Clifford. *Americans for Democratic Action.* Washington, D.C.: Public Affairs Press, 1962.

Brown, C. Edgar, ed. *Democracy at Work.* Philadelphia: Local Democratic Committee, 1948.

Burner, David. *The Politics of Provincialism: The Democratic Party in Transition, 1918–1932.* New York: Alfred A. Knopf, 1968.

Byrnes, James F. *All in One Lifetime.* New York: Harper & Co., 1958.

Carr, Robert K. *Federal Protection of Civil Rights: Quest for a Sword.* Ithaca, N.Y.: Cornell University Press, 1947.

Clark, Tom C., and Perlman, Philip. *Prejudice and Property.* Washington, D.C.: Public Affairs Press, 1948.

Congressional Quarterly Almanac, Vol. VI, 1950. Washington, D.C.: Congressional Quarterly News Features, 1951.

Dalfiume, Richard. *Desegregation of the U.S. Armed Forces: Fighting on Two Fronts, 1939–1953.* Columbia: University of Missouri Press, 1969.

Daniels, Jonathan. *The Man from Independence.* Philadelphia: J. B. Lippincott & Co., 1950.

Davies, Richard O. *Housing Reform During the Truman Administration.* Columbia: University of Missouri Press, 1966.

Dorsett, Lyle, *The Pendergast Machine.* New York: Oxford University Press, 1968.

Duffield, E. S., and Millis, Walter, eds. *James Forrestal's Diary.* New York: Viking Press, 1951.

Emerson, Thomas I., and Haber, David. *Political and Civil*

Rights in the United States. Buffalo: Dennis & Co., 1952.

Ernst, Morris, and Loth, David. *The People Know Best.* Washington, D.C.: Public Affairs Press, 1949.

Evans, Rowland, and Novak, Robert. *Lyndon B. Johnson: The Exercise of Power.* New York: New American Library, 1966.

Flynn, Edward J. *You're the Boss.* New York: Viking Press, 1947.

Franklin, John Hope. *From Slavery To Freedom: A History of American Negroes.* New York: Alfred A. Knopf, 1956.

Freidel, Frank. *FDR and the South.* Baton Rouge: Louisiana State University Press, 1965.

Galloway, George. *The Legislative Process in Congress.* New York: Thomas Y. Crowell Co., 1953.

Garfinkel, Herbert. *When Negroes March.* Glencoe, Ill.: Free Press, 1959.

Greenberg, Jack. *Race Relations and American Law.* New York: Columbia University Press, 1959.

Harris, Robert. *The Quest for Equality.* Baton Rouge: Louisiana State University Press, 1960.

Hays, Brooks. *A Southern Moderate Speaks.* Chapel Hill: University of North Carolina Press, 1959.

Heard, Alexander. *A Two Party South?* Chapel Hill: University of North Carolina Press, 1952.

Howard, J. Woodford Jr., *Mr. Justice Murphy: A Political Biography.* Princeton, N.J.: Princeton University Press, 1968.

Hughes, Langston. *Fight for Freedom.* New York: W. W. Norton & Co., 1962.

Huthmacher, J. Joseph. *Senator Robert Wagner and the Rise of Urban Liberalism.* New York: Atheneum, 1968.

Kesselman, Louis. *The Social Politics of FEPC: A Study in Reform Pressure Movements.* Chapel Hill: University of North Carolina Press, 1947.

Key, V. O. *Southern Politics in State and Nation.* New York: Alfred A. Knopf, 1949.

Kirkendall, Richard, ed. *The Truman Period As a Research Field.* Columbia: University of Missouri Press, 1967.

Konvitz, Milton. *Expanding Liberties: Freedom Gains in Postwar America.* New York: Viking Press, 1966.

Lee, R. Alton. *Truman and Taft-Hartley: A Question of Mandate.* Lexington: University of Kentucky Press, 1966.

Longaker, Richard P. *The President and Individual Liberties.* Ithaca, N.Y.: Cornell University Press, 1961.

Lubell, Samuel. *The Future of American Politics.* New York: Harper & Co., 1956.

————. *White and Black: Test of a Nation.* New York: Harper & Row, 1966.

MacDougal, Curtis D. *Gideon's Army.* 3 vols. New York: Marzani & Munsell, 1965.

McCoy, Donald. *Landon of Kansas.* Lincoln: University of Nebraska Press, 1966.

McWilliams, Carey. *Brothers under the Skin.* Boston: Little, Brown & Co., 1951.

Matusow, Allen J. *Farm Policies and Politics in the Truman Years.* Cambridge, Mass.: Harvard University Press, 1967.

Milligan, Maurice. *Missouri Waltz.* New York: Charles Scribners & Sons, 1948.

Mitchell, Franklin. *Embattled Democracy: Missouri Politics, 1919–1932.* Columbia: University of Missouri Press, 1968.

Moon, Henry Lee. *Balance of Power: The Negro Vote.* Garden City, N.Y.: Doubleday & Co., 1948.

Murray, Florence, ed. *The Negro Handbook, 1949.* New York: Macmillan Co., 1949.

Myrdal, Gunnar. *An American Dilemma.* New York: Harper & Brothers, 1944.

Negro Yearbook, 1952. New York: Wm. H. Wise, 1952.

Nichols, Lee. *Breakthrough on the Color Front.* New York: Random House, 1954.

Odum, Howard. *Race and Rumors of Race.* Chapel Hill: University of North Carolina Press, 1943.

Patterson, James T. *Congressional Conservatism and the New Deal*. Lexington: University of Kentucky Press, 1967.

Phillips, Cabell. *The Truman Presidency: The History of a Triumphant Succession*. New York: Macmillan Co., 1966.

Porter, Kirk, and Johnson, Donald B. *National Party Platforms: 1840–1964*. Urbana: University of Illinois Press, 1966.

Pritchett, C. Herman. *Civil Liberties and the Vinson Court*. Chicago: University of Chicago Press, 1954.

Record, Wilson. *The Negro and the Communist Party*. Chapel Hill: University of North Carolina Press, 1951.

Redding, John M. *Inside the Democratic Party*. Indianapolis: Bobbs-Merrill Co., 1958.

Rosenman, Samuel, ed. *The Public Papers and Addresses of Franklin D. Roosevelt*. Vol. II. New York: Harper & Brothers, 1950.

Ross, Irwin. *The Loneliest Campaign: The Truman Victory of 1948*. New York: New American Library, 1968.

Ross, Malcolm. *All Manner of Men*. New York: Reynal & Hitchcock, 1948.

Ruchames, Louis. *Race, Jobs, and Politics*. New York: Columbia University Press, 1953.

Schmidt, Karl. *Henry Wallace: Quixotic Crusader*. Syracuse, N.Y.: Syracuse University Press, 1960.

Stevenson, Adlai E., ed. *Major Campaign Speeches of Adlai E. Stevenson, 1952*. New York: Random House, 1953.

Truman, Harry S. *Memoirs*. Vol. I: *Year of Decisions*. Vol. II: *Years of Trial and Hope*. Garden City, N.Y.: Doubleday & Co., 1955, 1956.

Vose, Clement. *Caucasians Only*. Berkeley: University of California Press, 1959.

Westin, Alan F., ed. *The Uses of Power: 7 Cases in American Politics*. New York: Harcourt, Brace & World, 1962.

White, Walter. *A Man Called White*. New York: Viking Press, 1948.

———. *How Far the Promised Land*. New York: Viking Press, 1955.

Woodward, C. Vann. *The Strange Career of Jim Crow*. New York: Oxford University Press, 1957.

Articles

Ader, Emile. "Why Dixiecrats Failed," *Journal of Politics* XV (August, 1953), 356–69.

Aronson, Arnold, and Spiegler, Samuel. "Does the Republican Party Want the Negro Vote?", *Crisis* LVI (December, 1949), 364–68.

Bendiner, Robert. "Civil Rights—Fresh Start," *Nation* CLXIV (May 10, 1947), 536–38.

———. "Rout of the Bourbons," *Nation* CLXVII (July 24, 1948), 91–93.

Brearley, H. C. "The Negro's New Belligerency," *Phylon* V (4th Quarter, 1944), 152–89.

Cushman, Robert. "Our Civil Rights Became a World Issue," *New York Times*, January 11, 1948.

Dabney, Virginius. "Nearer and Nearer the Precipice," *Atlantic Monthly* CLXXI (January, 1943), 94–100.

Jones, Lester M. "The Editorial Policy of the Negro Newspapers of 1917–1918 as Compared with That of 1941–1942," *Journal of Negro History* XXIX (January, 1944), 24–31.

Kenworthy, E. W. "The Case Against Army Segregation," *Annals of the American Academy of Political and Social Science* CCLXXV (May, 1951), 27–33.

Kesselman, Louis C. "The Fair Employment Practice Movement in Perspective," *Journal of Negro History* XXXI (January, 1946), 30–46.

Maslow, Will. "FEPC—A Case History in Parliamentary Maneuver," *University of Chicago Law Review* XIII (June, 1946), 407–45.

Moon, Henry Lee. "What Chance for Civil Rights," *Crisis* LVI (February, 1949), 42–45.

———. "The Negro Vote in the Presidential Election of 1956," *Journal of Negro Education*, August, 1957, pp. 219–30.

Reynolds, Grant. "Triumph for Disobedience," *Nation* CLXVII (August 28, 1948), 228–30.

Shannon, Jasper B. "Political Obstacles to Civil Rights Legislation," *Annals of the American Academy of Political and Social Science* CCLXXV (May, 1951), 53–60.

————. "Presidential Politics in the South," *Journal of Politics* X (1948), 464–89.

Sherman, Richard B. "The Harding Administration and the Negro: An Opportunity Lost," *Journal of Negro History* XCIX (July, 1964), 151–68.

Stone, I. F. "Where There Is No Vision," *Nation* CLXII (February 9, 1946), 111–19.

Van Auken, Celia. "The Negro Press in the 1948 Presidential Election," *Journalism Quarterly* XXVI (December, 1949), 431–35.

White, Walter. "Will the Negro Elect Our Next President," *Colliers Magazine* CXX (November 22, 1947), 25–26.

INDEX

Abrams, Charles, 75
Acheson, Dean, 232
Agriculture, Department of,
    36 n. 107
Alabama, 101
Alexander, Sadie T., 55
Allen, George, 54
American Civil Liberties Union
    (ACLU), 168, 189
American Council on Human
    Rights, 212
American Federation of Labor
    (AFL), 28, 160, 189
American Jewish Congress,
    116 n. 126

American Veterans Committee,
    116 n. 126
Americans for Democratic Ac-
    tion (ADA), 106, 108,
    148, 160
Amicus curiae brief, 5–6, 74–75,
    172–73, 232, 240. *See
    also* Justice, Depart-
    ment of
Anderson, Clinton, 190
Arvey, Jacob, 107
Associated Negro Press, 76
Axtell, Enos A., 37–38

Baldwin, Raymond, 155

Baltimore Afro-American, 124
Baltimore, Md., 124–25
Baltimore Sun, 118
Barkley, Alben, 16, 87, 113, 147, 149
Batesburg, S.C., 44
Biddle, Francis, 211
Biemiller, Andrew J., 110
  civil rights plank, 111–12
Biffle, Leslie, 113
Bilbo, Theodore, 54
Birmingham News, 21
Bowles, Chester, 106
Boyle, William, 178
Bradley, Omar, 100, 119–20
Brown v. *Board of Education*, 240
Burton, Harold C., 208–9
Byrd, Harry, 190, 197
Byrnes, James, 13, 16, 54, 190, 198, 222–23

Caldwell, Millard, 89, 187
Calendar Wednesday, 170–71
California, 129–30
Capital Transit Company Strike, 29–31
Carbondale, Ill., 124
Carey, James, 50, 55
Carr, Robert K., 56, 61, 82
Celler, Emanuel, 140–41, 157
Centrist: *See* Truman, Harry S.
Centrist faction, 139, 203, 239
Charleston News and Courier, 223
Chavez, Dennis, 25
Cherry, Gregg, 93
Chicago Defender, 42, 172
Childs, Marquis, 148 n. 38
Civil liberties, 134 n. 181
Civil rights
  and Cold War, 61, 63, 77–78, 85, 240
  and Franklin Roosevelt, 4–8
  as issue in 1944 election, 17–22
  in 1948 election, 79–134
  in 1952 election, 195–232

Negro political strivings for, 6–7, 33–34, 41–44, 47, 50–54, 65–66, 74, 78, 97–100, 107–8, 117, 120, 123, 133, 159–60, 168, 179–80, 186–89, 195–96, 201–3, 212, 217–20, 224–25, 239
  and Republican party, 34, 59, 87–88, 103–4, 121–22, 130, 138, 153–56, 174, 178, 190, 208–10, 221, 223, 224 n. 130, 225
  and Harry S. Truman
  administration's action on, 45, 49, 53, 66, 74–75, 165–67, 172, 176–77, 192, 232–34
  contributions to, 235, 240
  executive action on, 29–31, 38, 51, 55, 74, 116–17, 165, 175, 185, 192
  legislative program for, 82–85, 157–59, 238–40
  during pre-presidential career of, 8–23
  public advocacy of, 25, 27, 32, 34, 35, 47–48, 52–53, 57–58, 60, 62–63, 72, 82, 83–85, 114, 120–21, 125–27, 140, 148, 164, 167, 175, 176, 184, 191, 194–95, 206–7, 225–29
  tactics concerning, 26–27, 29, 32–33, 51–52, 72, 77–78, 81–82, 108, 123, 161, 168, 237–40
  See also Fahy Committee; NAACP; President's Committee on Civil Rights; Truman, Harry S.; White, Walter; Wilkins, Roy
Clark, Tom C., 45, 47–48, 53, 66, 73–74, 177
Cleveland, Ohio, 126
Clifford, Clark M.
  as adviser to Truman, 73
  as political strategist, 80–82, 108, 128, 160, 165–66
Cloture vote, 33, 174, 178
Colmer, William, 92, 162
Columbia, Tenn., 45
Committee against Jim Crow in

the Military Service and Training, 97–98
Commission on Equality of Treatment and Opportunity in the Armed Forces. *See* Fahy Committee
Communists, 115
Congress of Industrial Organization (CIO), 55, 160
Conservative congressional coalition, 32, 35, 138, 153–56, 190
Connelly, Matthew, 28
Connor, Eugene, 112
Cox, Eugene, 86, 140, 169
Crisis, the, 64

Dabney, Virginius, 43
Daniels, Jonathan, 43, 51 n. 41
Davis, Benjamin, 15
Dawson, Donald, 123
Dawson, William, 29, 201, 212, 216
Defense, Department of, 99–100
Democratic National Committee, 33, 79, 162, 174, 178, 190, 202
Democratic party
  and civil rights plank, 102, 111, 213, 214
  national conventions of, 16–18, 108–14, 211–17
  and Negroes, 4, 18–19, 22–23, 49, 54, 77–78, 81, 90, 96, 102, 105, 108, 129–31, 133, 159, 180, 201–2, 207, 212–17, 222–25, 230–31
  and North-South split, 7, 17–18, 72, 83, 86, 88–89, 92–94, 100–102, 104, 189–90, 196–98, 201–3, 216–17, 222, 237–38
  See also Roosevelt, Franklin; Stevenson, Adlai; Truman, Harry S.; Wallace, Henry; White, Walter; Wilkins, Roy
Dewey, Thomas, 23, 72, 80–81,

103–5, 116, 125, 128–30, 132, 208
Dickey, John S., 55
Dixiecrats, 101–2, 114–15, 132–33. *See also* Thurmond, Strom
Dixon, Frank, 115
Donahue, Alphonsus J., 123
Douglas, Helen Gahagan, 130 n. 168
Douglas, Paul, 155, 199
Douglas, William O., 113
Driscoll, Alfred E., 209
Du Bois, William E. B., 22, 65, 115

Eastland, James O., 86, 88, 93, 115, 161
Eaton, Charles, 71
Einstein, Albert, 52 n. 43
Eisenhower, Dwight D., 106, 204–5, 208–11, 221, 223–24, 226–28
Eisenhower Democrats, 106–7
Ellender, Allen, 200
Elman, Philip, 172 n. 116
Elsey, George, 82, 95
Ernst, Morris, 55, 142
Ewing, Oscar J., 79, 95
Executive Orders
  Number 8802, 6
  Number 9364, 24
  Number 9664, 31
  Number 9008, 55
  Number 9980, 116–17
  Number 9981, 116–20, 175, 230, 239
  Number 10210, 185
  Number 10308, 192

Fahy Committee, 118, 123–24, 140, 175, 230
Fair Deal, 179–80
Fair Employment Board, 117
Fair Employment Practices Committee (FEPC), 6–7, 24–28, 32–33, 35–37, 158, 161, 168–71, 173, 184–87, 188–89, 198–99, 207, 208, 238. *See also* Civil rights;

Fair Employment (*Continued*)
    Randolph, A. Philip;
    Roosevelt, Franklin;
    Truman, Harry S.
Farm Security Agency, 4
Federal Housing Authority, 166–67
Filibuster, 33, 121, 141, 146–47, 154, 174
Final Report, 35–36
Florida primary, 199–200
Flynn, Edward J., 16–17, 107
Folsom, James, 88, 101
Forrestal, James, 99
Freedom to Serve, 175. *See also* Fahy Committee
Fulbright, J. W., 148–49, 194 n. 38
Fulton, Hugh, 14

Gabrielson, Guy, 189
Galloway, George (quoted), 146
George, Walter, 194
Gittlesohn, Ronald, 55
Government Contract Compliance Committee, 192–93
Graham, Frank, 55
Granger, Lester, 99–100, 123
Graves, John Temple (quoted), 7
Green, Theodore F., 212
Green, William, 28, 189

Hagerty, James A., 91
Hannegan, Robert, 11, 17, 33
Hardy, Porter, 180
Harlem, 126, 225, 227
Harriman, Averell, 203, 211, 216, 220
Haas, Francis, 55
Hastie, William, 28, 38, 165
Hayden, Carl, 141, 155
Hayden-Wherry Resolution, 141–42, 147. *See also* Senate Resolution Fifteen
Hays, Brooks, 160, 201
Heard, Alexander (quoted), 162
Herbert, F. H., 194

Henderson, Elmer, 177 n. 129, 186 n. 9, 212
Henderson v. *United States*, 172–73, 176–77, 233
Hill, Lister, 101
Hinton, Harold, 46
Holifield, Chet, 71
Holland, Spessard, 144
Hoover, Herbert Clark, 4
House Appropriations Committee, 25
House Education and Labor Committee, 161, 169
House Judiciary Committee, 140
House Rules Committee, 25–26, 32, 37, 139, 162, 169
Houston, Charles, 30
Howard, Lankin M., 115
Humphrey, Hubert H., 107, 108, 109 n. 104, 111, 146, 155, 163–64, 189, 196, 200–201, 206, 211, 214

Illinois, 129–30
Isacson, Leo, 90–91
Ives, Irving, 96, 143, 189, 209

Johnson, C. A., 126
Johnson, Charles, 22
Johnson, Lyndon, 183, 195
Justice, Department of, 5–6, 46, 48–49, 74, 165–66, 172–73, 232–34. *See also* *Amicus curiae* brief; Clark, Tom C.; Perlman, Philip

Kansas City, Mo., 8–9, 14
Kansas City Call, 8, 20, 64
Kefauver, Estes, 196, 198–200, 211, 216
Kennon, Robert, 223
Keyserling, Leon, 80
Knowland, William, 143, 145
Knowland Resolution. *See* Senate Resolution Thirteen
Konvitz, Milton (quoted), 118
Korean War, 178–80, 184–85, 192, 196, 230

Krock, Arthur, 86, 101–2, 112, 170, 190
Ku Klux Klan, 9, 20–22, 44, 46

Labor, Department of, 185
La Follette, Robert M., Jr., 34
Lawrence, David, 107
Lehman, Herbert H., 107, 179, 188, 196, 211, 218
Lesinski, John, 169–71
Lewis, Ira, 15
Liberal party, 22, 222
Lincoln Memorial, 61
Lippmann, Walter (quoted), 122
Los Angeles, 21, 76
Lubell, Samuel, 17
Lucas, Scott, 71, 138, 146, 151–53, 161, 163–64, 168, 173–74, 178, 179
Luckman, Charles, 56, 123

McCarran, Patrick, 161
McCarthy, Joseph, 180
McCarthyism, 230
McClellan, John, 141
McConnell, Samuel K., 171
McCormack, John, 139, 212–13
McFarland, Ernest, 183, 189, 195
McGranery, James P., 232
McGrath, J. Howard, 90, 92–93, 94–95, 120, 166, 172
McKinney, Frank E., 190, 201–2
McLaurin v. *Oklahoma State Regents*, 172, 176–77, 233
McNutt, Paul V., 113
Madison Square Garden, 33
Magnuson, Warren, 211
Malcom, Rodger, 46
March on Washington Movement, 6
Malin, Patrick Murphy, 189
Marcantonio, Vito, 170
Marshall, Thurgood, 45, 172 n. 116
Matthews, Francis, 56
Milgram, Morris, 19–20

Mitchell, Clarence, 96, 180 n. 142, 194, 218 n. 112
Mollinson, Irvin C., 29, 38
Monroe, Georgia, 46
Montgomery Advertiser, 118
Moody, Dan, 110
Moody Plank, 110
Moon, Henry L., 133, 224–25
Morse, Wayne, 62, 98, 145, 154–55, 189
Mundt, Karl, 189–90
Murphy, Charles, 80, 177
Murphy, Frank, 5
Murry, Esther, 110
Myers, Francis, 107–8, 138, 143, 179, 201

Nash, Philleo, 95, 193
National Association for the Advancement of Colored People (NAACP), 9, 37 n. 10, 96, 98, 108, 166 n. 126, 148, 168, 202–3, 217
  and Special Senate Committee Investigating the National Defense Program, 13–14
  petitions U.N., 65–66
  supports Truman (1948), 105
  criticizes Truman (1949), 159–60
  and May, 1951, conference, 187–88
  and civil rights mobilization, 195–96
  endorses Stevenson, 222
  See also Truman, Harry S.; White, Walter; Wilkins, Roy
National Citizens Council on Civil Rights, 142
National Colored Democratic Association, 12
National Committee for a Permanent FEPC, 179
National Conference of Christians and Jews, 164
National Conference on Lynching, 52
National Council of Negro Women, 164

National Emergency Civil
    Rights Mobilization, 168
National Emergency Committee
    Against Mob Violence,
    45, 50
National Negro Newspaper As-
    sociation, 231
National Negro Press Associa-
    tion, 205–6
National Urban League, 52–53,
    99, 179
Neely, Matthew, 156
Negro migration, 7
Negro Newspaper Publishers
    Association, 47
Negro press and Truman, 17–20,
    64, 90, 128, 165 n. 94,
    172. *See also Norfolk
    Journal and Guide;
    Pittsburgh Courier*
Negro vote
    in elections of 1928, 1932, 1936,
        1940, 4
    of 1944, 23
    of 1946, 53–54
    of 1948, 129–33
    of 1950, 179–80
    of 1952, 230–31
    See also Civil rights; Demo-
        cratic party; National
        Association for the Ad-
        vancement of Colored
        People; Stevenson, Ad-
        lai; Truman, Harry S.;
        Wallace, Henry; White,
        Walter; Wilkins, Roy
Neustadt, Richard, 71
New Deal, 4, 122
New Hampshire primary, 196
New Orleans, La., 223
New York Herald Tribune, 193
New York Post, 201
New York Times, 46, 59, 86, 91,
    96, 102, 134–35, 146,
    151, 156, 171, 195, 198,
    206, 212, 214, 222
Niles, David, 37, 51, 60–61, 90,
    159
Nixon, Richard M., 208 n. 82, 211
Norfolk Journal and Guide, 18–
    19, 56–57, 72, 197, 218–
    19, 230

Northern Democratic coalition,
    240
Norton, Mary, 26, 157

Odum, Howard, 43, 51 n. 41
Ohio, 129–30
Oxnam, G. Bromley, 28

Palmer, Dwight, 123, 193
Patterson, Robert, 142
Pendergast, James, 37
Pendergast, Tom, 8, 11 n. 26
Pepper, Claude, 86, 106
Perlman, Philip, 74–75, 166–67,
    172, 215
Philadelphia, Pa., 125
Phillips, Cabell (quoted), 81
Pittsburgh Courier, 19–20, 28,
    42, 64, 177, 192, 194,
    199, 218, 230
PM, 85
Powell, Adam Clayton, 99, 157,
    169–70, 215 n. 107, 217,
    219, 222
President's Committee on Civil
    Rights
    background of, 43, 50–52
    establishment of, 55–57
    membership of, 55–56
    meets with Truman, 60
    report to president, 66–71
    See also Civil rights; *To Se-
        cure These Rights;*
        Truman, Harry S.
Progressive Party, 76, 115–16
Propper, Karl G., 91

Racial violence, 42, 44–46. *See
    also* Justice, Depart-
    ment of; President's
    Committee on Civil
    Rights; Truman,
    Harry S.
Ramspeck, Robert, 187
Randolph, A. Philip, 6, 28, 32,
    43, 97–99, 117, 119, 184,
    186–87, 189, 239
Rankin, John, 104
Rayburn, Sam, 112, 138–39, 214,
    238

Reconstruction Finance Corporation, 54

Reeves, A. L., 38

Republican party, 3–4, 34, 54, 59, 72, 87–89, 114, 121–22, 125, 128, 130–31, 133, 135, 147–48, 151, 163, 180, 189–90, 223, 226, 230

and civil rights plank, 103, 210

and national conventions, 103–4

See also Civil rights; Conservative congressional coalition; Dewey, Thomas; Eisenhower, Dwight; Taft, Robert; Wherry, Kenneth

Reston, James, 197–98

Restrictive covenants, 74–77, 166–67

Reynolds, Grant, 97, 98, 119–20

Richards, Franklin, 166

Richardson, Thomas, 59–60

Richmond Times Dispatch, 43

Richmond, Virginia, 223

Ridgeway, Matthew, 192

Robeson, Paul, 52, 115

Rosenwald, Lessing W., 224 n. 130

Roosevelt, Eleanor, 43, 45–50, 51, 62, 189

Roosevelt, Franklin D., 4, 7, 11, 17, 22–23, 43, 64, 92, 189, 239. *See also* Civil rights; Democratic party; FEPC; Justice, Department of; Negro press

Roosevelt, Franklin D., Jr., 50 n. 37, 56

Roosevelt, James, 107

Ross, Malcom, 29, 35

Rowan, Carl T., 124

Royall, Kenneth, 100

Ruchames, Louis (quoted), 26–27

Russell, Richard B., 106, 113, 121, 143–44, 149, 152–53, 160, 184, 185, 198, 200, 238

Russell Amendment, 24, 185–86

Sabath, Adolph, 25–26, 139, 161

Saint Louis, Mo., 14

St. Louis Star, 65

Saltonstall, Leverett, 143

Schwellenbach, Louis, 32–33

Screws v. *United States*, 49 n. 33

Selznick, David O., 21

Senate Armed Services Committee, 125, 152, 204–5

Senate Democratic Policy Committee, 183–84

Senate Judiciary Committee, 161

Senate Labor and Public Welfare Committee, 87–88, 152, 163, 207, 220

Senate Resolution Thirteen, 143–45

Senate Resolution Fifteen, 141–42, 151–53

Senate Resolution Seventy-five, 13–14

Senate Rule Twenty-two, 121–22, 134, 142, 146, 188, 195, 211

Senate Rules and Administration Committee, 141–46, 188, 195

Sengstacke, John, 123

Shelly v. *Kraemer*, 74–77

Shelton, Willard, 85

Sherrill, Henry Knox, 56

Shreveport Times, 118

Sindler, Allan (quoted), 203

Sims, Cecil, 110

Slaughter, Roger, 37

Smith, Alfred E., 4

Smith v. *Allwright*, 44 n. 10

South Bend, Indiana, 126

Sparkman, John, 134, 165, 201, 212, 215, 217–20, 224–25, 228–29

Sparks, Chauncey, 21

Spingarn, Steven J., 165–66, 177–78

Spivack, Robert, 201–2

Stark, Lloyd, 11

Stassen, Harold, 72

Stevenson, Adlai E.
    as centrist politician, 197–98,
        216
    on FEPC, 198, 219–20
    receives Democratic nomina-
        tion, 216
    meets with Roy Wilkins, 220–
        21
    and 1952 campaign, 222, 223,
        228
    and Negro vote, 230–31
Stennis, John, 162
Stewart, Milton, 61
Styles, Hal, 21
Supreme Court (U.S.), 75, 172,
    176–77, 232–34, 240
Swope, Herbert Bayard, 142

Taft, Robert A., 72, 88, 148–49,
    174, 204–5, 208
Taft-Hartley Act, 144, 145, 156
Talmadge, Herman, 214
Taylor, Glenn, 116
Thompson, Marvin E., 88–89
Thurmond, Strom, 89, 92–93, 100,
    106, 114–15, 162
Tilly, M. E., 56
Tobias, Channing, 22, 45, 50, 56,
    193–94
To Secure These Rights, 67, 70,
    72, 74, 126
Truman, Harry S., 34, 39, 47, 74,
    76–78, 80, 89, 91–93, 95–
    97, 100–101, 105–6, 108,
    114, 120, 134–35, 142,
    156–57, 160–61, 164,
    181, 195–96, 217, 225,
    231–32, 234
    and Tom Pendergast, 8, 10
    and Negro vote before 1944,
        8–11
    civil rights views of, pre-1945,
        10–13, 19–20
    voting record on, 10, 15–16
    senatorial reelection campaign
        of, 10–11
    and Special Senate Committee
        Investigating the Na-
        tional Defense Pro-
        gram, 13–14
    receives vice-presidential nom-
        ination, 16–18
    as centrist politician, 17, 29,
        197, 203, 240
    in 1944 campaign, 20–22
    becomes president, 23
    and FEPC, 24–27, 32–36, 160–
        61, 170, 179, 185, 186
    and relations with Congress,
        25–26, 29, 32, 50, 57–58,
        82, 120–21, 141, 156–57,
        161, 167, 168, 170, 173,
        184, 187, 194–95, 238
    civil rights tactics of, 26–27,
        29, 32–33, 51–52, 72, 77–
        78, 81–82, 108, 123, 161,
        168, 237–40
    Negro appointments of, 29, 38,
        105
    and Senate filibuster, 33–34,
        174, 178
    on poll tax, 35
    and purge of Roger Slaughter,
        37–38
    and racial violence, 45, 47–48
    relations of, with NAACP, 45,
        61–63, 105, 159–60, 187,
        207
    and the South, 50, 86, 95, 102,
        104, 124, 160, 189, 194
    and origins of Civil Rights
        Committee, 50–52
    report of (*To Secure These
        Rights*), 70–73
    civil rights message to Con-
        gress (1948), 83–85
    receives presidential nomina-
        tion, 113
    issues Executive Orders 9980–
        9981, 116–18
    creates Fahy Committee, 123
    1948 campaign of, 122–27
    in Harlem, 126–27
    wins election, 128
    and Negro vote (1948), 129–31
    leadership qualities of, 137–38
    and Rule Twenty-two, 148
    submits civil rights program,
        157
    refuses compromise on FEPC,
        160
    receives Fahy Committee re-
        port, 175–76
    supports cloture, 178
    issues Executive Order 10210,
        185–86
    vetoes H.R. 5411, 191–92

issues Executive Order 10308, 192–93
announces retirement, 196–97
addresses ADA convention, 200–201
speaks at Howard University, 206–7
in 1952 campaign, 225–30
speaks in Harlem, 225–26
attacks Eisenhower, 227
defends Stevenson and Sparkman, 229
makes farewell address, 234–35
contributions of, to civil rights progress, 235, 240
Truman, Mrs. Harry S., 215 n. 107
Twenty-one-day rule, 139, 169, 184
Tuck, William, 93
Trussel, C. P., 86
Tydings, Millard, 180

United Nations, 65, 193
United Nations Commission on Human Rights, 66
United Public Workers, 59

Vandenberg, Arthur, 121–22, 147, 150
Vaughn, Harry, 15
Veterans Bureau, 36 n. 107
Vinson, Fred, 62, 75
Voice of America, 85

Wagner, Robert F., 13
Wakulla Springs, Fla., 88
Wallace, Henry, 16–18, 22, 51
and 1948 election, 76, 80–81, 83, 86, 90, 96, 105, 116, 119, 124, 131–32

Warren, Earl, 72, 103
Wheeling, W.Va., 223
Wherry, Kenneth, 122, 154, 163, 188
Wherry Amendment, 153–56
White, Hugh, 214
White, Walter, 24, 28 n. 82, 54, 134, 239
on Senate Resolution 75, 14
on Klan issue (1944 campaign), 21–22
and Capital Transit strike, 30
as spokesman against violence, 50–52
and Truman's NAACP speech (1947), 61–63
on restrictive covenants, 74
and politics in 1948, 78, 85, 104, 107–8
on civil rights program (1949), 140
and Senate rules fight, 142–43, 150
and FEPC, 186
disillusionment of, 187–89
on Truman's withdrawal, 197
and politics of 1952, 201–2, 212, 217–18, 224–25
Wickersham Committee, 55
Wilkins, Roy, 8–9, 15, 33, 150 n. 45, 159, 171–72, 173, 174 n. 124, 211, 214–15, 220–21, 221–22, 234
Williams, Aubrey, 218 n. 112
Williams, John Bell, 86
Wilkie, Wendell, 4
Wise, Stephan J., 28
Wilson, Charles, 55, 70
Woodward, Issac, 44
Workers Defense League, 19
Works Progress Administration, 4
Wright, Fielding J., 83, 88, 114
Wyatt, Wilson, 224–25